ARMENIA
A Journey Through History

ARMENIA
A Journey Through History

by
Arra S. Avakian, Sc.D.

Poetry
by
Ara John Movsesian

Cover Design
by
Ara John Movsesian

The Electric Press®
Fresno, California
1998-2008

Library of Congress Cataloging in Publication Data

Avakian, Dr. Arra S. 1912-
      ARMENIA: *A Journey Through History*; poetry written by Ara John Movsesian;
      interior illustrations from various sources
      Fresno, California: The Electric Press ©1998-2008

xiv, 338p

Bibliography: p335
Index: p327

1. History. 2. Armenia.
I. Title

ISBN-10 0-916919-24-2   (POD Softcover)
ISBN-13 978-0-916919-24-5

ISBN-10 0-916919-22-6   (POD Hardcover)
ISBN-13 978-0-916919-22-1

Library of Congress Catalog Card Number 98-88113

Printed in the United States of America

First Printing, December 1998
Second Printing, January 2000 (Expanded Version)
Third Printing, June 2003 (Expanded Version)

First POD Version July 2008

Preface

The nearly 3,000 years of Armenian presence on the world scene has given rise to a tremendous variety of significant events in the history of the people, with the development of a rich cultural heritage and the appearance of outstanding figures.

In preparing this book our aim was to offer our readers an appropriate and representative sampling of stories, concise and easy-to-read, of people, places, events, and facts.

No claim is being made, in any sense, that the 131 entries make for a comprehensive collection, nor that all of the most important elements in Armenian history have been included. Such an undertaking is tantamount to producing a multi-volume encyclopedia. Indeed, the production of a new, multi-volume (post-Soviet era) encyclopedia is being pursued in the Republic of Armenia.

It is our hope that this book, with its condensed stories, with its poems offering the essence of the story, and with an appropriate illustration will offer our readers not only enjoyable reading, but also a very useful quick-reference work on the Armenian people. The index will lead the reader easily to all references made to persons, places, events, etc.

The sources used for the material contained in the book are varied and many. The information given has been gleaned from numerous individual books, newspaper and magazine articles, personal contacts, general encyclopedias in the English language, and the *Haykakan Sovietakan Hanragitaran* (Armenian Soviet Encyclopedia) published in Armenia in the 1970's and 1980's.

We have sought to be diligent in our efforts to present condensed stories that are accurate in their content, and that present the most notable aspects of the subject. Any errors in the stories, serious omissions, or bias that may be perceived, are unintended.

Arra S. Avakian

Dedication

To My Wife
Georgia

Introduction

The topics in this compilation include the land of Armenia and its geography, the culture of the inhabitants over the centuries, their religion and Church, significant historical events, folklore and popular traditions, places, outstanding individuals, and the nation.

The entries have been grouped by their nature. Within each group, their order placement has been either chronological, or alphabetical, or in other ways, as appropriate. The Table of Contents shows this. In any case, the Index will enable the reader to find the information desired on any specific detail.

Proper nouns, the names of persons and places that arise in Armenian (or in other foreign languages), have been transcribed generally in two ways. The transliteration formula from the Armenian has been based essentially on the alphabet equivalence of classical times. However, when a name is very well known in a spelling that departs from the classical equivalence, the popular and familiar spelling has been used. In many cases, the internationally known form has been used, such as found in encyclopedias, for example, Tigranes instead of Tigran or Dikran. The following table is the classical alphabetical equivalence used in most cases.

Ա ա	a	Լ լ	l	Շ շ	sh	Ւ ւ	u/ v
Բ բ	b	Խ խ	kh	Ո ո	o	Փ փ	p
Գ գ	g	Ծ ծ	tz	Չ չ	ch	Ք ք	k
Դ դ	d	Կ կ	k	Պ պ	p	Օ օ	o
Ե ե	e	Հ հ	h	Ջ ջ	j	Ֆ ֆ	f
Զ զ	z	Ձ ձ	ds	Ռ ռ	r		
Է է	e	Ղ ղ	gh	Ս ս	s	ու	u
Ը ը	e	Ճ ճ	j	Վ վ	v	եա	ya
Թ թ	t	Մ մ	m	Տ տ	t	իւ	iu
Ժ ժ	zh	Յ յ	y/ h	Ր ր	r		
Ի ի	i	Ն ն	n	Ց ց	ts		

The Armenians

Sky plunges to earth; communes with stone;
  A jagged union so formed by God
That in its eerie polychrome,
  This land served as the seedling pod.

With hardened lines of massive rocks,
  Confronting gentle wisps of grass,
Whose tenacity to live and grow,
  Depends on roots to hold on fast.

And river valleys cleft in stone,
  Meander through this land of old;
While meadows full of Alpine life,
  Keep God's creatures in their fold.

Such a land of wide expanse -
Of monoliths with weathered face
A battleground 'tween life and death
Is home to a proud and noble race.

First to grasp the Christian life,
And fight to keep it their very own -
Great works attesting to their faith,
They built to rise from sculpted stone.

For ages, hordes of conquerors
Trampling o'er their ancient ground -
Killed, defaced, destroyed, disgraced -
Yet never was their spirit bound.

Adversity did not deter
This people from their will to be;
And nurtured by their faith in God,
They hung on quite tenaciously.

Today, they still exist on Earth,
While other peoples have come and gone
Armenians - with their hardy roots
Are waiting for another dawn.

And as their mighty, symbol grand -
Always watching from on high -
As if to lend a helping hand
Rises Ararat to meet the sky!

&

A Word about the Illustrations

The illustrations appearing in this work have been gleaned from numerous sources. Some are real, being true photographs of the persons and the places. They may be contemporary, or preserved from quite early times. Some are drawings, either objectively done intending to be true representations of the subject, or done in caricature. Others, especially of very early figures in Armenian history, are the traditionally accepted likenesses that have established themselves and reused over and over again, in most cases being no more than an early illustrator's imagined likeness. When variants exist, and they do, we have chosen what we felt is appropriate.

The sources of the illustrations are generally well known books, magazines, calendars, posters, etc. We have copied the chosen illustrations without seeking specific permission for their use, because in virtually all cases, the 'originals' from which we made copies have no easily determined 'owner,' or have been in nearly universal use for decades, if not centuries. In any case, we express our thanks and appreciation for having had the opportunity to use these illustrations.

In particular, the sources have been the following: a) published books and pamphlets on Armenian history, art, culture, etc., b) periodicals such as the Ararat Quarterly, The Armenian Digest, Hay Endanik, c) personally taken on-site photographs, and d) personally created items such as charts, maps, tables, etc.

We would like to especially thank the Melikian Studios of Worcester, Massachussets for providing photographs of Hagop Deranian (p78), American Steel Wire Trust Mill (p81), and Armenian Martyrs' Evangelical Church (p83).

Table of Contents

CHAPTER 3: Mythology and Folklore

CHAPTER 4: Christianity and the Church

CHAPTER 5: Political Events

CHAPTER 6:   Language and Literature

CHAPTER 7:   Fine Arts

CHAPTER 8:   Other Contemporary Figures

Chapter 1

THE LAND
AND
ITS PEOPLE

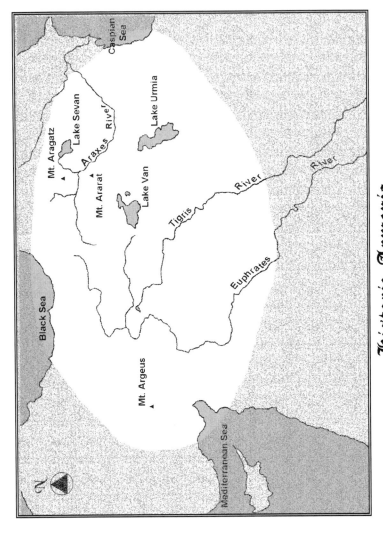

Historic Armenia

"The Land of Three Mountains, Three Rivers, Three Lakes & Three Seas"

The Geography of the Lands of Historic Armenia

𝖂here is historic Armenia?

Historic Armenia is where the "Garden of Eden" was. It is where Noah's Ark landed, and where he planted a vine in Nakhichevan. It is in the triangle of three seas: the Black (Sev), the Caspian (Kaspits) and the Mediterranean (Micherkrakan). It contains the triangle of three lakes: the Van (Bznunyats), the Sevan (Geghama), and the Urmia (Kaputan). It surrounds the eternal mountain Ararat (Masis). It was the "cradle of civilization." Today, part of it is in Turkey.

Historic Armenia, at its greatest extent (65 B.C.) stretched from "Sea to Sea" - from the Caspian to the Mediterranean. It had an area of about 240,000 square miles (approximately California and Utah combined). The present-day Republic of Armenia has an area of about 11,600 square miles (approximately Maryland and Rhode Island combined), or about 4.8% of historic Armenia at its largest.

The population of historic Armenia (at its greatest extent, under Tigranes II, all resident races included) may have been five to ten million. The present-day Republic of Armenia has a population of 3,500,000. With a world population of 5.5 billion, Armenia's population represents about 0.06%.

Throughout its area, historic Armenia is mountainous. Forming its northern border is the Pontus range of mountains that parallel the shore of the Black Sea a short distance inland. Along the south and in the west is the Taurus range, and to the east is the Anti-Taurus. Embracing Mt. Ararat is the range of mountains known in Armenian writings as "Haykakan Par" (Armenian chain).

Historic Armenia encompasses the regions drained by the Euphrates, Tigris, and Araxes Rivers, with their complex of tributaries. Each of these three river systems creates a well-defined watershed area.

Centrally located and surrounded by these three watershed areas is a fourth watershed area with land-locked Lake Van as its catch basin. Being land-locked, Lake Van is heavily laden with mineral salts, especially phosphates that are extracted and used commercially, industrially and agriculturally.

The evolution of Armenian culture undoubtedly developed in a way that was responsive to a certain level of isolation created by the watersheds.

3

Since the line of division between two such areas is a mountain ridge, communication and interaction between inhabitants of different watershed areas was impeded. As a result, cultural exchange would be diminished, and language variations and customs would develop along lines unique to each area.

Minerals and agriculture are and have been the main factors in the economy of the area, although neither has been developed and exploited to the extent possible with modern capitalization and technology.

The only mineral that has had a significant economic impact on the area is chromium, and to a lesser extent, petroleum.

The main agricultural products of economic importance have been cotton, other fibers, and dried fruits.

Agriculture, despite the mountainous character of the area, has a great potential for development because of the abundance of water and sunshine, as well as fertile soil. Until only very recent times, agriculture was confined to a relatively narrow band along the banks of streams and rivers that cover the land. The plentiful water was being exploited only by artificially diverting portions of streams along man-made canals, and irrigating by gravity flow.

Today, a very extensive system of dams has been and is currently being built in Turkey to store water and maintain higher hydraulic heads. Such water management systems will increase the area of agriculturally productive land, and at the same time provide hydro-electric power not only for commercial and industrial use, but also for driving pumps to lift and distribute the stored water for irrigation purposes.

The new water management and storage systems will enable the lands of historic Armenia to become a new, fruitful, modern-day "Garden of Eden."

છ

Armenia
"Cradle of Civilization"

The lands of Armenia spawned civilization as we know it, we are told. What is the basis for this assertion? The answer lies in two principal factors. One is the findings of archeological excavation and study. The other is the geographical and climatic conditions that exist there.

Historians have identified an area called the "Fertile Crescent," conducive to the advancement of civilization. The area extends northward up the Tigris and Euphrates river valleys into the mountains of historic Armenia, westward into Syria, and then southward to the Mediterranean into Israel. In that region, the favorable climate, soil, and water make for bountiful agriculture, an essential ingredient for the development of civilization.

A richly annotated map issued by the National Geographic Society (1967) entitled "Lands of the Bible Today" includes the following notes, as examples: *"Man's earliest known metal tools - cold hammered copper pins - were used here about 9000 years ago"* (southwest of Harput). *"Excavations reveal more than ten centuries of culture preceding the rise of the Hittite Empire about 2000 B.C."* (north of Kayseri). *"Archeological evidence here reflects man's transition from stone to metal tools...(around 4100 B.C.)"* (south of Diyarbekir). *"One of the oldest established villages yet unearthed. Here, more than 7000 years ago, nomadic man turned from hunting and fishing to agriculture"* (northern Iraq). *"Quarries in this area supplied Sumer and Elam with obsidian for tools and weapons in 1500 B.C."* (southwest of Tiflis).

Throughout the region of historic Armenia and northern Iran and Iraq, numerous archeological sites have been excavated and intensively studied. Even now, new sites are being discovered with names such as Karmir Blur (near Yerevan), Chavush Tepé (near Van), and Chatal Hoyuk (near Konya, southwest of Kayseri).

Obsidian, a widely occurring volcanic glass, was used in ancient times for making tools, weapons, household utensils, and jewelry. Its composition varies greatly, and an examination of an ancient artifact made of obsidian can disclose where the material had been quarried. Such studies reveal much information on trade between regions, and they have shown that trade was carried on between the ancient people of Armenia and remote peoples.

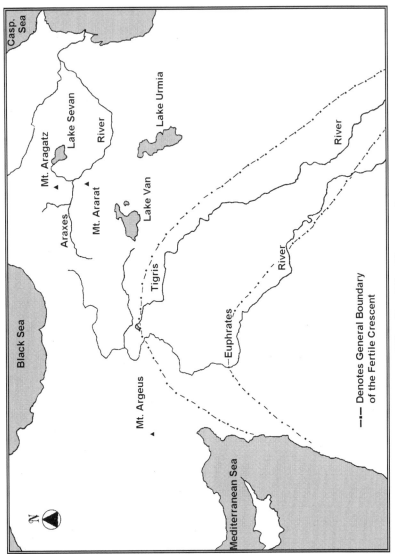

The Fertile Crescent

— Denotes General Boundary of the Fertile Crescent

When the level of the waters of Lake Sevan in Armenia was allowed to fall during the mid-20th century, ancient wheeled vehicles were revealed, buried in the sands near the shore. Two of those wagons are now on display at the historical museum in Yerevan. The magazine, Scientific American (July 1968) stated, *"The earliest examples of wheeled vehicles have all been found within a region no more than 1200 miles across, centered between Lake Van ... and Lake Urmia ... indicating that wheeled transport came into existence somewhat more than 5000 years ago."*

Four-Wheeled Wagons from Lake Sevan

When the nuclear power plant in Medzamor, Armenia, was to be built, construction work disclosed the remains of an ancient metallurgical site. Crucibles and other artifacts found there indicate that the art of making steel out of iron ore had already been developed more than 3000 years ago. An entry in the Encyclopedia Britannica says, *"... a distinctive iron metallurgy seems to have developed about 1400 B.C. in Anatolia ..."*

Undoubtedly, mankind's evolution from primitive, nomadic existence to a civilized one with a developed culture took place at more than one location on the face of the earth. But it is clear that western civilization, as we think of it, was cradled in the lands of historic Armenia. Further, the "Creation" (as set forth in the Judeo-Christian Bible) took place where *"A river flowed out of Eden to water the garden, and there it divided and became four rivers."* (Genesis 2:10) Two of the rivers are identified as the Tigris and the Euphrates. Also, Noah's *"...ark came to rest upon the mountains of Ararat."* (Genesis 8:4). These Scriptural texts tell us that Jewish tradition also regards civilization to have had its origin in the lands of historic Armenia.

෨ඓ

Mt. Ararat (as seen from the Republic of Armenia)

Ararat

As the light of day returns once more,
    To the ancient land of Urartu;
Off in the distance, a mountain looms
    Beckoning all for a rendezvous.

Rising up from surrounding soil,
    Its twin peaks always covered in white,
Ararat, the sentinel,
    Stands aloof both day and night.

Since before recorded history,
    Ararat has witnessed all;
The Flood and Noah and his Ark -
    And watched countless martyrs fall.

As the light of day slowly fades away,
    The symbol of Armenia stands;
As a beacon of hope for the future,
    And guardian of all Armenian lands.

෩

Ararat

"... the ark came to rest upon the mountains of Ararat."
(Gen. 8:4; RSV)

Since time immemorial, the eternal mountain has stood sentinel over the heartlands of the Armenian people, its twin peaks standing apart from other mountain masses and thrusting high into the sky from the surrounding elevated table-lands.

Steeped in ancient tradition of man's re-emergence to form a new civilization on earth, Mt. Ararat has witnessed the ceaseless ebb and flow of man's forces seeking to control the indigenous people. Standing astride a fault in the earth's mantle the mountain itself has felt nature's forces whenever the earth has shuddered.

In its Scriptural use, Ararat, derived from Urartu, the name of the land of the proto-Armenians, means the country. Armenians have their own special name for the mountain - Masis, identifying the twin peaks as the Greater and the Lesser.

One of the wondrous traditions of the mountain is that of St. James (Hacob) of Nisibis, beloved fourth century patriarch of the Armenians, who braved the insecure steep slopes of the mountain to find the Ark, believed to have been abandoned there by Noah. With his ascent only partial, and overcome with fatigue, Patriarch St. James would fall asleep, awakening to find himself at the foot of the mountain. After the third day of a failed ascent an angel confronted the aged patriarch, conveying God's word of forbidding about climbing the holy mountain, but giving the venerable saint a piece of the Ark to carry off. That fragment, a treasured relic of the Armenian Church, remains today at Holy Echmiadzin.

Others, though, have gained the perpetually snow-bound summit. The explorer-historian Parrot made the ascent in 1829 with Khachatur Abovian. Lynch and still many others have followed. Today, many mountaineers and historiophiles go to ancient Armenia to "climb Ararat."

For Armenians, Ararat, the mountain, continues as a symbol of their identity, even though today its peaks lie in a foreign country. Appearing as the central design on numerous issues of postage stamps of Armenia, the twin peaks always depict the lesser Masis to the left. That tells us that the view is from the east looking westward which gives the mountain a grander, loftier look. Armenian poets and artists throughout the ages have found their inspiration from Ararat, the Eternal Mountain.

ℰℴ

Karmir Blur
(Red Hill)

𝕬rcheologists around the world call it " Karmir Blur." They know they are giving the name of the site in Armenian, and that the name means " Red Hill."

Karmir Blur is just outside the city of Yerevan, to the west, toward Echmiadzin, on the left bank of the Hrazdan River that is the outlet of Lake Sevan.

It, along with the other archeological site in Yerevan, Erebuni (also known as Arin-Berd), is what establishes the date for the founding of Yerevan, earlier called Erebuni. The acknowledged date for the founding of Erebuni (and therefore Yerevan) is 782 B.C., with Karmir Blur about a century later. Together they laid the foundation of Yerevan.

To bring honor to Yerevan, the Soviet Union issued a pair of commemorative stamps, in 1968, to proclaim the 2750th anniversary of the founding of Yerevan, a city older than Rome.

The founding of Yerevan (Erebuni) occurred during the Proto-Armenian period of Urartu. The principal figures and events of the times have been well studied and recorded, as a result of the excavations at Karmir Blur and Erebuni, as well as in the Lake Van basin.

The excavations at Karmir Blur were undertaken as a result of a chance discovery by a geologist. He had found a stone bearing a cuneiform inscription. He had taken it to the Yerevan Museum of Natural History where it was deciphered.

That discovery led to excavations on the site disclosing the fact that the hill had an ancient habitation, on the hilltop and on its slopes. The covering soil, being reddish in color, gave the site its name. It turned out that for years local inhabitants had been using hewn stone blocks found there for their own buildings. Also, they had been using the red soil to enrich the soil of their farms. They had also been finding pottery fragments.

The archeological site of Karmir Blur turned out to be a rich find.

Excavation on the hilltop disclosed the vestiges of a fortress, now known as the Citadel of Teishebaini. The site provided numerous artifacts of bronze, gold, and pottery. Included were a bronze statuette of the god Teisheba, a bronze horse-head, bronze helmets and shields, and gold jewelry.

Cuneiform Writing Found on the Inscription Stone

Visitors to the Museum of Natural History in Yerevan can view many of the artifacts found at Karmir Blur.

Commemorative Stamps on the 2750th Anniversary
of the Founding of Yerevan

Armenia From 'Sea to Sea' Under Tigranes II

The lands of the Armenians over the nearly three millennia of their history ranged in size from tiny to gigantic.   At one time they extended from "Sea to Sea" (meaning the Caspian and the Mediterranean).

How and when did they get so large?

During the first millennium before Christ, several peoples and tribes occupied the lands of Asia Minor, consisting of the Anatolian Peninsula and continuing eastward to include the highlands of the sources of the Euphrates and Tigris Rivers, the regions of the lakes Van, Sevan, and Urmia, and reaching beyond the River Araxes.

Amalgamation of the tribes of the highlands gave rise to the people of Urartu (Ararat) who formed a powerful kingdom during the period of the ninth to seventh centuries B.C. Peoples akin to the Phrygians of central Anatolia migrating eastward brought with them an Indo-European language, and mingled with the Hayasa-Azzi tribes.   The resulting amalgamation enabled the people to absorb the weakened Urartu nation and to impose their Indo-European language and customs on the inhabitants.

This was the mechanism, it is believed, of the origin of the Armenian people.

The new nation grew strong and was able to establish a ruling dynasty, the Orontid (Yervantian), that remained in power until about 215 B.C., when it came under the more powerful Seleucid dynasty (successor to the Greek Alexander the Great).

A new Armenian dynasty, the Artaxid (Artashesian), under Artashes I was able to regain power and autonomy in about 190 B.C., as a result of the defeat of the Syrian Antiochus III at the hands of the Romans in the Battle of Magnesia.

Successor kings of the Artaxid dynasty to Artashes I (190-157 B.C.) were Artavazd I (159-149 B.C.), Tigranes I (147-123 B.C.), Artavazd II (123-94 B.C.) and Tigranes II (the Great, 94-54 B.C.).

Armenian power and rule had grown continuously under these rulers of the Artaxid dynasty.

It was during the reign of Tigranes II that the lands under his rule reached their greatest extent. Favorable alliances with neighboring rulers, marriages, internal troubles in Persia, along with victorious military campaigns enabled Tigranes to continue to extend his realm. He declared himself "King of Kings," and occupied northern Mesopotamia. Turning to the west he occupied northern Syria and advanced into Phoenicia and Cilicia.

By the year 70 B.C. Tigranes II had become a very powerful ruler, with his empire extending "From Sea to Sea" (the Caspian and the Mediterranean).

Tigranes II founded a new capital city, more central to his realm. The new capital city was named Tigranakert (built by Tigran), but its actual site is uncertain. The modern city of Diyarbekir (Amida) is usually called Tigranakert by Armenians, but it is probable that the fortified capital city built by Tigranes II is located on another branch of the Tigris River.

Tigranes' successful rise to power did not escape Rome's attention and concern. A Roman army under the command of Lucullus laid siege against Tigranakert and broke down its defenses. The loss of his capital city spelled the loss of Tigranes' empire to the west. Fresh attacks under Pompey inflicted further losses, and Tigranes II was obliged to sue for peace, in 66 B.C.

By the year 10 A.D. the Artaxid dynasty had come to its close. Armenia fell under the control of Medes, Parthians, and Romans.

℘

Greek Historians on Armenia

𝕬cademic scholarship during the earliest centuries of Armenian history was concentrated within the Greek culture. Greece was the center of western learning at that time, and its historians chronicled the world events as they observed them, and very much participated in them.

Several Greek scholars recorded events concerning Armenia and Armenians. These historical records form a critically important resource for Armenian scholarship. It should be added, however, that careful analysis has shown that these Greek scholars were not always without some bias.

Named below are five Greek scholars, listed chronologically, whose works include significant reference to Armenia and Armenians.

HERODOTUS (5th century B.C.), historian who wrote extensively of the conflict between Greece and Persia. His history is important to Armenians because he was the first to record material on Armenia. He describes Armenia under the Persian Achaemenids, the taxes collected, Armenians serving in the Persian armies, their garments, Armenian geography, and Armenia's relationship with other countries.

Herodotus

Xenophon

XENOPHON (c.430-c.355 B.C.), historian and military mercenary. Cyrus the Younger, Persian governor, had marshaled an army of Greek mercenaries to help him overthrow his brother Artaxerxes, ruler of Persia. When Cyrus was killed in battle, the 10,000-man army of Greek mercenaries, left without their commander, was led by Xenophon through Armenia (401 B.C.). In his "Anabasis" Xenophon describes passage through Armenia, reporting on the land, the people, and the rulers.

STRABO (c.63-c. 23 B.C.), geographer and historian, born in Amasya. His works on the geography of Asia Minor, especially to the southeast of the Black Sea where he traveled, is important source material for studies in the early history of Armenia. He covers the geography, the history, including interesting details on Armenian cities, economy, military power, religion, and the breeding of horses.

PLUTARCH (c.46-120 A.D.), biographer and philosopher. He provides information on Armenian rulers and military commanders. He tells of the building of Artashat, the Armeno-Roman wars, Tigranes II, the Great and his defeat by Lucullus, Artavasd II. Armenian studies make it abundantly clear that he was biased against Armenians.

Plutarch

EUSEBIUS of Caesarea (c. 260-339 A.D.), ecclesiastical historian. His history is the primary source of the early history of the Christian Church. Out of his voluminous material he compiled his "Chronicles," an epitome of the church history. It has been strikingly noted that the original Greek text is non-extant, but it is only the Armenian version that remains from earliest times, and is generally recognized as such.

৪০

Yerevan
(782 BC -)

Yerevan: Capital, Republic of Armenia; Pop. 1,250,000;
Elev. 865-1390 m. (2840-4560 ft.); Area 230 sq. km. (89 sq. mi.)

ounded in 782 BC (as attested to in a cuneiform inscription) it was the fortified capital city Erebuni built by King Argishti of the then powerful kingdom of Urartu, on the plains approximately 80 km. (50 mi.) north of Mt. Ararat. Archeological excavations at the site (within the present-day boundaries of Yerevan) and a museum offer the visitor a visual history.

About one century later, a second fortified site, Teishebaini, (also within Yerevan) was established, being the present archeological site known as Karmir Blur.

It was in the fifth to fourth centuries BC that the weakened nation of Urartu gave way to the rise of Armenian dominance in the area.

Mostly through changes in the phonetic values of letters, the name Erebuni transformed into Erevan, becoming Yerevan.

These are the circumstances, simply put, that led to the common assertion that Yerevan is older by 29 years than the "Eternal City" Rome.

Commemorative stamps were issued in 1968 to mark the 2750th anniversary of the founding of Yerevan.

Early Armenian historians have connected the name Yerevan to Noah. Accordingly, it would have been that as the waters of the Deluge were receding and dry land began to appear, Noah might have said (in Armenian?), "Yerevats" (it appeared), and so the name stuck! Others have connected the name to an early Armenian ruler named Yervand. Be all that as it may!

Though much of present-day Armenia is rocky and mountainous, the plains around Yerevan are fertile, and they are watered by the flow from Lake Sevan through the River Hrazdan which skirts the city of Yerevan.

Yerevan served as the capital of the first Republic of Armenia (1918-1920). Today, once again, it serves as the capital of the second Republic of Armenia. Yerevan's population has grown steadily from the 1913 village of 30,000 to the 1,250,000 metropolis that it is today. Published population figures show the following growth pattern:

1913	30,000
1926	65,000
1939	204,000
1959	518,000
1970	775,000
1977	967,000
1997	1,250,000
2007	1,100,000

The city administrators recognized the need for planning city growth and construction. Architect Alexander Tamanian (who also built the Opera House, 1935) was called upon to create the city plan. An appropriate monument stands in the city; it shows the architect standing above and pouring over a layout of the city carved in stone.

Within the city and in its vicinity are many regions and nearby towns named after historic Armenian cities, such as Nor Arapkir, Nor Sebastia, Nor Kharberd, Nor Malatya, etc.

Yerevan today is a tourist city with its many parks, fountains, monuments, statues, museums, theaters, and historic sites. It also touts its "Metro," an underground rapid transit system.

೫೧

Van
(The City and the Lake)

Van (the city, known also in ancient times as Tospa, Tushpa, Shamiramashen, and Yervandashen) lies at an elevation of 5600 feet above sea level, just east of the southeast corner of the lake of the same name. Founded during the early Urartian period (proto-Armenian, before 800 B.C.) it is the capital city of the Vilayet, or Province of Van, earlier known as Vaspurakan. As a walled city, it lay immediately to the southwest at the foot of the Citadel of Van, the long and narrow, free-standing rock about three-quarters of a mile long and 360 feet high, that had been made into a fortress during the Urartian realm, also known as the Vannic Kingdom.

The Fortress of Van Rising above the Site and Remains of the Old City

Beyond the ancient walled city to the south and east were the fertile fields and farms called "Aygestan" (Gardenland).

The walled city was destroyed during the upheavals at the turn of the century and the first two decades of the 20th century. The site, at present, is desolate except for some ruins of churches, mosques and public buildings.

Prominent on the smooth wall built on the Citadel is an ancient (8th century B.C.) cuneiform inscription.

The population of the city in about the year 1900 was approximately 30,000, of which two-thirds were Armenian. But the present-day city, just to the east has a population of about 60,000, most of whom are Kurds.

Throughout its turbulent history, Van and the region surrounding it fell under the dominion of Medes, Persians, Byzantines, Arabs, and Seljuk Turks (Battle of Manzikert, 1071 A.D.). Van was finally conquered in 1543 by Suleyman I, after which it came under the control of the Ottoman Empire. Today, it lies in the secular Republic of Turkey.

Catholicos Mkrtich I "Khrimian Hayrik" was Van's most famous son. He was a very progressive educator, and during his years there, he founded a girl's school and published a periodical "Eagle of Vaspurakan." This much-loved churchman, when Patriarch of Constantinople (before his election as Catholicos of All Armenians), became famous for his remark about Armenia not having an "iron ladle" with which to share in the "herriseh banquet" along with the European powers - referring to the land grabbing by the Europeans that took place at the Berlin Conference of 1878 following Turkey's defeat in the Russo-Turkish war.

The Armenians of Van, during the time of the massacres instigated by Sultan Abdul Hamid in 1895-1896, stubbornly held off a Turkish seige.

Lake Van (known in much earlier times as Bznunyats Dzov) is land-locked, at an elevation of 5400 feet above sea level. It is heavily laden with mineral salts that give the clear water a distinctive blue color. Unfortunately, the water is unfit for drinking. Vestiges of early waterworks indicate that fresh water was being brought into the city from mountain sources in conduits as early as the Urartian period. Credit is usually given for that ingenious system to the fabled Assyrian Queen Shamiram.

A ferry plies the 60-mile width of the lake, between Tatvan in the west and Van (at the nearby port of Iskele) in the east. It carries, in addition to people and vehicles, a railroad train over this segment of the east-west railroad across Anatolia. As such, this ferry is an important link, through Van, of international trade.

About three kilometers off the southern shore of the lake is the island of Aghtamar with its Holy Cross Church, at one time the Cathedral of the Holy See of the Armenian Church. The site is touted by the Ministry of Tourism as one of the most important tourist attractions in east central Turkey.

℘

Moush

Moush, ancient city in middle Armenia, is often cited to have retained a purer form of popular Armenian speech that is less adulterated by external influences.

One tradition has it that the city got its name from the fact that it is often enshrouded in mist, or fog (in Armenian, "Mshoush"). More particularly, some versions of tradition have it that the Armenian Goddess of Love, Astghik (Venus) would bathe each morning in the Aradzani (Meghraget, Murat, southern branch of the Euphrates) River, and a mist or fog would arise to conceal her from prying eyes.

Another tradition has it that it was named by Moushegh Mamikonian who rebuilt the city.

Moush is situated about 50 miles west of Lake Van, astride a tributary of the river called Meghraget ("honey river"). An earlier name of the city, Taron, applies to a larger area, part of the ancient province of Turuberan. To the south lies the Anti-Taurus mountains, sometimes called the Armenian Taurus.

In the vicinity are numerous historical monuments, including bridges, churches and ancient fortresses. Their vestiges are still evident.

Ancient Bridge over the Aradzani (Meghraget) River near Moush

Moush was the winter home of the Mamikonian clan during the fifth century. After the popular revolt against the Arab Caliphates (775) the region came under the Bagratids.

21

During the late nineteenth century, at the time of the intense revolutionary activity, the people of Moush played a significant role in support of the Zeitun uprising against Ottoman tyranny.

The population of Moush in 1900 was approximately 20,000 (Armenian, Turk, and Kurd), of which nearly half were Armenian.

The deportations and massacres of 1915 totally denuded the area of Armenians.

The route of Xenophon's retreat with the 10,000 through Armenia is believed to have passed through Moush.

Although agriculture (tobacco, dried fruit, wine) was the primary produce of the area, Armenians were more involved in commerce and crafts (leatherwork, textiles, jewelry).

A Boulevard in Moush - 1994

Among the several parish churches of Moush, the most resplendent one was St. Marine, which was regarded as the cathedral. One of the churches has been converted into a mosque.

Not far to the south is the mountainous village of Sasoun, home of numerous epic events that have taken place throughout its history.

℘

Tigranakert/Diyarbekir

Diyarbekir (ca. 1867) with the St. Kirakos belltower (rear left of center)

$\mathfrak{A}$long the left bank of a branch of the historic (and Biblical, Gen. 2:14, some versions) Tigris River lies the ancient walled city of Amida. The city today, in historic Armenia, is called Diyarbekir. Armenians have lived there from earliest times, and have been calling it, and still do call it, Tigranakert (or Dikranagerd), meaning built by Dikran (Tigranes II, the Great, King of Armenia, 94-54 B.C.). However, modern scholarship places Tigranes' capital city that he built not at Diyarbekir, but at a site about 45 miles to the northeast, at Silvan.

As recently as 1970 Diyarbekir had the largest Armenian population (more than 1,000) of the eastern cities of Turkey. The community has its own cemetery, which still may be visited. The gravestones, however, bear inscriptions in the Turkish alphabet, not Armenian.

The main church (St. Kirakos, with its five altars, built in 1883 to replace a smaller structure that had been destroyed by fire) had been in regular use, with a resident pastor until about 1980, when the marked thinning of the Armenian population brought that to an end. In more recent years the roof has collapsed, and it is not possible to use the church. The remaining handful of Armenians hold religious services once every few months with a visiting priest in a separate room of one of the residences in the courtyard of the church complex.

The new St. Kirakos included a tall bell tower that had been destroyed by lightning in 1913. It had been replaced by an even taller bell tower (see illustration), but that was destroyed in 1915 by Turkish cannon fire, leaving the church with no bell tower.

The Destroyed Steeple for the Main Church at Diyarbekir (Left Spire)
The Original Steeple (Right Spire)

Diyarbekir has grown into a large city, extending far beyond the ancient walls. One of the bridges over the Tigris River, still in use for vehicular traffic, was originally built by the Romans.

The Ancient Bridge Over the Tigris River

The current population consists mainly of Kurds.
Diyarbekir is famous for its watermelons.

℘

Kharberd/Meziré
(Harput, Kharpert, Mezré, Mamouret-ul-Aziz, Elazig)

𝕶 harberd, principal city of the vilayet (province) of Mamouret-ul-Aziz in east central Asia Minor, was a thriving commercial and agricultural center during the 19th century. The "Kaghak" (city), Kharberd, was located on a hilltop (elevation 4,500 feet) surrounding the old fortress (*berd*). It was the site of the Euphrates College (originally named *Armenia College*), founded in 1857 by the American Board of Commissioners for Foreign Missions. The population of Kharberd (ca. 1900) was Armenians: 15,000 and others (Turks, Kurds, Armenian-speaking Assyrians, etc.): 15,000.

Kharberd (ca. 1880) with St. James Armenian Church (center) and
Euphrates College (top center)

Below the city, on the fertile valley floor (elevation 3,000 feet, and about four miles distant) was the city's adjunct called Meziré, the craft and trade center of the area, as well as the government center of the vilayet. The population (ca. 1900) was Armenians: 20,000 and others: 20,000.

Kharberd and Meziré were completely denuded of Armenians during the 1915 era. Euphrates College was closed, and its entire complex of buildings was demolished. The total population of Kharberd declined to hardly 1,000, though today, it is growing once again with modern multi-family residences. Its present name is Harput.

Meziré, presently called Elazig, has become a thriving center of nearly 200,000 (with only a dozen or so Armenian families). Elazig, also the name of the vilayet (province) is situated on the main east-west rail line, and it has a new university and an airport.

A very substantial dam has been built at the confluence of the southern (Murat) and northern branches of the Euphrates River, at the small village of Keban (about 15 miles from Elazig to the northwest, and half way to the small city of Arapgir). The Keban dam has a height of 500 feet. It has formed a large lake extending upstream along the two major branches of the river and its feeder streams. The lake, which now provides hydroelectric power and irrigation (and recreational opportunities) to a very large area, has submerged as many as 75 ancient villages. The fertile valley floor, once called the "Golden Plains of Kharberd," has the potential to be as productive as the San Joaquin Valley in California. The new lake twists around Harput/Elazig, and its waters can be seen from Harput.

Villages in the area (during the pre-1915 era) with significant Armenian populations were: Hiusenik, 4,500; Kesrik, 4,600; Sursuri, 3,000; Habusi, 3,000; Khuylu, 3,000; Bazmashen, 4,700; Hoghe, 1,800; Tadem, 1,300; Ichme, 1,200; and many others with less than 1,000.

Euphrates College was the pride of Kharberd. Its first president was Dr. Crosby Wheeler. It included departments of theology, languages, mathematics, history, geography, philosophy, and natural sciences. The college was co-educational. In its days, it enjoyed the services of dedicated teachers, many of whom went on to become famous. Many of its graduates, likewise, went on to gain national reputations in their specific fields of endeavor.

Famous and unique for central Asia Minor, was the Fabricatorian establishment. Founded in about 1870 by Krikor Fabricatorian, and developed by his five sons, this large silk textile factory employed as many as 300 persons. Having won medals in industrial fairs in Europe, the firm won the praise of the Sultan. The firm imported American and British looms, and produced brocades in silk and cotton, as well as finished textile goods. No vestiges exist today of this fine operation.

Three major books (in Armenian), by Vahé Haig (1,500 pp) Manoug Gismegian (750 pp), and Hagop Deranian (323 pp) provide in-depth information about the region -- history, geography, demography, language, culture, and customs.

ജ

Through the Cilician Gates

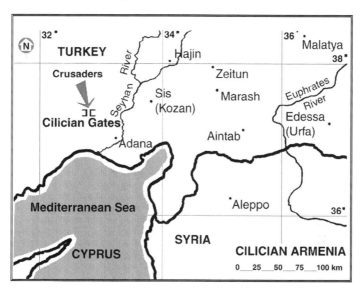

𝕿his erstwhile Roman province of Cilicia, bordering around the northeast corner of the Mediterranean Sea, has repeatedly played a significant role in the life of the Armenian nation, politically, spiritually, and culturally.

Initially as an Armenian principality, founded as a result of the replacement mainly of the Armenians from Ani, it became a kingdom and boasted a royal house, a dynasty, recognized by the crowned heads of Europe. It became a center of religious training and learning where much of the religious literature of the Armenian Church was created.

Later, it became a crucial element in the Crusade movement. On their way to the Holy Lands, the Crusaders passed through the Cilician Gates (a strategic mountain pass) and through Cilician Armenia where they received much-needed replenishment of supplies.

Still later, Cilicia became an important marshaling area for the Armenian Revolutionary movement. It even became an "independent Armenian Republic," for "one day."

During the repressive days of Communist rule in Armenia, the religious hierarchy of the Catholicate of the Great House of Cilicia was able to continue the much-needed role of preparing clergy for the Armenian Church.

27

Were all of Armenia's long history to be pressed together in time, it would show a triune Armenia: the East (beyond Mt. Ararat in the valley of the Araxes); the West (over the heartlands of Armenia in the regions of the Tigris and Euphrates); and the farther West – Cilicia (southeast of the Cilician Gates and bordering on the Mediterranean).

Despite the Persian threat during the Vardanants wars of the fifth century, the Arab threat during the seventh century, and all the other countless assaults upon the nation by hostile outside forces, Armenia continued to maintain its national identity.

But it was the invasion of the Turkic (Seljuk) forces in the eleventh century, coupled with hostile, destabilizing Byzantine actions against the Armenian nation, which caused a mass movement of the people out of the traditional Armenian homeland and into contiguous regions, especially Cilicia.

The emergence of an Armenian government there began with the Rubenid Dynasty headed by Prince Ruben in 1080 AD. There followed the Lusignan lineage during which tenure Prince Leon II became recognized as King Leon I by the monarchs of Europe.

During modern times, several major Armenian population centers played significant roles in the Armenian cultural and economic presence in the Near East. They were mainly in the cities of Adana, Aintab, Hajin, Marash, and Aleppo. Today, all (except Aleppo in Syria) are a part of Turkey, and have a negligent Armenian population. The Armenian population of Syria (Aleppo) may be estimated at about 150,000.

Before the upheavals early in the twentieth century, the Armenians living in the Cilician Armenian cities enjoyed a relatively peaceful life, with their own seminaries, churches (Apostolic, Protestant, and Catholic), and elementary schools. A significant portion of the Armenian population, however, was Turkish-speaking (especially in Aintab, where Armenians were forced to do so). These people had Bibles and other published materials in the Turkish language that was written with Armenian letters.

The Armenian populations of the major Cilician cities at the start of the twentieth century have been estimated to be as follows:

Adana: Armenians numbered 13,000 out of a total population of 45,000. Their churches were built as early as the thirteenth century. It was there in 1909 that the twentieth century genocide of the Armenians began.

Aintab (today's Gaziantep): Armenians numbered 20,000 out of 50,000. It was in Aintab that the largest Armenian Church in Asia Minor (St. Mary) was built in the 1800's. Today, it still stands attesting to the Armenian historical presence, although it is now used as a mosque.

St. Mary Armenian Church – Aintab (Gaziantep) - 1994

<u>Hajin</u> (today's Saimbeyli): Armenians numbered 25,000 out of 35,000.

<u>Marash</u> (today's Karamanmarash): Armenians numbered 40,000 out of 70,000.

View from the Citadel – Marash (Karamanmarash) - 1994

<u>Sis</u> (today's Kozan): Armenians numbered 10,000. Sis was the site of the Holy See of the Armenian Church from 1283 to 1441, when the Holy See was returned to Echmiadzin. However, in about 1443, it was declared to be a counter-See, and it remained so, in Sis, until 1929 when it was transferred out of Turkey to Antelias, Lebanon.

The Citadel - Sis (Kozan)

Former Armenian Quarter - Urfa (Sanli Urfa) - 1994

Zeitun (Sulymanli) - 1994

Descendents of early Cilician families found throughout the Armenian dispersion can often be recognized through their names: Adanalian, Aintablian, Hajinlian, Marashlian and Sislian.

෯

New Names for Old
(Present-Day Names & Their Historic Counterparts)

𝕿ime takes its toll. As peoples and nations move across the lands and occupy new places, they cast aside the old labels attached to the cities, rivers, lakes, and mountains, replacing them with new ones.

So it was in Armenia. Armenians, themselves, applied new names, choosing what they felt were more descriptive or appropriate. Also, other peoples, having trampled over Armenia's hills and valleys, chose to rename things as they saw fit.

Sometimes, confusion or uncertainty led to discrepancies in names. For example, the name, Tigranakert. What city did Tigranes II, the Great, build during the first century B.C. as the capital of his Armenia from "sea to sea?"

Today, Diyarbekir (Amida in Roman times), a large walled city (but today grown far beyond its walls) has been called Tigranakert by Armenians. But modern scholarship identifies the city of Silvan, about 45 miles up the Batman River as Tigranes' city.

Here is a partial list of New Names for Old.

Cities & Provinces

Present-Day Names	Earlier or Other Names
Bitlis	Baghesh
Diyarbekir	Tigranakert, Amida
Elazig (city)	Meziré, Harput
Elazig (province)	Mamuret-ul-Aziz
Erzurum	Garin, Theodosiopolis
Harput	Kharberd
Kayseri	Gesaria, Caesarea, Mazaca
Maku	Artaz
Malatya	Melitene
Moush	Taron
Nisibis	Mtzbin
Sivas	Sebastia
Suleymanli	Zeytun
Sanli Urfa	Edessa
Van (city)	Tushpa, Shamiramakert, Yervandashen
Van (province)	Vaspurakan

31

Rivers

Present-Day Names	Earlier or Other Names
Araxes	Arax, Yeraskh
Arpa	Akhurian
Akh	Spitak
Euphrates	Murat, Aradzani
Firat	Euphrates
Kizilirmak	Halys
Tigris	Dicle

Lakes & Seas

Present-Day Names	Earlier or Other Names
Black	Euksinian, Sev
Caspian	Vrkana, Gasbidz
Mediterranean	Mare Internum, Micherkrakan
Sevan	Geghama
Urmia	Kaputan
Van	Bznunyats

Mountains

Present-Day Names	Earlier or Other Names
Ararat	Masis, Agri
Agri	Ararat
Aragatz	Alagyaz
Erciyes	Arkeos
Suphan	Sipan

࿐

Armenian Terms of Kinship

𝕿he traditional, old-world Armenian family was an extended one, of usually three or four, sometimes even five, generations. A girl taken as bride by a son in a family simply entered that family and became a member of it.

A Portrait of an Extended Armenian Family

Such a closely knit, extended family would have many kinds of relationships, and the Armenians had a distinctive term for each kind.

Here is a listing of them. Often, some of the terms were slightly contracted.

father's	brother	hor-yegh-payr, a-mou
"	brother's offspring	hor-yegh-por-vor-ti
"	sister	ho-ra-kouyr
"	sister's offspring	hor-kouyr-vor-ti
mother's	brother	mor-yegh-payr, ke-ri
"	brother's offspring	mor-yegh-por-vor-ti
"	sister	mo-ra-kouyr
"	sister's offspring	mor-kouyr-vor-ti
grandfather		medz-hayr, hav
grandmother		medz-mayr, ha-ni
stepfather		ho-rou

husband's	father	ges-rayr
"	mother	ge-sour
"	sister	dal
"	brother	dakr
wife's	father	a-ner
"	mother	zo-kanch
"	sister	ke-ni
"	brother	a-ner-tsak
sister's husband		ke-rayr
husbands of two sisters		ke-ne-gal, ba-ja-nakh
wives of two brothers		ner
bride in the family		hars
groom (to wife's family)		pe-sa

ഔ

What's in an Armenian Surname?

*A*rmenian surnames, virtually all, are easily recognized, both by their "ian" suffix and by their familiar roots. Few would fail to pick out an Armenian name from a general list.

The "ian" suffix (sometimes written "yan," usually after a vowel, or in the common transcription of names of those who are from present-day Armenia) is an Indo-European suffix meaning "of" or "from." It is essentially comparable to its use in "Bostonian," or in "librarian." It is recognized also in the forms "an" and "ean," meaning "relating to," as in "sacristan" and "Mediterranean."

Other peoples, such as Persians, have surnames ending in "ian."

It is the root of Armenian surnames that is of greater interest. Roots of Armenian surnames are typically given names, trades, physical or other traits, and geographic origins.

Surnames based on given names are quickly self-evident, such as Hagopian, Minasian, Aramian, Ohannesian, etc. Doubled names, such as Garabed Garabedian are common.

Surnames based on trades arise from both Turkish (and other foreign sources) and Armenian words, and usually both forms exist. Examples are Tashjian and Kardashian (mason), Boyajian and Nergararian (dyer), Kuyumjian and Vosgerichian (jeweler), Chobanian and Hovivian (shepherd), Demirjian and Yergatagordzian (smith), Terzian and Tertzagian (tailor), Najarian and Adaghtzagordzian (carpenter), etc.

If a name used by Armenians ends in "jian," then one can be sure that the name is based on a trade with its description given in Turkish, such as Demirjian (Demir, meaning iron, and "ji" meaning "worker of") and Boyajian (Boya meaning dye, and "ji" meaning doer).

Surnames based on physical and other characteristics can occur in both Armenian and Turkish roots. For example, Takvorian and Melikian both mean king, Sevhonkian and Karakashian both mean black eyebrows, and Avakian and Bashian both mean chief or senior.

Some surnames have a prefix "Der" (or Ter). It arises out of the practice of addressing a clergyman with the title Der (Lord), as in Der Sarkis. A family arising from a priest of the name Sarkis would lead to following generations using the name Der Sarkisian. It follows that since the root of such a name must be a given name there cannot be a name such as Der Tashjian, or as Der Nergararian.

35

Although the written form of surnames used by Armenians is always the same in Armenian, the transcription using the English alphabet results in great variations. The result can be distressful when seeking an Armenian name in the telephone book. The name Khachadurian might appear in more than fifty different spellings. Instead of "Kh" some will write "K" or "H." For the "ch" some may write "tch." For the "d" some may write "t." For the "u" some may write "oo" or "ou."

Some names are based on the geographical origin of the family. Examples are Broussalian (from Broussa), Msirlian (from Msir, Egypt), Stambulian (from Istanbul), and Adanalian (from Adana). Such names usually end in "lian."

Some whose family name was based on a Turkish root, having disdained that fact, have changed their name to the Armenian equivalent. A famous example may be found in the renowned Durian (Tourian) family of churchmen and writers. With the ancestral name of Zumbayan (meaning a carpenter's tool) they changed it to the Armenian form "Dur."

In modern times Armenians often change their names to English-language "equivalents," phonetically or in meaning: Bedrosian becomes Peters, Boyajian becomes Dyer, Erganian becomes Long, Elmasian becomes Mason, Hovagimian becomes Vagim, Atamian Becomes Adams, Berberian becomes Barber, Kaprielian becomes Gabriel, Simonian becomes Simon, Karakashian becomes Kashian, and on and on.

Even so, a sharp-eyed observer can often make a good guess.

ℰ⌒

Homely Wisdom

Wield an adage that's apt. The Armenians have more than an ample supply of them to fit every situation. Here below find a good sampling of them. They offer folksy wisdom, out of the heart and mind of simple folk. Use them, and you will get your point across.

Call them adages, aphorisms, sayings, maxims – all peoples have them. They very succinctly, and pointedly, offer a wise message concerning human nature. In Armenian, the word is առած (aradz). Usually, the saying has been boiled down to a pithy, pungent, lyrical phrase.

Many of the Armenian adages have their equivalent, and sometimes identical, version in English (and, in fact, in all languages universally), and they are a part of common, everyday speech. Examples are "Don't put off till tomorrow what you can do today;" "Keep your door locked, and don't accuse your neighbor of burglary;" "Whatsoever you sow, so shall you reap;" "Better a wise enemy than a stupid friend;" "Where there's a will, there's a way." Some sayings arise directly out of the Bible. But most sayings arise out of normal, human experiences.

Armenian sayings are often in rhyme, rhythm, and alliteration, just as Armenian riddles are usually phrased.

Here is a selection of Armenian adages, along with their phonetic transcriptions and literal translations. The deeper, philosophical meanings are pretty self-evident.

Note: Pronounce "**e**" as in "get" and "**e̲**" as in "giv**e̲**n." Also pronounce "**a**" as in "far," "**i**" as in "fin," "**o**" as in "for," and "**u**" as in "sure."

Երեք չափէ, մէկ կտրէ։
> Ye-rek cha-pe, meg gd-re.
>> Measure thrice, cut once.

Դանակն իր կոթը չի կտրեր։
> Ta-na-gn ir go-te̲ chi gd-rer.
>> A knife cuts not its own handle.

Ի՞նչ է մեղրէն քաղցր. քացախը՝ եթէ ձրի է։
> Inch e megh-ren kagh-tsr? Ka-tsa-khe̲, ye-te tzri e.
>> What is sweeter than honey? Vinegar, if it's free.

Լաւ է մաշիլ, քան ժանգոտիլ։
> Lav e ma-shil kan zhan-ko-dil.
>> 'Tis better to wear out than to rust away.

37

Մատդ խրած փուշը չի ձգեր որ ուրիշ բանի վրայ մտածես:
Madt khradz pu-she chi tzker vor u-rish pa-ni vra mda-dzes.
A thorn in your finger blocks out other thoughts.

Մեծ լեռը մեծ մշուշներ կ՛ունենայ:
Medz le-re medz mshush-ner gu-ne-na.
A big mountain has big fogs.

Շունը շան միս չ՛ուտեր:
Shu-ne shan mis chu-der.
A dog will not eat the meat of a dog.

Ուրիշին չուանով հորը մի իջ՛ներ:
U-ri-shin chva-nov ho-re mi ich-ner.
Don't go down a well with another's rope.

Նեղն ինկած կատուն վագր կը դառնայ:
Neghn in-gadz ga-dun va-kr ge tar-na.
A cat in trouble becomes a tiger.

Ջուրը չտեսած՝ մի բոպիկնար:
Chu-re chde-sadz mi po-big-nar.
Don't bare your feet before seeing the water

Սրտիդ ուզածն է գեղեցիկը:
Sr-dit u-za-dzn e ke-ghe-tsi-ge.
It's what your heart craves that's beautiful.

Պտղառատ ծառին քար նետող շատ կ՛ըլլայ:
Bd-gha-rad dza-rin kar ne-dogh shad gel-la.
A tree heavily laden with fruit will attract a host of stonethrowers.

Ցեխին քար մի նետեր, որ վրադ չաղտոտրի:
Tse-khin kar mi ne-der, vor vrat chagh-do-di.
Don't throw stones into mud, so you won't get dirty.

Քամիին բերածը քամին կը տանի:
Ka-mi-in pe-ra-dze ka-min ge da-ni.
What the wind brings, the wind will blow away.

Oձին խայթը կ՛աղեկնայ, լեզուինը կը մնայ:
O-tzin khay-te ga-gheg-na, lez-vi-ne ge m-na.
The sting of a snake heals, that of the tongue remains.

ℰᴑ

Fit for a King!

Dinner is served; and it's fit for a king! Armenian cuisine provides the best in dining.   And that is because it is not only tasty for its choice of ingredients and for the way many dishes are prepared, but also because they are prepared with tender loving care, and, we might add, with patience.

The basic staple of the food is *tsoren* (wheat). Converted into *aliur* (flour), it provides "our daily bread." Converted into *tsavar* (aka *bulgur*, with variant spellings), it is made into *yeghints* (aka *pilav*, with variant spellings). Converted into *dzedzadz* (aka *gorgod*, the whole-hulled wheat), it is made into soups and stews.   And so it is apparent that *wheat*, evolving into several forms and creating numerous eatables, is indeed the primary staple.

What, in fact, is *tsavar*? *Tsavar* is whole wheat that has been boiled, sundried, ground, and graded to produce the three or four sizes of *bulgur*.

Very characteristic of the raw elements that go into Armenian cookery is that they are converted into forms that allow for long-term storage without refrigeration. To name some: *tsavar*, itself, (and other grains, especially rice and barley); breads (*lavash* and cracker bread); milk converted into cheeses or *madzun* (aka *yogurt*); vegetables and fruits sun dried as well as in preserves (*bastegh* and *rojig*); meats, as *khavurma*, braised and stored deep in their own congealed fats as well as *yershik* (aka *sujuk*) and *apukht* (aka *basterma*); pickled (salted) vegetables (*tourshi*); wines; confections, etc.

These remarks on Armenian cuisine are hardly to serve even as a foreword to an Armenian cookbook (of which there are many, and of high quality).   But the mainstays of Armenian dishes are the following: *hats* (breads, such as *lavash*); *khorovadz* (aka *kebab* of lamb, pork, or beef); yeghints (aka *pilav*, of *tsavar* or *printz*); *letsvadzk* (aka *dolma*, meaning stuffed, with fillings of grains, meats, onions, and other taste enhancers); *derevapatat* (aka *sarma*, meaning wrapped, usually in grape leaves or cabbage, and with the filling essentially as in *dolma*); *gololag* (aka *kufta*, in a great variety of forms, and with spellings generic to the geographical area); *gjij* (aka *geovej*, an endless variety of stews); *abur* (thick soups); *khmoreghen* (pastries, both plain and sweetened); *gat* (milk, yielding *banir* (cheese), *madzun* and *tan*, a refreshing drink); *havgit* (also *tsu*, eggs, yielding a very large variety of dishes).

Very important and characteristic of Armenian cuisine is what is prepared and eaten during the Christian season of Lent (and some other shorter periods of abstinence). Since animal products are forbidden during Lent, grains and legumes become the major food elements. Lentils come into their own at that time and the reader will see the word "lent" buried in "lentil." "Lentil" is the source of the word "lens," and the same relationship exists in the Armenian; lentil is *vosp*, and lens is *vospniak*.

Well, how shall we characterize Armenian cuisine? It is a queen among foods, fit for a king!

TABLE OF ARMENIAN FOOD TERMS

Armenian Name	AKA
tsa-var	bulgur
ye-ghints	pilav
dze-dzadz	gorgod
ma-dzun	yogurt
yer-shik	sujuk
a-pukht	basterma
kho-ro-vadz	kebab
lets-vadzk	dolma
de-re-va-pa-tat	sarma
go-lo-lag	kufta
gjij	geovej

℘

Chapter 2

HISTORICAL
EVENTS
AND
FIGURES

Bronze Figurine of Winged Gryphon from Erebuni - 9th Century B.C.

Chronology of the Armenian Nation

The nearly three millennia of history of the Armenian people follows the pattern of the natural evolution of organic systems. In the initial period there is the convergence of the elements that create the body, followed by physical growth and development, attaining physical maturity. That is followed by intellectual growth and maturity.

The chronological chart identifies the principal events that mark salient points throughout the entire history.

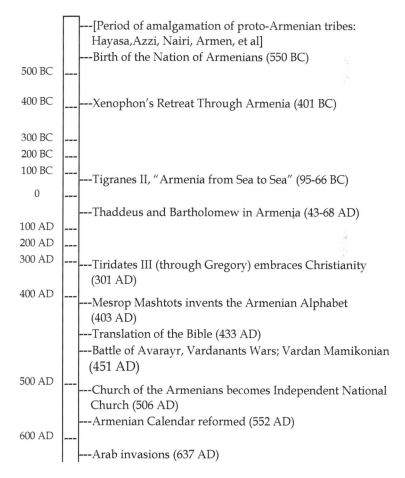

	---[Period of amalgamation of proto-Armenian tribes: Hayasa,Azzi, Nairi, Armen, et al]
	---Birth of the Nation of Armenians (550 BC)
500 BC	---
400 BC	---Xenophon's Retreat Through Armenia (401 BC)
300 BC	---
200 BC	---
100 BC	---
	---Tigranes II, "Armenia from Sea to Sea" (95-66 BC)
0	---
	---Thaddeus and Bartholomew in Armenia (43-68 AD)
100 AD	---
200 AD	---
300 AD	---Tiridates III (through Gregory) embraces Christianity (301 AD)
400 AD	---Mesrop Mashtots invents the Armenian Alphabet (403 AD)
	---Translation of the Bible (433 AD)
	---Battle of Avarayr, Vardanants Wars; Vardan Mamikonian (451 AD)
500 AD	---Church of the Armenians becomes Independent National Church (506 AD)
	---Armenian Calendar reformed (552 AD)
600 AD	---
	---Arab invasions (637 AD)

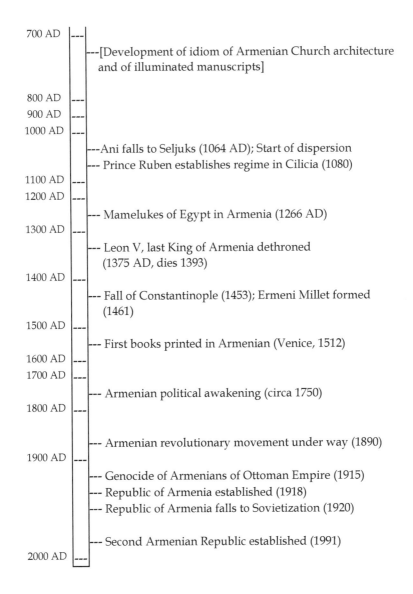

700 AD	---[Development of idiom of Armenian Church architecture and of illuminated manuscripts]
800 AD	
900 AD	
1000 AD	---Ani falls to Seljuks (1064 AD); Start of dispersion
	--- Prince Ruben establishes regime in Cilicia (1080)
1100 AD	
1200 AD	
	--- Mamelukes of Egypt in Armenia (1266 AD)
1300 AD	
	--- Leon V, last King of Armenia dethroned (1375 AD, dies 1393)
1400 AD	
	--- Fall of Constantinople (1453); Ermeni Millet formed (1461)
1500 AD	
	--- First books printed in Armenian (Venice, 1512)
1600 AD	
1700 AD	
	--- Armenian political awakening (circa 1750)
1800 AD	
	--- Armenian revolutionary movement under way (1890)
1900 AD	
	--- Genocide of Armenians of Ottoman Empire (1915)
	--- Republic of Armenia established (1918)
	--- Republic of Armenia falls to Sovietization (1920)
	--- Second Armenian Republic established (1991)
2000 AD	

ℰᴐ

Moses of Khoren
(Khorenatsi)

With the invention of the Armenian alphabet at the beginning of the fifth century, there began 100 or so years of feverish literary activity that included the translation of the Holy Bible into Armenian. This period is called "The Golden Age of Armenian Literature."

Among the many writers of that Golden Age was one Moses, of the village of Khoren (west of Lake Van) who wrote a "History of the Armenians." Moses of Khoren (Movses Khorenatsi, in Armenian) is so notable that he is usually identified only by "Khorenatsi."

Khorenatsi's History is clearly a compendium or collection of all the popular legendary beliefs and folklore concerning the ancient history of the Armenian people, in the same way that the Judeo-Christian Bible is, in part, the history of the Jewish people.

Indeed, Khorenatsi begins with Noah and his three sons, Shem, Ham and Japheth and their succeeding generations. In the Bible, the genealogical line of the Jewish people is established by carrying eleven generations from Noah and Shem to Abram (Abraham), the father of the Jewish people. Khorenatsi, recognizing that the Bible does not do the same for the generations following Japheth, feels the need to supply the names of his succeeding eleven generations. Thus, he extends the genealogical line from Noah, to Gomer, to Togarmah (all named in the Bible, but with Tiras placed before Togarmah), and on to Haik, Armenak, Aramayis, Amasia, Gegham, Harma, Aram and Ara (the handsome).

The entire History of Khorenatsi may be regarded as an Armenian adjunct to the Judeo-Christian Bible.

Khorenatsi wrote the History as a series of separate stories, as he recognized them from the prevailing beliefs and understandings by the Armenians concerning their past.

The nearly two hundred separately titled stories are grouped in three books. Below is a sampling of several of the titles of the stories. Many of them will be recognized by Armenians, with the stories often believed literally.

Book I   (32 titles) **Genealogy of Greater Armenia**

4.   On the fact that other historians do not agree about Adam and other patriarchs
10. On the rebellion of Haik
12. On the races and generations descended from Haik, and actions of each
15. On Ara and his death in the war with Semiramis

Book II   (92 titles) **The Intermediate Period of Our Ancestral History**

2.   The reign of Arshak and his sons
14. On the reign of Tigranes
22. On the reign of Artavazd and his war against the Romans
27. On the building of Edessa and the family of our Enlightener
31. Abgar's letter to the Savior
33. On the martyrdom of our Apostles
74. On the arrival of Anak and the birth of St. Gregory

Book III (68 titles) **The Conclusion of Our Fatherland's History**

10. Death of Khosrov and the war with the Persians
35. On the misfortunes brought about by the death of Arshak
42. On the division of Armenia into two
47. On the blessed Mesrop
51. Sahak the Great's journey to Ctesiphon, and his return with honors
53. On Mesrop's letters, granted from on high
54. On the letters of the Armenians, Georgians, and Albans
61. On the Council of Ephesus, because of the heresy of Nestorius

Moses of Khoren's History is considered by Armenians as the "good book."

ℰℭ

Haik
(The Eponym[1] of Armenians)

here is a popular legendary account of the origin of the Armenian people.   The immediate source of that account comes from the *History of the Armenians,* a work written by Moses of Khoren. But, in truth, the source of that source is nothing more than the popular legend that had arisen in ancient times among the Armenian people.

The work of Moses of Khoren, who was regarded as the "first Armenian historian," is in fact primarily a compendium of the popular beliefs of the people, which were kept alive as "oral history," handed down from generation to generation, for centuries upon centuries.

Moses of Khoren's history was written probably in the fifth century, during the Golden Age of Armenian Literature, that 100 or so years of feverish literary activity immediately following the "discovery" of the Armenian alphabet.

According to the Moses of Khoren account, Haik, the leader of a tribe of people who sought freedom from the despot Bel, fought the tyrant in order to establish the right of his people to live in freedom. Haik slew Bel and took his people from the lands of Assyria into the highlands that became Armenia. Thus was the beginning of the Armenian people.

The Moses of Khoren account also declares that Armenians call themselves "Hai", in Armenian, after their patriarch, Haik.

Further perusal of the Moses of Khoren history identifies Haik as the son of Togarmah, who may be found mentioned in the Judeo-Christian Bible (Gen. 10:3) as the son of Gomer, who was the son of Japheth, who was the son of Noah.

---

[1]Eponym: the person for whom something is or is believed to be named

Thus Haik, not named in the Bible, would be the great, great grandson of Noah.

Moreover, Moses of Khoren identifies Bel probably as Nimrod (Gen. 10:8), the "mighty hunter," as the grandson of Ham, or great grandson of Noah.

Using Biblical chronology (with the Creation set at 4004 B.C.), the date for Haik's rebellion would come at 2942 B.C. (with some minor inconsistencies).   That date, 2942 B.C., is designated as year "1" in the "Original Armenian Calendar," *(boun tvakan hayots)* a dating still in parallel use in the Calendar of the Armenian Church. Thus, 1995 A.D. would be 4487 O.A.C (Original Armenian Calendar).

The above is the legendary (Moses of Khoren) account of the origin of the Armenians, of their name having been taken from the eponym, Haik, and of the date of their origin being several generations after the Deluge, in consonance with the Judeo-Christian Bible. That has remained the popular account, and is as any typical Armenian school child would learn it.

Prevailing historical records and studies, not surprisingly, give a different account.

It is quite likely that the Armenians call themselves "hai" from a pre-Armenian tribe called "Hayasa", one of several regional tribes that amalgamated into the Armenian people.   Also, the international name "Armenian" probably arose from another of the amalgamating tribes called the "Armens".

It is generally accepted that the first recorded use of the name Armenia appeared in a work by the Greek historian Hecateus of Miletus (ca. 550 B.C.) and in the inscription of Darius I at Behistun (ca. 520 B.C.). It must be said that the earlier people of Urartu (Ararat, as mentioned in the Bible), were the original Armenians.

It is probable that the name "Haik" (a personification of the people) is nothing more than the plural (in Classical Armenian) of the name "Hai."

Moses of Khoren's History adds to the genealogical line following Haik by naming succeeding generations as follows: Armenak, Aramayis, Amasia, Gegham, Harma, Aram, and Ara (the handsome). He undoubtedly did so to parallel the same number of successive generations of the Biblical genealogy of Shem (of the Semitic people) going down to Abram (Abraham), the father of the Jewish people.

The names in the genealogical sequence from Haik to Ara, as given by Moses of Khoren, provide a strong indication of what were regarded as true Armenian names.

ॐ

Ara the Handsome

Shamiram Attempting to Revive Ara the Handsome

The History of Armenians, by Moses of Khoren, is the primary source of this much-loved Armenian legend concerning Ara the Handsome. According to Khorenatsi, this is the account:

Ara, son of Aram, was the seventh generation after Haik who was the fifth generation after Noah. Ara had inherited his father's lands (Armenia) and was its admired and loved king.

Semiramis (Shamiram) was queen of Ninevah (Assyria), a neighboring nation to the south. She had learned of Ara's beauty and coveted him for herself. She sent messengers with gifts inviting him to marry her and reign over the combined lands, or have union with her and then return to his own country in peace and with riches.

Ara continued to reject the repeated entreaties. Semiramis, in her sensual want, then sent her armies against Ara, but only to take him alive. However, in the battle, Ara was felled by her generals. The queen then sent her agents to recover Ara's lifeless body from among the slain, and take it to her palace.

When the Armenian army recouped and tried to reclaim the body, the queen said that her gods would bring Ara back to life. That attempted revival having failed, she tried to pass off one of her consorts as Ara brought back to life. She was able to beguile the people of Armenia into believing her ruse. She called Ara's land Ararat, after his name.

Ara-Les (near Van)
Legendary Site of Shamiram's Attempted Revival of Ara

This much-condensed account from Khorenatsi concerning the event clearly has its parallel in a number of ancient legends among the peoples of the Middle East. A common element of the legend that can be likened to other peoples' legends is bringing the slain body back to life by the gods, or by the licking of beasts (dogs).

The Armenian legend concerning Ara the Handsome has grown and been adorned above the telling by Moses of Khoren. As popularly believed, Ara was married to Nevart, and his firm refusal to assent to union with Semiramis is taken to substantiate the chastity of marriage as an Armenian institution.

As with other legendary figures, such as Haik and David of Sasoun, Ara is essentially a personification of the people. The 'personal' behavior of these figures, being nothing more than the actions and the happenings to those people, serves to tell their story of the times.

The legend of Ara the Handsome serves most of all to confirm the sanctity of the Armenian family.

⧤

The Ancient Armenian Calendar

$\mathfrak{A}$ll the world conducts its business according to a common calendar, which happens to have its years numbered from about the time of the birth of Christ. But many peoples have a concurrent year-dating system based on some event of their own histories.

Armenians have not one, but two, different year-dating systems, in addition to dating based on the " Christian Era."

The strong national tradition for Armenians is to consider their origin to be the rebellion of Haik against Bel. The commonly accepted date for that event is 2492 B.C. Thus, that year is numbered year "1", and may be designated 1 O.A.C. (Original Armenian Calendar, "<u>Boun</u> <u>Tvakan</u> <u>Hayots</u>.") There is an anachronism in that choice of the " origin," because the rebellion by Haik (great great grandson of Noah) would have to be after the Deluge. Yet, Scriptural chronology, which traditionally puts the Creation at 4004 B.C., sets the date of the Deluge to be 2347 B.C., 145 years <u>after</u> Haik's rebellion. Be that as it may!

According to this Armenian dating, the year 1996 A.D. would be the year 4488 O.A.C.

Another dating system used by Armenians is based on a variety of calendar and ritual issues that led to the restructuring of the calendar by the Armenians. Thus, the year 552 A.D. was designated year 1 E.C.A. (Epochal Calendar of the Armenians, "<u>Tomarakan</u> <u>Tvakan</u> <u>Hayots</u>.") According to this dating, the year 1996 A.D. would be considered the year 1445 E.C.A. But that's not quite true, for it is customary in certain cases (such as in E.C.A. dating and in the numbering of chapters in books, especially in the Bible) to use letters instead of numerals. Thus, the 36 letters of the original Mesropian (Armenian) alphabet stand for numbers as follows: The first nine letters stand for the numbers 1 to 9; the next nine for numbers 10 to 90; the third nine for numbers 100 to 900, and the last nine for numbers 1000 to 9000. Thus, the date 1444 would be written as follows:

Ռ Ն Խ Դ

The small but thick pocket calendar for the services of the Armenian Church, published annually at Echmiadzin, lists all three dates. The calendar for 1996 shows the following (in Armenian): 1996 A.D. (new style); 4488-4489 O.A.C.; and 1445-1446 E.C.A.

Why are there two numbers for the additional two calendars? The ancient calendars started not on January 1, but on "Navasard 1," equivalent to August 11.

Incidentally, the Armenian Church changed from using the Julian calendar (old style) to the Gregorian calendar (new style) in 1924. However, the Armenian Patriarchate in Jerusalem remains on the Julian calendar to match the practice of the Greek Orthodox Church. The purpose in doing so is to safeguard the complex pattern of Armenian rights and practices in the Holy Places.

The Original Armenian Calendar consisted of 12 months of 30 days each, with an "Excess" period of 5 (or 6) days. The month names were Navasard, Hori, Sahmi, Tre, Kaghots, Arats, Mehekan, Areg, Ahekan, Mareri, Margats, Hrotits, and Haveleats (Excess).

Unexpectedly, each of the 30 days in the months had its own name, rather than a numbered date. Those names were Areg, Hrand, Aram, Margar, Ahrank, Mazdegh, Astghik, Mihr, Tzopaber, Mourts, Erezkan, Ani, Parkhar, Vanatour, Aramazd, Mani, Asak, Masis, Anahit, Aragadz, Grgour, Kortouik, Dzmak, Lousnak, Tsron, Npat, Vahagn, Sein, Varag, and Gisheravar.

Even the hours of the day had names. But we shall withhold them.

It appears that Armenians took their time seriously.

ဆ

Anania of Shirak
Mathematician

He told of the movements of the Celestial Spheres

Erudition in Armenia in the seventh century was virtually all in the discipline of religion, but one name stands out uniquely in the then disdained field of secular learning.

Anania of Shirak, 7th century mathematician, cosmologist, geologist, and historiographer was abreast of the scientific knowledge of the world of his times. Having looked upon mathematics as the "mother of all sciences," he earned the title of "mathematician."

Anania, known also a Shirakatsi, was born in the region of Shirak (Gyumri, Ani). Having shown love for learning at an early age, he was able to go to Trebizond where he studied with a renowned scholar for many years. He became versed in astronomy, mathematics, and physics, authoring works in those fields.

Anania was called upon in the year 667 by the Catholicos Anastas to develop a perpetual calendar for the Armenian Church that would prescribe the date for the fixed and movable feasts, a challenging task. Catholicos Anastas portrayed Anania as being "eloquent and skilled, thoroughly knowledgeable" ("Azgapatum," Ormanian). Anania's solution to that requirement is reflected today in the repeating cycle of 532 years, after which there is a repetition of all the factors that affect the designation of dates for feasts: namely, the solar cycle (occurrence of leap years each 4th year), lunar cycle (matching the solar cycle after 19 years), and the days of the week, 7. The product of 4, 19, and 7 is 532.

Though probably subscribing to the Aristotelian theory (4th century, BC) of a geocentric universe instead of a heliocentric one, Anania understood that the world was round, along with a few others of his time who had the courage to reject the flat earth belief.

He also believed that the Milky Way consisted of distant stars.

As a mathematician, Anania delved deeply into arithmetic, algebra, and some trigonometry. He dwelled on the nature of integers that as a discipline would today be called Number Theory. His works, originally in manuscript, of course, contain countless numerical tables for addition, subtraction, multiplication, and division, as well as other numerical relationships. Such works are on display at the Matenadaran in Yerevan (see separate story).

With an Armenian alphabet in hand for only two hundred years, writing in Armenia in the seventh century used letters of the alphabet to represent numerals, when they were needed, as was being done in Rome with the Roman notation. Arabic numerals were adopted later. The 36 letters of the alphabet at that time represented numbers as follows: the first nine letters represented the numerals one to 9; the second nine letters, 10 to 90; the third nine, 100 to 900; and the remaining nine, 1000 to 9000. Thus, the number 562 was written ֆԿԲ (500+60+2). As is done in Roman notation, the letters are placed in order of descending value, starting with the highest. Their numerical values are simply added together. Again, as in Roman notation, when a smaller numerical value is placed to the left, it means to subtract.. Thus, ԷԽ ("take 7 away from 40") represents the number 33 (which could also be written ԼԳ). In Roman notation, while "vi" represents 6, "iv" represents 4. Such a subtraction notation was needed to enable carrying out arithmetic problems.

The chart on the next page, a fragment of a much larger chart of several pages, appears to be an overly simple arithmetic table. Why bother? It must be remembered that arithmetic using that awkward notation needed that kind of help. Such a table is comparable to multiplication tables we use in schools. As an aside, we would say that doing arithmetic in Roman notation was even more difficult than Shirakatsi's math!

Representing numerals with letters is still in common use by the Armenians today, as in numbering chapters in a book. Even in English, we often write "Chapter XL." In Armenian we might see a biblical reference as "Լուկ, ԺՄ: 2-4" (Luke 11:2-4).

Anania Shirakatsi was Armenia's first scientist.

54

Simple Arithmetic Table

(See transcription below)

5-2=3	10-5=6-1	10-8=9-7	30-10=20	90-40=50
4-2=2	10-5=5	10-8=8-6	20-10=10	
3-2=1	9-5=4	10-8=7-5		
10-3=9-2	8-5=3	10-8=6-4		
10-3=8-1	7-5=2			
10-3=7	6-5=1			
9-3=6				
8-3=5				

Arithmetic Table (fragment, transcribed), **from Anania of Shirak**

Note: The upper left entry is actually 500-200=300. All of the "00"s have been omitted for convenience. [5-2=3 would be written ք҄բ҄ գ, and 10-3=9-2 would be written ժ ҄դ ҄ թ ҄ բ]. The original chart was, of course, hand lettered. But as you can see, it lacked a careful proofreading. The reader might like to find the errors. Hint: in the second and in the fourth columns.

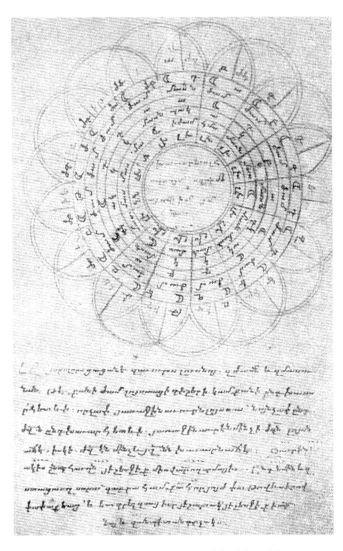

Shirakatsi's Cyclic Designation of the Moon Phases

"Anabasis"
(Xenophon's Retreat, Through Armenia)

yrus the Younger of the Persian Achaemenid dynasty, sought to overthrow his brother Artaxerxes, the King. As governor of a province he was able to assemble a 10,000-man army of Greek mercenaries, ostensibly to put down a revolt in a neighboring province.

But he turned treacherously on his brother, and was killed in the ensuing battle (401 B.C.).

With the Persian army having killed the major Greek generals also, the 10,000 Greek mercenaries were left in great danger.

Xenophon, a Greek volunteer, emerged as a new leader and convinced the remaining leaders to an armed retreat.

That retreat, along with a number of military encounters along the way, took place along the Tigris River valley, through Armenia, and to the Black Sea, enabling a safe evacuation by the ten thousand.

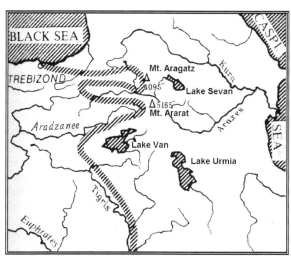

Map of Xenophon's Retreat through Armenia (401 B.C.)

"Anabasis" is Xenophon's detailed account of that retreat. It includes descriptions of Armenia, its people, its geography, and its life.

Scholars have tried to reconstruct the exact route followed in the retreat. No universal agreement exists on it, but the following, as it pertains to Armenia, is highly probable.

Entry into Armenia was along the Tigris River valley. At about Siirt, the route continued northward, passing to the west of Bitlis. Continuing northward it passed to the east of Garin (Erzurum) to some point west of Kars and Ardahan, and then turned westward along the southern slopes of the Pontus Range. The path then turned approximately to the northeast to Trabizond on the Black Sea.

There are several places in Anabasis describing encounters with Armenians. As the ten thousand leave the Tigris River valley, going north, Xenophon writes, "*...the prisoners said that after passing through the country of the Carduchians [probably forerunners of Kurds] to the north they would come to Armenia, the large and prosperous province of which Orantes was ruler...*"

As they approach the river that separates them from Armenia "*they caught sight of horsemen at a place across the river, fully armed and ready to dispute their passage, and likewise foot-soldiers drawn in line of battle upon the bluffs above the horsemen, to prevent their pushing up into Armenia.*"

However, entry into Armenia was accomplished, and in a village where the troops were bivouacked, Xenophon describes some homes in which there "*... were goats, sheep, cattle, fowls, and their young; and all the animals were reared and took their fodder there in the houses. Here were also wheat, barley, and barley-wine [probably beer] in large bowls ... in it, were straws, some larger and some smaller ... and when one was thirsty he had to take these straws into his mouth and suck. It was an extremely strong drink unless one diluted it with water, and extremely good when one was used to it.*" The next day Xenophon took the village chief to visit the troops "*.. and found them faring sumptuously and in fine spirits. There was no place from which the men would let them go until they had served them a luncheon, and no place where they did not serve on the same table lamb, kid, pork, veal, and poultry, together with many loaves of bread, some of wheat and some of barley.*"

At another point the village chief was asked about a horse being reared. The answer was that it was for the King. Xenophon wrote, "*The horses of this region were smaller than the Persian horses, but very much more spirited.*" The village chief advised Xenophon about wrapping small bags round the feet of horses and beasts of burden "*when they are passing through snow, for without these bags the animals would sink up to their bellies.*"

Xenophon's "Anabasis" is the earliest non-Armenian detailed account of personal interaction with Armenia and Armenians.

[*Quoted passages are from Brownson's translation*]

෨

Avarayr

The morning air so fresh and sweet -
  The verdant valley full of life -
The flowing river clear and swift -
  Quietly waiting for death and strife.

Amassed on either side of glade;
  Tensed like Tigers stalking prey;
Two armies stood prepared to clash,
  To see whose strength would thus outweigh.

Yazdegerd and his Persian horde,
  Determined to confront and win;
To force upon Armenians all
  A god that was not genuine.

And Vardan and his army small;
  With Cross and Ghevond at his side;
Stood prepared to fight till death
  Against oppression from outside.

Thus, as the Sun's rays filled the sky,
  A thunderous roar disturbed the scene;
And suddenly, this peaceful place
  Became a hellish sight, obscene.

Avarayr, this valley faire,
  Was blessed with Vardan's blood that day,
And even though Armenians lost,
  Yazdegerd never got his way.

&

Commander Vardan with Ghevond Yeretz Blessing the Armenian Army
on the Eve of the Battle of Avarayr

The Battle of Avarayr

*A*rmenia, in the fifth century, was a feudal state. Without a king, the country consisted of principalities, each with its own prince and its own military force.

The powerful Persian State to the south held a ruling hand over Armenia, having named one of the princes, Vasak of Siunik, as "marzpan" (governor) of Armenia.

The Persian ruler, Yazdegerd, was a fanatical believer in the fire-worshipping (Zoroastrian) faith. He wanted Christian Armenia to give up its faith and embrace his, thus he exerted tremendous pressure on Armenia to gain this end.

Initially, there were exchanges of notes between Yazdegerd and the Armenian bishops. Each claimed to believe in the true faith and called the other's false.

Eventually, Yazdegerd summoned the Armenian princes to his palace on the Tigris River at Tizbon (Ctesiphon), imprisoning them and demanding that they yield to him. The princes feigned agreement in order to be released from captivity. Yazdegerd was overjoyed.

However, on their return to Armenia, the wives of the princes (historians call them "delicately reared ladies") showed greater resolve, and belittled their husbands for having acted without courage.

On realizing that he had been deceived, Yazdegerd marched on Armenia with an army of 300,000 men, reinforced by elephants (military "tanks" of the times).

The Armenian princes, now unified in their resolve to resist the Persian attack, rallied their militias, producing an army of 66,000 men, including archers and lancers.

The combined Armenian forces were put under the command of Vardan Mamikonian, of the family that in earlier times had provided the military leaders for Armenia.

On the eve of the battle, Vardan addressed his men with a stirring message about their commitment to "their heavenly king".

The men then took communion from Ghevond Yeretz, Chaplain of Vardan's Army.

The two forces collided on May 26, 451 AD, the day of the Pentecost, on the field known as *Avarayr*, located on the banks of the river Teghmut (believed to be south of Khoy now in northwest Iran).

The Persian and Armenian armies fought fiercely, however, the result was indecisive at best. On that day, the Armenians lost 1,036 men, including Commander Vardan himself, as well as several princes. The Persians lost 3,000 men.

Having tasted the intense Armenian resistance, Yazdegerd withdrew.

During the next thirty years, there were sporadic military engagements, with the Armenians being led by Vahan Mamikonian, Vardan's nephew.

Eventually, in the treaty of Nouarsak, 484 AD, the Persians agreed to allow the Armenians to worship the faith of their choice.

The battle of Avarayr could thus be considered the first battle in history in which a people fought to defend their Christian faith.

℘

Vardan Mamikonian
(ca. 400-451 AD)

"From this faith no one can shake us, neither angels nor men; neither sword, nor fire, nor water, nor any nor all horrid tortures ..."

In the middle of the fifth century, Bishop Hovsep I, Catholicos of All Armenians, with such words in a long message directed to the Grand Commander of the Persians, Mihrnerseh, declared the unwavering faith of the Armenians. That bold and courageous declaration was signed by all the bishops of the church.

It was Vardan Mamikonian, Commander of the Armenian forces, who buttressed that declaration with action. He led the resistance against the ever-intensifying pressure being applied by the Persian monarch, Yazdegerd, who was demanding that the Armenians deny their Christian faith and embrace his fire-worshipping faith of Zoroastrianism. A climactic, one-day military confrontation took place at Avarayr, on May 26, 451 AD. In that battle, Vardan was slain.

Who was Vardan Mamikonian, and how did he come to play this most crucial role in Armenian history? It may justifiably be said that without his committed leadership, the term "Armenian" today might have referred to no more than an obscure, one-time, Christian people of long past.

In fifth century feudal Armenia, the Mamikonian clan was one of the princely families that ruled over the several loosely united principalities under the control of Persia. One of the princes (or "Nakharars," rulers),

Vasak Siuni, had been appointed "marzpan" (governor) by the Persian monarch.

The Mamikonian clan had been providing military leadership for Armenia. They had established themselves in Armenia several generations earlier, having come from the east, from regions of China. Their early history can be gleaned from the writings of Moses of Khoren and of Sebeos.

The role of Vardan Mamikonian in Armenian history is a powerful one. His standing in the people's minds has been elevated above the level of an ordinary mortal human, to a height wherein he is taken to be the embodiment of all the positive attributes - devoutness, courage, leadership, patriotism, integrity, righteousness and virtue.

His positive character is enhanced by the existence of his antithesis, another Armenian prince, Vasak Siuni, the Persian-appointed governor, who, like Judas, traitorously turned against his people by supporting the Persian position for personal aggrandizement. In Armenian tradition, Vardan and Vasak are the two antipodes of human character. No Armenian couple would ever name a son Vasak, while Vardan as a name was highly prized. "Kach Vardani torrn em es" (I am the grandchild of brave Vardan), are words to a poem young children were taught to recite.

Two major sources tell of the events leading up to and immediately following the climactic clash between the Persian army and the Armenians at Avarayr. The two authors are Elisaeus (Yeghishe), who wrote "The War of Vardan and the Armenians," and Ghazar of Pharbe (Parbetsi), who wrote "The History of the Armenians, and Discourse on Vahan Mamikonian."

The combined militias of the several Armenian principalities had formed an army of 66,000 under the command of Vardan when the clash occurred. That force was to repulse the attacking Persian army of 300,000 (see separate story on Avarayr).

The Armenian Church has designated Vardan as a saint, as well as the "1036 witnesses," those who were martyred at Avarayr. A religious feast day, Vardanants, has been marked in the church calendar.

One of the sharakans (hymns) of the Armenian Church !s dedicated to Vardan and his commanders It is the sharakan "Norahrash." written by St. Nerses Shnorhali. Each of the eight verses of the sharakan contains one name of a commander, starting with Vardan and continuing with Khoren, Artak, Hmayak,Tajat, Vahan, Arsen, and Garegin.

According to early Armenian tradition, a person would celebrate his "name day" rather than the anniversary of his birth. That name day would correspond to the feast day in the church calendar set aside for a saint of that name. However, the name day for those with names for which there were no designated saints was the feast day of Vardanants, for surely all male names could be found among those 1036 martyrs. In the church calendar, the Vardanants feast falls on the Thursday preceding the start of Lent.

The personality of Vardan continues to be a powerful symbol of patriotism for the nation of Armenians. A nation-wide fraternal organization, the Knights of Vartan, has chosen that name to reflect its aims.

Vardan Mamikonian was killed in the Battle of Avarayr, but he did not die; he lives today as a true patriot in the minds and hearts of all genuine Armenians.

Great Rulers of Armenia

ARTASHESIAN DYNASTY

ARSHAKUNIAN DYNSTY

King Tigranes II
(the Great)

King Tiridates III

BAGRATUNIAN DYNASTY

RUBINIAN DYNASTY

King Gagik

King Leon I

The Royal Dynasties of Armenia

Armenia, throughout its history of nearly 3,000 years, has experienced dramatic rise and decline repeatedly, from being a regionally powerful state to a land of enslaved people (with various intermediate levels of foreign domination), each time to rise and become a strong sovereign state once again.

The principal reasons for the Armenian people to have experienced such extreme vicissitudes are twofold: 1) the geographic location made Armenia a battlefront and prize to be won by the great powers to the east and to the west, and 2) the people were resolute, indestructible, and courageous, enabling them to reassert themselves when the time was propitious and in so doing regain sovereignty over their native lands.

Ruling over their ancestral lands, throughout the history, have been royal dynasties, each having left its mark on the nation.

Here is a listing of those dynasties.

THE ROYAL DYNASTIES OF ARMENIA

Name of Dynasty	Dates	First Ruler	Last Ruler	No. of Rulers	Principal Events
Yervandian (Orontid)	320 BC - 215 BC	Yervand I (Orontes I)	Yervand II (Orontes II)	10	
	215 BC - 190 BC				Local Princes Under Seleucid Rule
Artashesian (Artaxid)	190 BC - 10 AD	Artashes I (Artaxes I)	Erato	19	Armenia "from Sea to Sea" Under Tigranes II (The Great, 94-54 BC)
	10 AD - 193 AD				Domination by Medes, Parthians, Romans
Arshakunian (Arsacid)	193 AD - 430 AD	Trdat I (Tiridates I)	Artashes IV (Artaxes IV)	24	Adoption of Christianity (301 AD) Under Tiridates III, Armenian Alphabet

THE ROYAL DYNASTIES OF ARMENIA
(Continued)

Name of Dynasty	Dates	First Ruler	Last Ruler	No. of Rulers	Principal Events
	430 AD - 860 AD				Domination by Arabs, Persians, Byzantines; Armenian Governors, Vardanants Wars
Bagratunian (Bagratid) Ani	860 AD - 1080 AD	Ashot I	Gagik II	10	Fortified capital city of Ani: Fall under Seljuk & Byzantine incursions
Bagratunian (Bagratid) Kars	960 AD - 1080 AD	Moushegh	Gagik	3	
Bagratunian (Bagratid) Van	910 AD - 1020 AD	Gagik	Senecherim	6	Church of the Holy Cross built on Aghtamar Island
Rubinian (Rubenid)	1080 AD- 1375 AD	Ruben	Leon V	23	Cilician prominence; interaction with Crusades; Prince Leon II crowned King Leon I

The Seventh Century Arab
Aggression into Armenia

The newly emergent Islamic faith (founded by Mohammet, born 570 A.D. in Mecca, on the Red Sea) was growing and spreading rapidly toward the north, out of the Arabian Pennisula into Asia Minor. Mohammet's successor, Abubekr (632), compiler of the Koran (as "revealed" to Mohammet) declared a holy war. His forces completely defeated the armies of the powerful ruling Sassanid dynasty of Persia (c 637).

During the early part of the seventh century Armenia was a divided state, with part under the control of Persia, and part under Byzantium.

The areas under Persia were the provinces of Mok, Korduk, Vaspurakan, Parskahayk, Dvin, Siunik, Paytakaran, Uti, and Artsakh, being the region extending east of the Tigris River, through Lake Van, continuing northeast to the Kura River, to the Caspian Sea, and southwest through the northern parts of Lake Urmia.

The areas under Byzantium were the provinces of Tayk, Ayrarat, Turuberan, and Aghtznik, being those regions of Armenia to the west of the provinces under Persia, as well as extending northward to the Black Sea.

With the Arab defeat of Persia, those regions that had been under Persian control had come under the control of the Arab Caliphates.

Thus, during the second half of the seventh century, those regions that had been historically Armenia had come to be partly under Byzantine control and partly under Arab control.

Armenia under the Arabs, for a time, enjoyed certain benefits it did not have under the Sassanid Persians, nor under the Byzantines.

The Arab Caliphs imposed reduced taxes (tribute) on Armenia, allowed them to keep an armed force with a much reduced occupational force, and gave assurance of Arab military aid should Byzantium attempt any incursion beyond the regions already controlled.

Thus, the Arabs were allowing Armenia to enjoy a greater level of autonomy than was being allowed by Byzantium. Such an arrangement by the Caliphs was even more assured by appointing an Armenian, Grigor Mamikonian, as governor, with royal titles.

However, that arrangement ceased when an internal movement arose in Armenia to turn toward Byzantium. As a result, the Arabs tightened their control, converting the region into a police state.

It was not until about two centuries later that Armenia regained a semblance of being an autonomous state, with the rise of the Bagratid dynasty of Ani (c 860).

જી

Armenia and the Crusades
(The Cross versus the Crescent)

It was 1097 AD. Two threads of history intertwined to cast Armenia into a role it could hardly have expected to fill.

It was the role Armenia (Cilicia) played in support of the Crusades.

European monarchs, devout Christians, were stirred with indignation at stories of wanton destruction at the Holy Sepulchre in Jerusalem by Seljuk Turks, and at the brutality being committed against Christian pilgrims in the Holy Lands. Moreover, they recognized that the Seljuks formed an impassable barrier to eastward trade. It became a compulsion for them to liberate the Holy Lands. They would mount a crusade.

The Bagratid Armenian Prince Ruben had taken his people, driven out of their native lands by the onslaughts of Seljuks and Byzantines, to establish a new Armenian kingdom (a principality) in Cilicia where an Armenian colony had already been formed by Armenian pilgrims to the Holy Places.

It was these two threads of history that intertwined.

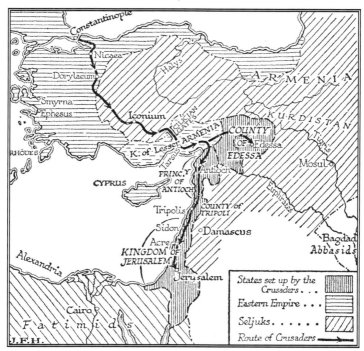

Map of the First Crusade

71

The Crusaders, as they were called, crossed from Europe into Asia Minor. To reach Jerusalem, they would need to cross Asia Minor and go through the "Cilician Gates" of the Taurus Mountains. That would bring them into Cilician Armenia, but in a fatigued and famished condition.

The Armenian ruler, Prince Constantine I, son of Prince Ruben, gave them a warm welcome and provided generous funds and rations. Thus, fed and rested, the Crusaders were able to continue on their quest.

It was in this manner that Cilician Armenia was brought into close contact with Europe, the consequence of which having had great bearing on the fortunes of the Armenian nation.

Prince Constantine I entered into an alliance with the Crusaders, and used his

The Citadel at Edessa (Sanli Urfa) built by the Crusaders and held by the Armenians

own army and resources to fortify the Crusaders in their attack against Antioch, which had to be taken in order to proceed to Jerusalem.

It was this tie with Europe that led, one hundred years later, for Cilician Armenia to be recognized by the European monarchs as a kingdom. Prince Leon II had assumed the throne of Cilician Armenia in 1187. But through negotiations with the European monarchs, and with the intercession of the Church, Prince Leon II became recognized in 1196 as King Leon I.

ഇ

The Armenians of India
and the Far East

With their strong penchant for carrying on trade with people in distant lands, Armenians reached out in a southward sweeping arc into India and continuing to the remotest reaches of the Far East. In doing so from very early times they established outposts in the main centers of each of the countries in their sweep, maintaining small, but prosperous, colonies at each center.

Though the colonies remained quite small, their people clung firmly to their cultural heritage, building churches, schools, and all kinds of cultural and social institutions. In the process they produced significant numbers of individuals who became prominent in intellectual life, in commerce, in philanthropy, and in civic affairs.

Countries that include this chain of commerce outposts that became vibrant Armenian cultural centers, as well as commercial ones, are India, Burma, Singapore, Indonesia, Manchuria, and Japan, as well as Australia and New Zealand.

Although these colonies in recent times have continued to wane, in most cases, the vestiges of their luminous pasts remain in the churches, schools, and monuments they built.

INDIA

There is some evidence of an Armenian trading presence in India from 1500 years ago, but the earliest material evidence of their permanent presence there is the church built in Agra in 1562, and the cemetery marker there giving the date 1630.

Churches were built thereafter in Chinsurah (1695), in Calcutta (1707, with address '2 Armenia Street'), in Madras (1712, and a second one in 1772 at '2 Armenia Street'), in Dacca (1781), in Bombay (1796), and in Saidabad (1860).

An Armenian college was opened in Calcutta in 1821; it is now a very large school and currently offers educational opportunities for young Armenians from other countries, because with a significant decrease in the Armenian population of India there is

The Armenian Church of Kolkata (Calcutta)

space available in that large educational facility. In addition, other income-producing properties are held in the name of the Armenian community (apart from substantial private holdings).

BURMA

The Armenians of Rangoon built their church in 1862, on land graciously presented to them by His Majesty, the King of Burma.

The Armenian Church of Singapore

SINGAPORE

Travel folders of Singapore always feature a picture of the Armenian Church, identifying it as the 'First Christian Church in Singapore,' built in 1835. It is on a main street, with 'Armenia Street' on the back side.

INDONESIA

The early Armenian traders in Indonesia (Java) arrived at the end of the 18th century. An Armenian merchant built a simple church in Djakarta in 1831, later replaced with a substantial structure in 1854. The Armenian community in Surabaya built a church there in 1927.

MANCHURIA

The widespread displacement of Armenians after World War I led to many settling in Harbin, Capital of Manchuria. It was not long after their arrival that they built their church.

AUSTRALIA

The first Armenians arrived in Australia in the middle of the 19th

The Armenian Church of Manchuria (China)

century, in the era of the gold rush, many from India and some from Constantinople. A small migration to Australia occurred after World War I, but a much larger one occurred after World War II. Churches were built in Sydney (1957, and a large one in 1966) and in Melbourne (1962).

The sun never sets on an Armenian Church.

℘

The "Lost" Armenian Community of Poland

$\mathfrak{T}$he fall of the Bagratid dynasty and the Armenian capital city of Ani in 1061 led to the forced dispersion of its people away from their native lands. Probably about 50,000 of them travelled north of the Black Sea and to the east through Slavic lands into Poland where they established a new Armenian community.

The community was centered in the Polish city of Lwow, but with significant numbers of Armenians making their homes in many other cities of Poland.

The Armenian Cathedral of Lwow, Poland

The new arrivals were received warmly. Polish kings granted them religious freedom and certain political rights. The Armenians were permitted to form a governing council to rule over themselves, in accordance with traditional Armenian laws and customs.

Not long after their settlement in Poland the Armenians had their own church.

The Polish Armenian community prospered culturally and economically, eventually reaching a population of about 200,000.

However, about 500 years after their first arrival in Poland, trouble began to brew in a rising conflict between the Apostolic Church of the Armenians and the Roman Catholic Church of the Poles. The conflict was precipitated mainly through the acts of certain church leaders who sought personal aggrandizement and influence.

The conflict led to a rapid decline of the spiritual well-being of the Armenians, so that about 700 years after their arrival the Armenians had all but lost their religious and political privileges. As a result, their identity as a distinct community in Poland no longer existed as a viable one.

The 700-year presence of an Armenian community in Poland did not disappear without leaving some traces. Armenian influences can still be detected in present-day Polish foods, art, architecture, music, crafts, and family names.

Churches formerly belonging to the Armenian community are now Roman Catholic Polish churches.

There are present-day Polish families that know that their origin is Armenian, though they have altogether lost the use of the Armenian language.

ℰᴑ

EXODUS: Armenian Style
The Aftermath of the Genocide

ubjected to oppression by invading hostile forces, or by internal tyranny, the Armenian people, throughout their history, have been repeatedly persecuted. Along with the consequent death and destruction has come forced dispersion, being driven away relentlessly from their ancestral homelands in the highlands of eastern Anatolia, in the broad regions of Mt. Ararat. They were ruthlessly dispossessed of their property and goods over the centuries, and were forced to abandon their native lands.

Major historical events that led to the exodus are as follows:

With the Seljuk invasion in the eleventh century, Armenians were forced out of their Eastern Highlands (Ani, principally). They moved north of the Black Sea into Europe, and eastward into the former Roman province of Cilicia.

With the continuous persecution by the Ottoman overlords, and the massacres toward the close of the nineteenth century, Armenians began a significant exodus into Europe, the Near East, and the Americas.

With the wholesale slaughter of the 1915 era, Armenians of the western regions of historic Armenia were decimated, and virtually to the last man, woman, and child were annihilated or driven out of their homeland, denuding Armenia of the people that gave it its name, one that it had borne for two and one-half millennia. That action was clearly an attempt to annihilate the race and its culture.

In more recent times, the political and sociological enslavement of the Armenian people under Communism has led to still another exodus.

Genocide, defined as the systematic killing or extermination of a whole people or nation, was perpetrated on the Armenian people and nation, and its vestigial effect has been to create a "nation in dispersion."

Today, Armenians throughout the world number more than they have been at any time previously in their long history. They live in all the important countries of the world. They contribute more than their proportionate share to the well-being of the countries of their abode. And they, themselves, are economically secure.

Let us see where they live today. On the following page, you will find a table that lists approximate population figures based upon a recent report prepared by the Armenian Church.

Armenians Worldwide
(Estimated 1999)

Region	Population	Percentage (%)
Armenia	3,984,000	41.0
Artzakh (Nagorno Karabakh)	221,000	2.3
Australia/New Zealand	39,000	0.4
Canada	90,000	0.9
Europe (excluding Russia)	456,000	4.7
Georgia	400,000	4.1
Middle East	218,000	2.2
Near East (Including Anatolia)	394,000	4.1
Russia (Including Ukraine)	2,578,000	26.5
South America	112,000	1.2
United States	1,200,000	12.4
All Others	20,000	0.2
Total Estimated Population	**9,712,000**	**100.0**

Source: *Armenian Church Ecclesiastical Assembly, 1999*

ဢ

Revival of a Nation in Dispersion

Though they were driven out of their native homelands and cast to the four corners of the world, they carried away with them the memories they cherished and the spirit with which they were endowed. Wherever they finally transplanted their roots they were able to re-create a bit of the motherland and savor its sweet memories.

Settled in new worlds, Armenians formed communities with churches, schools, compatriotic societies, cultural unions, sports clubs, etc. Their lives took on a dual character, one that kept their national heritage alive, and one that became part of the society of their new land of abode.

Armenians Participating in a Local Parade (ca 1919....)

In addition to the organizations and collective activities in which large numbers of the community's members participated, there is also a very important personal activity that played a significant role in recording and preserving the nation's recent history. Dozens of books were written describing the life and times, as well as the locale, of the old-world Armenian communities. Together, these volumes represent an invaluable reference library of knowledge about the life of the Armenian people in their native homeland. Without such a preserved record, knowledge of the recent history of the Armenians would in a short time be dissipated.

These books, in some cases exceeding a thousand pages in size, describe the old-world communities, in each case being dedicated specifically to a single community. Thus, they cover Kharberd, Hiusenik, Arapkir, Malatya, Tigranakert, Van, Tokat, Garin (Erzurum), Erzincan, Moush, Kayseri, Aintab, Marash, and on and on, including many obscure villages.

The books cover the geography, early history, recent history (especially the circumstances under which the Armenians were forced to abandon their homes), families (with their genealogical charts), culture, customs, regional dialects, educational institutions, religious bodies, folk songs and dances, recreational activities, famous sons, etc. Pictured often in the books are household utensils, farm equipment, craft tools, transport vehicles, costumes, etc.

| Vahe Haig | Kevork Sarafian | Hagop Deranian |
| on Kharberd | on Aintab | on Hiusenik |

Most important is the fact that the writers, usually taking on the task on their own, were themselves part of the community they wrote about and therefore knew first hand about what they wrote. Moreover, it has turned out happily that these writers were competent to undertake the task.

Nearly all of these books were orginally written in Armenian. Some of them such as Hagop Deranian's *Hiusenik* and Manoog Dzeron's *Village of Parchanj* have been translated and published in English.

Though dispersed and removed from their indigenous lands, Armenians can find comfort in having this very rich library of reliable and readily available information on the last years in their native homeland.

&

Armenians in America

They came and found what they wanted - Freedom!
    The first clearly documented Armenian to come to America, Khachig
Oskanian, a bright student, was sent to the
United States in 1834 by the American
missionaries to continue his education. He was
one of many young Armenians in
Constantinople who had taken advantage of the
opportunity offered by the Protestant
missionaries to gain an education, a benefit not
easily available to Armenians because of
Turkish restrictions. The missionaries, having
come initially to convert Moslem Turks to
Christianity and finding that to be an impossible
undertaking, had turned to offering Armenians
the chance to go to school, and, incidentally, to
converting them to Protestantism.

The Statue of Liberty
Symbol of Freedom

    Khachig Oskanian lost no time in his quest,
graduating from the College of the City of New York in Journalism, and
making a name for himself.

    Others followed him, mostly through missionary activity, and by 1854
there were about twenty Armenians in America. By 1870 the number had
risen to about seventy, most of them being in New York and Boston.

    Profitable employment opportunities in the wire mills of Worcester,
Massachusetts, attracted many to go there in the ensuing years, and it was
there that the first Armenian churches, both Apostolic and Protestant, were
established in about 1890 when all the Armenians in America numbered
about 2,000.

    During the last decade of the nineteenth century (1890-1899) about 20,000
Armenians came to America impelled by the growing intensity of Turkish
persecution against Armenians. Luckily, immigrants at that time were not
faced with many restrictions.

    In 1898 the Armenian Apostolic churches in America, previously under
the jurisdiction of the Patriarchate of Constantinople, became a separate
diocese.

The second wave of Armenian immigration (1900-1914) was very large, about 50,000, and by the time of the Balkan Wars (1912) in which Turkey was involved, and the outbreak of World War I, when even travel out of Turkey was virtually impossible, there were already about 100,000 Armenians in America.

The third wave of Armenian immigrants, starting after World War I and lasting up until 1924 numbered about 25,000. But new and more restrictive immigration laws in the United States (especially the Johnson-Reed Act setting up quotas) suddenly curtailed the flow of Armenians coming into America down to a trickle. Those who came after world War I until 1924 were mostly orphans, individuals, and chance groupings of people because after the forced marches and massacres, family groups were torn apart and chaos reigned. America had become a meeting-place for the reunion of groups and families that had lost track of one another.

From 1924 to the close of World War II the numbers of Armenians entering the United States were small, mainly because of the quota system in which Armenians who would come from Turkey came under that country's quota.

The McCarren-Walter Immigration Act of 1952 reaffirmed the national quota system, and gave preference to those who had relatives in the United States, or had needed skills.

But the Refugee Relief Act of 1953, the Refugee-Escape Act of 1957, and the World Refugee Year Law of 1960 provided some new easing of immigration restrictions.

The Immigration Act of 1965 provided further easing of restrictions.

A new era with a substantial increase in the number of Armenians entering the United States came about with the continuing unrest and turmoil in the Middle East, mainly in Armenia (Soviet), Iran, Lebanon, and Turkey.

As a result of this world unrest, the Armenian community in America has swollen to very substantial numbers. The recent immigrants, being mostly Armenian speaking, have brought about a revival in Armenian cultural life, displaying new vigor with more Armenian schools, newspapers, cultural societies and activities.

As of 2007, it is estimated that the number of Armenians in all of the Americas is as follows: United States, 1,100,000; Canada, 80,000; and South America, 175,000.

ഈ

Armenians in Worcester

"**W**orcester" and "America;" they were one and the same for thousands of Armenians who came to the United States during the first wave (1880-1900) of immigration. Having landed at Ellis Island in New York and being asked by immigration officials (according to a popular anecdote) where they were going, they gave the answer, "I go America." "But you are already in America," many an official would say. "No, No," would the Armenian reply "I go Ousdr."

Though the first wave entered at New York, Worcester, Massachusetts must be regarded as the earliest Armenian community in America. The following is an account of how that came to be.

An American missionary, Rev. George C. Knapp, stationed in Bitlis had a servent named Garo (Garabed). In about 1867, on returning back home, Rev. Knapp brought along servant Garo, after extracting a written agreement that Garo would continue as servant for two years, and at his previous wages of seventy-five cents a day. The missionary settled in Worcester, near relatives, with Garo at his beck and call. An Irish washerwoman incensed at the "slave labor" wages Garo was getting, finally persuaded the naive Garo to break his agreement and take another job where he could earn three times as much. Garo, who had been worried that breaking his agreement would get him into trouble, finally assented, and with the help of the Irish washerwoman got a job at the large wire mill (later, American Steel-Wire Trust). Elated at his increased pay, Garo wrote letters home exalting the wonderful work opportunities at the "vyre mil." That is the likely story of why the flow of Armenian immigrants to Worcester began.

The American Steel Wire Trust Mill

In 1880, when Melkon Markarian (whose son Krikor later became a prominent tobacconist) left New York for Worcester, he found about ten Armenians there, one of whom was Hagop Seropian, who, to find relief from his respiratory ailment, with his brother became Fresno, California's first Armenian resident (1881). In

1884, the Armenians in Worcester numbered thirty-five; in 1890 over 1,000; in 1910 about 1,600; and in 1920, more than 2,000.

The earliest Armenians in Worcester were of both Apostolic and Protestant persuasion.   Religious services were held jointly in rented or borrowed churches and halls.   Both Apostolic and Protestant clergy were available to fill the people's needs.   In 1889, the two groups separated and arranged for services of their own.   The need for their own church edifices led to their raising funds to fill that need.

The Apostolic community bought land on Laurel Street and built their church, Holy Saviour Armenian Apostolic Church, the first in the western hemisphere.   The church was consecrated on January 18, 1891, being the Feast Day of Nativity and Revelation of Christ (Note: January 6 is the proper date for the Feast Day of Nativity in the Armenian Church.   But until about 1924, the Armenian Church was still using the Julian calendar while the western world was using the Gregorian calendar.   Thus January 6 on the Julian was equivalent to January 18 on the Gregorian.).   The cost of building the church was $9,400 that included the price of the land ($1,275).   Some construction was voluntary.   The basement of the church was the National Library.

Sourp Purgich (Holy Saviour), Worcester, built in 1891

The Protestant Armenian community, during the same period, also built their own church, the Armenian Martyr's Evangelical Church, which was completed by 1893.

With the number of Apostolic churches in America having increased, a first assembly of parish priests and bishop was convened in Worcester on June 17-18, 1901. An Encyclical from the Catholicos, dated July 2, 1898, was read, declaring the establishment of the separate Diocese of the Armenian Church in America. For a time, the Diocesan headquarters remained in Worcester, until 1923, when it moved to New York.

In the early period, especially during the 1880's, the main constituency of the Armenians in Worcester was comprised of young, unmarried men, living together in cramped quarters in rooming houses. Most worked at the wire mill and a few knew English. One, named Azaria, who knew English and worked in the wire mill office as interpreter, selfishly exploited his advantageous position to the detriment of the other workers. In particular, in order to gain his boss's favor, Azaria led the young Armenian workers to believe that by joining the church of their "boss," they would be assured job security. Until this sordid matter was cleared up, many had become apostate, abandoning their mother church.

Armenian Martyr's Evangelical Church, Worcester, built in 1893

Another more serious problem arose in that early period. The Armenians, eager to be secure in their jobs and thus be able to send money back home, were willing to work harder, and for lower wages. That did not sit well with the considerable group of Irish workers, who, in turn, were finding the security of their jobs being threatened. The rising hostility between the two groups grew into virtual warfare between them. It did not help that each of the two groups lived in its own closely-knit region of town, with one region being adjacent to the other. The intensity of the clashes was further enhanced because the Irish believed that all Armenians were Protestants (which, of course, was not the case). The fact that the young men were single, without families, meant that they had little to do outside of their work and that made them ready to engage in those ethnic skirmishes.

That anti-Armenian attitude of the Irish led t o their looking upon

Armenians as Turks, even profaning them as "god-damn Turks."   One Armenian who hardly knew any English, in his wrath, had protested being so insulted. The case had gone to court. The judge had asked the Armenian how he understood what he was being called when he did not know English. The Armenian had answered, through an interpreter, "Any one knows what that means, even I."

But the passage of time, acquiring an education, the ever-increasing population, and the general acculturation has, of course, made the Armenian community of Worcester a prosperous and progressive community that shows high success in keeping its national heritage alive.

ℰ℧

Armenians in Fresno
"They Conquered Discrimination"

Chance brought the first Armenian settler. For his respiratory ailment he was in search of a warm, dry climate to replace the cold and moist climate of Worcester, Massachusetts, where he had settled only a short time earlier. Ailing Hagop Seropian, accompanied by his younger brother Garabed, arrived in Fresno in the fall of 1881.

The Fresno climate reminded him of the Armenian heartlands with the warm sun rising over the mountains to the east. The brothers were joined later by three younger brothers, and they engaged in the packing of figs and raisins.

More Armenian families came to Fresno, some directly from old Armenia, eager to be where there were "boat-sized" watermelons, "egg-sized" grapes, and "nine or ten-pound eggplants."

They soon made their presence felt in the county's agriculture and economy.

By 1906 the number of Armenians in Fresno was about 2,500, and together they farmed about 13,000 acres of land.

The Seropian Brothers Packing Shed (ca 1897)

The Armenians paced the Fresno economy as it grew more vigorous. They helped transform the packing industry so that it became the important link that it is between the growing of the area produce and the selling of it to the consumer.

The prosperous years of the early "twenties" saw the number of Armenians in Fresno at a peak. But the decline of the local agricultural economy at the end of the decade became the signal for a distinct exodus. Many Armenians moved to the Los Angeles area, there to engage in pursuits other than agriculture.

But the "twenties" saw the peaking of another phase of their existence in Fresno. Their presence in Fresno was strongly evident not only in their contribution to the area economy, but also in their sheer numbers. At the time they were more than ten percent of Fresno's total population. Many of the remainder of the population mistook Armenian traits of thrift for avarice, industriousness for aggres-siveness, gregariousness for segregationism, ambition for obduracy, shrewdness for guile, and tenacity for obstinacy.

First Armenian Presbyterian
Church (ca. 1901)

As a result, the Armenian became the object of irrational prejudices. He felt the sharp pain of discrimination. He was denied normal rights and privileges. His children grew up in a tense environment, unable to understand why they should bear the indignity of intolerance.

But times did change. The onset of national and universal economic stress of the early "thirties," followed by a world-wide war, broadened the social understanding of people.

More importantly, the Armenians themselves, undaunted by the malice shown toward them, lifted themselves by their bootstraps to better themselves in all ways. Without seeking help from any front they brought about tran-sition.

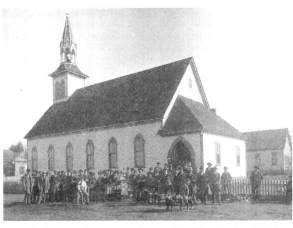

Holy Trinity Armenian Apostolic Church (ca. 1900)

Today, the social air is different. The Armenians of Fresno live there as a natural part of the commu-nity, without overt prejudice toward their rich cultural heritage. They are able to carry their full share of the community's life, and at the same time enrich the community by sharing their heritage.

෴

Chapter 3

MYTHOLOGY
AND
FOLKLORE

Anahit, Goddess of Nature and Family

Armenian Mythology

$\mathfrak{T}$he pre-Christian religion of the Armenian people was based on the worship of gods and goddesses, of whom there were many, forming a substantial Pantheon.

Temples dedicated to each of these gods and goddesses became sites for festive religious celebrations on the designated feast days. Great crowds would assemble, along with the members of their royal households. These very popular celebrations were marked by competitive sports. Enormous tabernacles were erected in fields and decorated with flowers and banners. These occasions were the most joyous times for the people.

When Christianity was replacing the pagan faith of the Armenians, it was necessary to displace both the pagan temples and the pagan worship with Christian churches and Christian worship. Temples could be destroyed (and they were) and replaced by churches. But replacing popular pagan practices was more difficult. In general, feast days of the pagan era were given a Christian meaning to erase the pagan meaning. But many pagan practices seeped through, and can today be recognized in some of the customs associated with the great present-day Christian church feasts.

When in 1958 the main altar at Holy Echmiadzin was to be replaced by a much heavier marble altar, it was deemed necessary to reinforce the foundation on which the new altar would be placed. Excavations made under the bema disclosed an ancient fire-pot, believed to have been the central point of worship in a pagan temple. Visitors to Echmiadzin can go beneath the altar bema to see that important relic of Armenian pagan times.

The gods and goddesses of the Armenian Pantheon can be equated to comparable deities in the Roman, Greek and Persian Pantheons. The table on the following page, with some approximations, shows the equivalences.

A word commonly used in Armenian to refer to gods and goddesses is to add the sound of the negative, "ch," as a prefix to the word for god, "Asdvadz." Thus the resulting new word becomes "chasdvadz," literally "non-god."

Pantheon of Gods and Goddesses
(Equivalences)

Armenian	Roman	Greek	Persian	Meaning
Aramazd	Jupiter	Zeus	Ormizd/ Ahura-Mazda	Omnipotence/ Air
Mihr	Vulcan	Hephaestos	Mitro	Sun & Fire/Art
Barshamin	Juno	Hera		Heaven/Mirth
Vahagn	Mars	Hercules/ Ares	Veretranga	War
Anahit	Diana	Artemis	Nahit	Nature/Family
Astghik	Venus	Aphrodite		Love & Beauty
Nané	Minerva	Athena		Heaven/ Wisdom
Tir	Mercury	Apollo/ Hermes	Tir	Rain/ Knowledge

These seven gods and goddesses (corresponding in number to the classical Pantheons), plus the Armenian eighth god Vahagn comprise the principal Armenian deities. Of course, there were many lesser deities, as well as spirits, monsters, dragons (vishaps), devs (devils), and other creatures, mostly of the nether world, that make up the collection of mythical creatures in Armenian folklore.

ℰℭ

Armenian Folklore
(Popular Tales, Legends, and Epics)

$\mathfrak{J}$t is an inherent quality in all peoples to have engendered a plethora of legends and beliefs concerning their origin and epic events in their history. Together these traditions form a vast body of folklore, which is an adornment of true history. What is significant is that each people's folklore bears the stamp of the character of the people.

What may be more significant is that an unreal event or myth that a people believe to be true, and hold dear, may be more influential in guiding their behavior than a real event which that people disclaim or repudiate.

Armenians are no exception. The vast body of their "oral history," handed down over countless generations, now exists in writing, as authors throughout the ages (from the fifth century to today) have chosen to record what had reached their ears.

By far, the main Armenian source for these ancient tales, legends, and epics, in large number, is Khorenatsi's *History of the Armenians*. Some authors of the classical period chose to record essentially only one major epic, and in detail. For example: Elisaeus (Yeghishe) and Lazar of Pharbe (Ghazar Parbetsi) have given a definitive account of the Vardanants Wars of the Armenians against the Persians. Koriun, Mesrop Mashtots' pupil, has written of his mentor's search for an Armenian Alphabet. Agathangelos has revealed the life of St. Gregory the Enlightener and the Christianization of Armenia.

In modern times the very popular and much loved prolific poet Hovhannes Toumanian has set down (at the turn of the century), nearly always in poetical form, legends and popular tales. Included in his tremendous output is his rendering of the major epic of David of Sasoun, as have a dozen or more other writers before and after him. Each of these authors set down the epic story of David of Sasoun (or the complete saga of four cycles of the revolutionary and freedom-loving people of Sasoun) as he heard the epic related. In most cases it has been possible to determine what the oral source was of each author's written account, that is, who the "teller of the tale" was.

The principal characters in epics are usually heroes, and their exploits in legend are heroic. But Armenian folklore also has its evil beings.

Heroic figures in folklore are often the source of names that are in popular use among the people. Examples out of Armenian folklore are, for men, Haik (the eponym of Armenians), Ara, Aramayis, Armen, Vahagn, Mihran, Tiran. For women: Astghik, Arousiak, Anahit, Hripsime, Gayane, Shoghakat.

In Armenia, as it was in most early cultures, there was not always a clear distinction between gods and mortals. In fact, in some legends a god has changed into a mortal, and conversely. Also, gods and goddesses had children. It was even so that a child was born of the union of a god and a mortal.

It was through popular belief that a mortal would become transformed into a god, an easy transition in the pagan mind. In modern thinking, such a transition would be to go from reality to myth.

An example is found in the legend concerning Artavazd. The legend is as told by Khorenatsi, essentially. When the much-loved King Artashes of Armenia died, many people were killed, or killed themselves, as was a pagan custom. His son, Artvazd, was wrathful for his father's having left him the land so desolate of people, and complained bitterly. In turn, his father (out of his death) cursed Artavazd, damning him to imprisonment in a cave, and bound in iron chains. Thus, Artavazd is popularly believed to still be confined in the cave. His two dogs continually gnaw at the chains to set their master free. But it was a custom for blacksmiths to strike their anvils a few times at the beginning of each week to re-strengthen the chains so that Artavazd would not go free and destroy the world.

౸

Yervand Kochar's Statue of
David of Sasoun - Yerevan, Republic of Armenia

David of Sasoun

With Jelali, his trusty steed
*   His armor and his lightning sword,*
David of Sasoun stands aloof
*   To slay the oncoming horde.*

So fearless, so courageous ...
*   So resolute is he,*
That all who come to face him
*   To this, they all agree.*

As the son of Lion Meher,
*   Under Ohan's guiding hand,*
David protects the livestock,
*   His people and his land.*   (Continued Next Page)

Thus, one day as fate decrees
        Melik and his horde arrive;
From Egypt, they descend
        To conquer and deprive.

With Jelali, his trusty steed,
        His armor and his lightning sword
David of Sasoun rides to Melik
        To attack the oncoming horde.

The fighting is fast and very fierce;
        He slays from left to right;
But Melik can't be found
        On that horrendous night.

Then someone shouts, "Why fight us?
        Your enemy lies there!
Within that tent asleep!
        Go slay him, if you dare!"

David calls to Melik,
        "Wake up and meet your fate."
And Melik calls to David,
        "Come in, let us debate."

As David enters Melik's tent,
        He falls into a pit;
But the Patroness of Sasoun
        Helps David to outwit.

Then Misra-Melik strikes a blow;
        A vicious dual begins.
But in the end with his mighty sword
        David of Sasoun wins.

With Jelali, his trusty steed,
        His armor and his lightening sword
David of Sasoun triumphs
        Over Melik and his horde.

ᔥ

96

David of Sasoun

℧he epic tale of David of Sasoun is the foremost and most-loved in Armenian folklore. It is the third of four cycles, separate sequential tales that have been joined together portraying the spirit of the people of Sasoun, a region located in the highlands of Armenia, west of Lake Van.

This poetic story pictures David as a person. But, in truth, he is the personification of all the people of Sasoun -- courageous, fearless, resolute, devout, and uncomplicated.

David's tale, transcribed metrically as well as in prose by many authors, relates to events in the 9th century when Arabs from the southwest tried to enslave the people of Armenia, exacting tribute. The people of Sasoun, however, resolutely resisted these efforts.

David's cycle begins with his birth which occurs in answer to his father's (Lion Meher of the second cycle) prayer for an heir to succeed him as ruler of Sasoun.

David grows big and strong under the care of his uncle, big-voiced "Tzenov"Ohan. When Misra-Melik (literally, Egypt's King) learns of Meher's death, he sends lieutenants to force the people of Sasoun to pass beneath swords to show submission, and also to collect gold and take slaves.

Even as a young boy, David refuses to submit. He then routs the would-be conquerors.

To keep him occupied, the elders give David the task of grazing the domestic animals of Sasoun. At each day's end, with his mighty call, David rounds them up, chasing them all over the hills. But so commanding is his call that the wild animals also submit to him. David drives them all into Sasoun where the people are frightened by the presence of the wild animals.

Tzenov Ohan gives David his father's horse (Jelali), his armor, and his Lightning Sword (Tur Gedzagin).

One day, all of Sasoun is surprised to find the stream that supplies their water has dried up. Tzenov Ohan goes to the hilltop to see what the problem is. To his dismay, he finds Misra-Melik's encamped army. So enormous are its numbers that the stream has been drunk dry.

Firebrand David, on learning of the Egyptian army's readiness to attack, rides Jelali in the early dawn to confront the army. He proclaims, *"If you are asleep, awaken! If you are awake, put on your clothes! If you are clothed, take up your arms! If you are armed, mount your horses! Do not let anyone claim that David came stealthily during the night and attacked."*

The fighting begins and rages fiercely. David slays left and right. A grey-haired swordsman pleads with David, *"Why are you fighting us? We are not your enemy. Your enemy lies over there, asleep in his tent."*

David rides to the tent and insists on awakening Misra-Melik from his seven-day sleep in order to confront him in battle. The guards awaken Melik from his deep sleep only by prodding him with a red-hot plowshare.

"O, David, come in. Let us talk," says Melik.   But as David steps on the carpet lying in front of Melik's throne, he falls into a deep pit - a trap that has been set for him. The pit is then covered with a heavy millstone.

In a dream, Tzenov Ohan senses David's plight. He rides quickly to the battlefield and shouts for David, entreating him from wherever he is to call on the Madonna, patroness of Sasoun, for help. David hears his uncle, complies with his request, and miraculously leaps out of the pit sending shattered pieces of the millstone flying up into the sky.

"My turn, first to strike," claims Melik. David, compliant, takes his stand in the field with his shield. The first blow is mighty, but David is unhurt. The second is even more powerful, but to no avail.   To gain more momentum, Melik rides his horse all the way from Egypt for a stupendous strike. The whole earth shudders, and the raised dust blocks out the Sun taking a week to settle. David cries out, *"I am still here. Now it is my turn!"*

But Melik's mother and then his sister plead for David to give up a turn for their sake. David nobly obliges.

Melik takes refuge at the bottom of a deep pit covered by forty millstones and forty hides of oxen. David rides his horse, Jelali, and with his Tur Gedzagin strikes his blow -- through the hides -- through the millstones, and through Melik.

"I am still here!" cries out Melik. David is astonished. He yells, *"Melik! Shake yourself!"*

When Melik shakes himself, to his horror, he breaks apart and falls into two pieces - one here and one there.

Chapter 4

CHRISTIANITY
AND
THE CHURCH

St. Gregory, The Enlightener

The Christianization of Armenia

$\mathbb{T}$he Armenian people, as a nation, embraced Christianity at the turn from the third to the fourth centuries. The sequence of dramatic events that led to the conversion, stand out very prominently in the people's history. Those events hold a very dear place in the heart of every Armenian, and their character has taken on the adornment and gloss of popular tradition and belief.

This is the story in its simplest form.

It was the middle of the third century. Armenia was ruled by the much-loved King Khosrov, of the Arsacid dynasty. The more powerful neighboring Persia was ruled by another branch of that dynasty. But Armenia, a border-buffer state, was being sought after as a prize by both Persia to the south and Rome to the west.

To gain an advantage, Anak, a ranking prince of the Persian royal household, slew Khosrov. Loyal followers of Khosrov, in turn, sought out and killed Anak. Khosrov had an infant son named Tiridates (Trdat), also a young daughter Khosrovidoukht (literally Khosrov's daughter). Anak had an infant son who would later be named Gregory.

Tiridates (Trdat)   Khosrovidoukht

The Roman royal family took Armenian heir-apparent Tiridates into its household to prepare him for the day when he would assume his rightful place. Gregory was kept by members of his family.

Armenia was thus reduced to a feudal state.

Tiridates grew into maturity in the pagan faith of the Romans.

Gregory grew into maturity in Christian centers, especially Caesarea.

When the time was right (probably in the year 301 A.D.), Rome seated Tiridates on the then empty throne of his popular father to serve as king and bring Armenia into the Roman sphere of influence.

Soon thereafter, Tiridates became aware of the existence of a highly learned member of his lineage named Gregory. In order to benefit by his knowledge, Tiridates appointed him secretary of the court.

It was the festival of the goddess Anahit. It seemed as though all of Armenia joined in the festivities. But in truth, not all partook because many were secretly Christian and as such would not worship that false deity.

The Interior Dungeon Walls of
Khor Virap ("Deep Pit")

Gregory, a devout Christian and in keeping with his faith, refused to participate in the pagan festival. In his rage, Tiridates had Gregory thrown into the "Deep Pit" (Khor Virap) which was inhabited by asps and scorpians, intending that banishment to be mortal punishment.

Some time later, a group of Christian maidens from Rome, under the leadership of abbess Gayane, escaping the unwanted attention of Emperor Diocletian, sought refuge in Armenia. One of the maidens named Hripsime was of rare beauty, and Tiridates sought her for his queen. When she refused his offer, Tiridates had all of the maidens (35 in number) put to death.

At about that same time, Tiridates lost his sanity. (Some say that it was as a consequence of the crime he had committed, and that he went about on all fours grunting like a hog.) No cure could be found to restore the king's sanity.

Christian followers of Gregory (who immediately after the banishment must have taken him from the "Deep Pit" and kept him in hiding waiting for the appropriate moment), brought him before the king. (Some say it was fourteen years after the banishment.)

The shock of discovering that Gregory was still alive cured Tiridates, who saw it as a miracle and recognized in it the revelation of the power and goodness of the new faith of Christianity.

Gold Cross at Echmiadzin
(Symbol of the New Faith)
Work of B. Arzoumanian and J. Chouloyan (1979)

King Tiridates III embraced the faith and declared it for his entire nation. (The date is usually taken to be 301 A.D.)

Thus, Armenia was the first of all nations to embrace Christianity as its state religion.

℘

St. Gayane Church (630 A.D.)

Hripsime and the Gayanian Maidens

⑥ne of the most loved, and even revered, traditions of the Armenian
people is that of the Christian maiden Hripsime and her companions
under the leadership of Gayane, and their role in the Christianization of
Tiridates III.

The prime sources of the details of this tradition are the writings of the
fifth century authors Agathangelos and Khorenatsi. In his monumental
work "Azgapatoum" (National History) Archbishop Ormanian has compiled
extensive references to this tradition. As a secondary source it is clearly the
most complete and easily used reference.

It appears that all non-Armenian references to this tradition go back to
Armenian sources only.

The Armenian Church has elevated Hripsime and her companions to
sainthood. Foreign churches defer to the Armenian tradition and recognize
St. Hripsime, St. Gayane, and their sanctified companions.

The tradition in its simplest form is the following.

Living in Rome was a group of Christian nuns, Gayane being their head.
In the group was the beautiful Hripsime.

Emperor Diocletian of the Roman Empire (c. 300 A.D.) sought to take as
wife the most beautiful woman in the Empire. It was found that the most

beautiful was Hripsime, who was of royal birth. Diocletian was smitten by her ravishing beauty, as shown by her picture. The Emperor would have her brought to the palace, to marry her at once.

But, unwilling to submit to the pagan monarch, Hripsime wanted to flee from Rome. To support her, Gayane and more than seventy of the Christian nuns together fled from Rome.

They arrived in Armenia by way of Alexandria, Jerusalem, and Edessa. In Armenia they reached Van, and after spending some time on Mt. Varag nearby, they reached Vagharshapat, the capital city. Their presence there became revealed to Tiridates, through word that reached him from Diocletian.

While on the Varag Mountain the maidens earned their livelihood by making and selling glass beads and jewelry. It is also believed that they had brought with them a valuable Christian relic, a fragment of the true Cross, which had been kept in a cave on Mt. Varag. That belief led to the miracle of the Cross of Varag.

The tradition continues that Tiridates, in his turn, lusted after Hripsime. When his invitation for her to come to him in honor was rejected, he had the maidens brought before him by force. Their continued refusal to yield to him enraged Tiridates, and he had them all put to death.

As a result of his brutal act Tiridates lost his reason.

Here, then, the stage is set for the rest of the tradition concerning Tiridates' conversion to Christianity. No cure being found for his ailment, his sister, Khosrovidoukht, secretly a Christian, brought Gregory before Tiridates. The king, in shock for seeing Gregory alive after fourteen years of banishment in Khor Virap (Deep Pit), was cured. Recognizing the miracle of the cure brought about the king's conversion.

The number of maidens killed is usually put at 35, according to tradition, but more had fled from Rome. Other traditions tell about what happened to the others.

Serious scholars of church history recognize the beauty in this tradition and the satisfaction the knowledge of it provides the faithful. However, the absence of any corroborative information from outside primary sources and certain impracticalities of some of the details, raise questions about the tradition.

Notwithstanding, the tradition of Hripsime and her companions remains a cherished belief in the minds of the Armenian faithful.

Khor Virap
(Deep Pit)

$\textbf{O}$nce a dungeon, a facility for the execution of a royal sentence of death, Khor Virap today is a highly venerated Christian pilgrimage site. Pilgrims come from the far corners of the world to visit this much-revered, sacred shrine, and experience a personal communion with their patron saint, St. Gregory the Enlightener.

Khor Virap, a half-hour's drive from Yerevan, near the site of the ancient Armenian capital Artashat, and virtually in the shadow of Mt. Ararat, is a pit carved into a stone promontory facing south toward the eternal mountain. The pit is circular, nearly 15 feet in diameter and about 20 feet deep. Today, a steel ladder fixed against the pit wall enables pilgrims to descend to the flat, stone floor. Cut into one part of the pit wall is an altar, affixed with religious votaries.

The site complex consists of a fortress-type wall containing cubicles, and surrounding a courtyard. Inside the courtyard is a small church. A tiny chapel is built over the entrance to the Deep Pit. The entire site once served as a monastery. Today, regular church services are held there. It also serves as a place where the devout can make an offering with a sacrifical lamb or fowl.

Khor Virap occupies a central place in the story of the Christianization of Armenia. It was into that Deep Pit that King Tiridates III in 287 A.D. banished St. Gregory the Enlightener, who as a Christian had refused to honor and venerate the pagan goddess whose feast was being celebrated.

The Church at Khor Virap (Deep Pit)

That banishment was tantamount to a sentence of death, because, as tradition has it, the Pit was inhabited by poisonous snakes and scorpions. But tradition has it further that St. Gregory survived in the Pit for 14 years, - had he been secretly removed and kept in hiding until some propitious moment, by other Christians? - was taken out and brought before the King. The King, in shock at seeing St. Gregory, was instantly cured of a severe, incurable ailment that had persisted. The miracle of St. Gregory's survival and Tiridates' cure brought about the King's conversion to Christianity.

ଛୀ

Echmiadzin

Son of God descending ....
With Golden Hammer in hand;
Striking ground - commanding
A church be built to stand.

St. Gregory could not ignore
A vision so profound,
And heeding Christ's command
Built a Church on that Hallowed Ground.

Echmiadzin, he called it .....
And he made it the Holy See;
Where the Catholicos of All Armenians
And the "Mayr Ator" would be.

And as the beacon of our Christian Faith,
Its light spread across the land;
Giving to all Armenians,
A spiritual helping hand.

From its simple and modest beginnings,
In the time of Trdat's reign;
The church was modified, embellished,
Destroyed and built again.

Beneath its arched and vaulted roof
The "Ijman Seghan" stands,
Showing all where His hammer struck
As He issued His commands.

Such stories could its walls recount
Of pagan and of darker days,
Of liturgies and sharakans ...
Of priests and deacons giving praise.

Today, there it stands as the symbol
Of Armenia's Christian past;
Proclaiming with its melodic bells,
The strength of a faith that will last.

৪৩

Echmiadzin

Echmiadzin

Էջ միածինն ՚ի ՀօրԷ՛ եւ լոյս փառաց ընդ նմա
"The Only-Begotten One Descended from the Father ..."

In the Armenian faith, it was the miracle of St. Gregory's (the Enlightener, "Sourb Grigor Lusavorich") that brought about the conversion of Tiridates III, King of Armenia, to Christianity, and with it the nation. After the King had embraced the faith, St. Gregory, who became the head of the Church, had a vision. In it, Christ was seen to descend from Heaven and strike the ground with a golden hammer, directing Gregory to build a church on that site, which he proceeded to do.

Based on this tradition, the name of the church became "Echmiadzin," meaning "the Only-Begotten One Descended." As the Holy See of the Armenian Church, the Cathedral, or Mother Church, it serves as the sanctuary of the center of hierarchical authority in the Armenian Church, and where the Supreme Patriarch, Catholicos of All Armenians resides. In Armenian: "Mayr Ator, Srbo Echmiadzni."

Within the cathedral, approximately central in the nave, is a separate altar known as "Ijman Seghan" (Altar of Descent), marking the traditional spot of Christ's descent in Gregory's vision.

As recently as 1958, when the main altar was to be replaced with a heavier, marble altar, and it was determined that a firmer foundation would be needed, excavation beneath the bema (raised altar platform) disclosed a previously buried relic believed to be the vestige fire-pot of a pagan temple. It is thus generally accepted that Echmiadzin was built to replace a pagan temple, which was razed.

Pagan Fire Pit Beneath the Altar

What would the original structure have been as built at the start of the fourth century?

Virtually nothing is known about that. What is known is that it probably had a roof built of timber, had no dome, and certainly no belfries.

---

* "Echmiadzinn I Hore ..." opening words of a sharakan (hymn), from the liturgy of the Armenian Church.

The structure had undergone numerous changes over the centuries, making use of masonry exclusively, adding apses, dome, porch, and belfries. It was not until the seventeenth century that the appearance resembled what shows today.

With the observation of the 1700th anniversary (in the year 2001) of the establishment of Christianity in Armenia, and with the Armenian claim that it was the first nation to embrace the Christian faith, it may be proper to assert that Echmiadzin is the first publicly built house of Christian worship in all history.

The rear facade of Echmiadzin Cathedral

The much-loved traditions surrounding the Christianization of Armenia include a part concerning Tiridates III. In popular belief, the king himself, personally joining the masons and laborers, bore heavy blocks of stone on his back in the actual construction of the edifice.

℘

The Doctrinal Position of the Armenian Church

In 325 A.D., shortly after Roman Emperor Constantine in his "Edict of Milan" (312 A.D.) declared that Christianity could be worshipped freely in the Roman Empire, he convened a council of church leaders. The purpose of the council, at Nicaea (today's Iznik, near Istanbul), was to prepare a clear, formal statement of what the new faith of Christianity was comprised.

Church leaders from all over Christendom attended.   Representing Armenia was Aristakes, older son of St. Gregory the Enlightener.

The council, now known as the First Ecumenical Council prepared the text defining the faith.   It is a very fundamental statement, "The Nicene Creed."   The Armenian name for it is "Hanganak Nikioy," or, popularly, the "Havatamk" (We Believe).

In arriving at the Creed the Council rejected a heretical concept being promoted by a church leader named Arius.   He declared that Christ was "created out of nothingness," and was only similar to God.   The Nicene Creed declares that Christ is "con-substantial" with God.

Հ ՍԻՍՍԱՄՔ Ի ՄԻ
Աստուած Հայր ա_
մենակալ, յարարիչն երկ_
նի և երկրի, երևելեաց
և աններևութից։

Եւ ի մի Տէր Յիսուս
Քրիստոս յորդին Աստու_
ծոյ, ծնեալն յԱստուծոյ
Հօրէ` միածին. այսինքն
յէութենէ Հօր։

*W*e believe in one God, the Father almighty, maker of heaven and earth, of things visible and invisible.

---

*A*nd in one Lord Jesus Christ, Son of God, begotten of God the Father, only-begotten, that is of the substance of the Father... .

The First and Second Passages of the Nicene Creed in Armenian

The First and Second Passages of the Nicene Creed in English

113

A Second Ecumenical Council, convened in Constantinople (381), rejected a modified form of Arianism, the heresy of Arius. Armenians attended.

A Third Ecumenical Council, convened in Ephesus (431), rejected a new heresy, that of Nestorius, who maintained that the divine Christ came to dwell in man (the Christ child), and that the Virgin Mary was not a "God-Bearer" ("Astvadzadzin," in Armenian). Armenians attended this Council and confirmed the rejection of the Nestorian heresy.

The Fourth Ecumenical Council was convened at Chalcedon (today's Kadikoy, near Istanbul), in 451. Armenians did not, and could not, attend, because they were busy at war defending their faith of Christianity at Avarayr, under the command of Vardan Mamikonian. The Council concerned itself with still another heresy, a concept proclaimed by Eutyches that Christ was a divine being and only appeared as man (one nature, or monophysite). In rejecting that heresy the Council declared that Christ was both divine and human (God and Man), both natures being blended into one person. This declaration by the Council is called the Chalcedonian formula, or the dyophysite nature of Christ.

However, the Council of Chalcedon also concerned itself with ugly jurisdictional disputes between the five regional Patriarchs (at Rome, Constantinople, Jerusalem, Antioch, and Alexandria), and their relative hegemony.

Displeased with that unchristianlike behavior at Chalcedon, Armenian church leaders in their own Council of Dvin (506) rejected Chalcedon. In doing so, the Armenians distanced themselves and their Church from the "One World of Christendom," and declared their Church to be an independent national church (the first nation to do so).

Other churches regarded the Armenian rejection of the Chalcedonian formula as a sign that Armenians accepted the Eutychean heresy, and therefore that their faith accepted the Monophysite doctrine. That perception of the Armenians by the rest of the world has had far-reaching effects. When Mehmet II took Constantinople and set up the Ottoman Empire, he divided his Christian subjects (being far greater in number than his Moslem subjects) into two bodies - the "ortodoks" millet (dyophysite sects) and the "Ermeni" millet (the monophysite sects, mainly Armenians, but including the Copts of Egypt, the Abyssinians, the Syrian Jacobites, and the Malabar Christians of India).

The fact of the matter is that the Armenian Church and its doctrine is dyophysite (not Monophysite), and the texts of the Armenian liturgies make that amply clear.

℘

The Holy See
(Its Peregrinations - Locations and Relocations)

he Holy See of the Armenian Church is the Cathedral. It is where the Catholicos-Patriarch of All Armenians sits in his hierarchical authority. It is called the "Throne of St. Gregory the Enlightener." It is where the Church keeps the relic that identifies and authenticates that hierarchical authority, which relic is the jewel encrusted gold and silver likeness of the hand and forearm of St. Gregory the Enlightener, believed to contain actual bones of his hand.

In the past, it was appropriate that the Holy See be physically wherever the center of civil authority was. If there was, in fact, a King of Armenia in authority, or sovereign, his site (whether it was a city, fortress or palace) would mark the center of civil authority. Then, that is where the Holy See would be. Throughout the centuries, since the establishment of Christianity in Armenia - from its earliest date (ca. 301 A.D.), that arrangement did in fact prevail.

It was as though the sovereign had an advisory council, a cabinet, and the Catholicos-Patriarch was his Minister of Religion.

But the fortunes of Armenian civil authority throughout its history were changeable, both in the level of sovereignty and in geographical location. Hence, the Holy See would change its geographical locations accordingly.

However, sometimes, due to political circumstances, it was not clear where that civil authority was, or if it existed at all. In such circumstances, the history of the movements or the peregrinations, of the

Right Hand of
St. Gregory the Enlightener
Relic From Echmiadzin
Sign of Patriarchal Authority

Holy See shows that it waited out the events until they became clear.

Thus, a study of the relocations of the Holy See, starting and returning to Echmiadzin, reflects the history of the Armenian nation.

Below is a table that displays the movements. Please note that the numbers after the names of the Catholicoi refer to their successive positions, according to Ormanian.

Dates shown are not universally agreed to. The total time of the wanderings of the Holy See is 513 years.

Peregrinations of the Holy See
(Locations and Relocations)

Place	Vicinity	Start	Length of Time	Catholicoi	No	Civil Ruler
Echmiadzin	Yerevan	A.D. 301	183	Gregory I	1	Tiridates III
Dvin	Yerevan	484	444	Hovhannes I	15	Persian
Tsoravank	Van	928	3	Hovhannes V	50	Ashot
Aghtamar	Van	931	13	Stephanos II	51	Gagik
Argina	Ani	944	48	Anania I	54	Abas
Ani		992	58	Sargis I	58	Gagik I
Sebastia	Sivas	1051	6	Petros I	59	Abussalah
Tavblour	Malatya	1057	8	Khachik II	60	Abussalah
Tzamndav	Amasia	1065	40	Grigor II	61	Abussalah
Shoughr	Cilicia	1105	20	Barsegh I	62	Toros I
Dzovk	Cilicia	1125	22	Grigor III	63	Toros I
Hromkla	Cilicia	1147	136	Grigor III	63	Toros II
Sis	Cilicia	1283	158	Grigor VII	73	Leon II
Echmiadzin	Yerevan	1441	557+	Kirakos I	88	

℘

The Four Hierarchical Centers
of the Armenian Church

The Armenian Church, as it is formally known in English, is an independent national church. The formal name in Armenian is "Hayastanyayts Ekeghetsi," translating strictly into "Church of the People of Armenia."

The Armenian Church also has several descriptors, sometimes used with the name: "One, Holy, Apostolic, Orthodox, and Universal (Catholic)," in Armenian, "Mek," "Sourb," "Arakelakan," "Oughghapar," and "Unthanrakan."

The two terms, One and Universal, imply that the Church has a single, monolithic structure. It is often said that the Church and its people are "One Flock and One Shepherd" ("Mek Hot ou Mek Hoviv"). As such, it should enjoy a hierarchical structure with one head, extending in echelons down to the entire flock of the faithful, the people.

Yet, the Armenian Church has four hierarchical thrones, each with an occupant with definite autonomous rights and privileges. There are two Catholicoi and two Patriarchs. (There was time when there were three concurrent Catholicoi.) Why this is so has its roots deeply implanted in historical events of world-wide scope, with many being outside of Armenian control.

The four hierarchical heads of the Armenian Church are the following.

- Catholicos of All Armenians, Echmiadzin, Armenia

- Catholicos of the Great House of Cilicia, Antelias, Lebanon

- Patriarch of Jerusalem, Jerusalem

- Patriarch of Constantinople, Istanbul

A. <u>Catholicos of All Armenians</u>: The Catholicate was founded at the present site in the year 301 AD by St. Gregory the Enlightener and King Tiridates III. In order for the Catholicate to be where the civil authority was, the Catholicate moved about from the year 484 to 1441 at which time it returned to Echmiadzin.

A. Echmiadzin

B. Antelias

C. Jerusalem

D. Constantinople (Istanbul)

B.   Catholicos of the Great House of Cilicia: With the return of the Catholicate to Echmiadzin in 1441, and the ensuing conflict and uncertainty of authority, a counter-Catholicate was established at Sis (in Cilician Armenia), which later (1930) moved to Antelias, Lebanon.

For centuries there was continuing conflict between the Great House of Cilicia and Echmiadzin regarding respective regions of jurisdiction. But with the Great House of Cilicia having played an effective role in redeeming the remnant Armenians of Syria, Lebanon, and Cyprus after the dislocations resulting from the 1915 massacres it was agreed that the Great House of Cilicia would have jurisdiction over the dioceses of just those countries.

However, as a result of further conflicts precipitated by the assassination of Archbishop Ghevond Tourian, in New York in 1933, some other dioceses have come under the jurisdiction of the Great House of Cilicia.

C. Patriarch of Jerusalem: Having established a strong presence in the holy places around Jerusalem beginning early in the fourth century as a result of trade and pilgrimages to the holy land, Armenians continued to increase their influence there. Their rights and privileges, confirmed by a series of decrees by the Sultans, established their position shared equally with the

Roman Catholic and Eastern Orthodox Churches. One corner of the old walled city of Jerusalem is the Armenian Quarter.

D.   Patriarch of Constantinople: When in 1461 Mehmet II divided the Christians in the Ottoman Empire into two millets (peoples forming nations within a nation) the "Ermeni" millet was to have a Patriarch serving as the civil as well as the religious head of the millet, governed by its own laws, but compatible with the laws of the Empire.

Most of the world's Armenians during the 19th century were within the Ottoman Empire. Thus, they came under the authority of the Patriarch of Constantinople, and as a result he was more influential in the lives and affairs of Armenians than the Catholicos of All Armenians.

ℰᗡ

Varag Monastary (ca. 1907)

Ruins of Varag Monastary (1994)

The Monastery of Varag
(Varaga Vank)

℟he annals of the Armenian Church tell of a unique and miraculous event that took place on Mt. Varag. That event gave rise to a special feast day which is regularly observed but only in the Armenian Church. The miracle is recorded as follows:

St. Hripsime and her companion maidens under the leadership of their abbess, St. Gayane, who had fled Rome because of persecution and unwanted attention by Emperor Diocletian, had found refuge on Mt. Varag in Armenia (ca. 300 A.D.). They had brought with them a relic (fragment) of the True Cross, which was believed to have remained concealed there.

In 653 A.D., long after the martyrdom of the Christian maidens, the hermit, Todik, believing that the relic must still be there on Mt. Varag, prayed for its presence to be revealed.

One day, together with his pupil, Hovel (Joel), they heard sounds. A light shone from a rock. Around the light, there arose twelve columns of light, and fragrance filled the air. Heavenly music lasted all day, and at the close of day, a cross rose from the stone and entered the chapel that had been built there, and rested on the altar.

The vision of the Cross and the luminous columns lasted for twelve days. People from near and far including members of the royal household and churchmen came to view the miracle.

Catholicos Nerses the Builder (Pontiff 642-661 A.D.) confirmed the miraculous event. Chapels were built at each of the twelve luminous columns, and the chapel where the Cross had come to rest was enlarged into a church and monastery complex (Varaga Vank).

A church feast day, "Cross of Varag" was declared to be observed on the Sunday occurring September 25 to October 1, the second Sunday after the Exaltation of the Cross.

The site of Varaga Vank is about ten miles to the southeast of Van. The monastery, no longer in use since the times of the great deportations of 1915, in partial ruin, lies in the center of a tiny village of Kurds. Because the church had seven sanctuaries built together in one complex, the present-day name of the village is Yedikilise, meaning "seven churches." The several standing chambers of the complex now serve mainly as storage rooms for the present population.

Travelers who go to the area of Van would do well to visit the village of

Yedikilise and enter what remains of the monastery. Its front has a very characteristic design of three pointed masonry arches side by side. Flanking the left side of the sanctuary entrance on the exterior wall is a row of carved crosses.

Detail of Exterior Wall Carvings at the Entrance

Khachkar Nestled in the Church Sanctuary Wall

The insides of the chapels all bear traits of Armenian Church architecture. Frescoes and inscriptions, no longer brilliant and sharp, adorn the walls, along with more contemporary graffiti.

The present inhabitants are reasonably hospitable toward visitors.

℅

St. James of Nisibis
(*Surb Hakob Medzbna Hayrapet*)

St. James of Nisibis, much-loved, esteemed, and revered fourth century Patriarch of the Armenian people, exists at once as a very popular figure in Armenian Church history, and as a vaguely identified person about whom very little is known.

However much doubt there may be about him as a specific individual, there is no doubt that his extreme popularity among the Armenian people has given him a very strong identity.

Armenian monasteries and churches throughout the world named St. James ("Surb Hakob") are named after this patriarch, not after others with the name James who also could be honored by naming a church.

St. James is one of the revered saints in the Armenian Church. His feast day occurs on the Saturday falling in the interval December 12 to 18.

His exact identity is shrouded in uncertainty. Some say he was an Assyrian bishop, the Patriarch of the Christians (or of the Armenians) of Nisibis (in Armenian, "Medzbin;" today's Nusaybin, about 60 miles southeast of Diyarbekir). Others relate him to an Armenian royal lineage.

The exact date and place of his birth are unknown. Nor is it known where and when he died, or where his remains have been interred.

It seems quite certain, however, that he attended the First Ecumenical Council, in 325, in Nicaea (today's Iznik, in Turkey) along with Bishop Aristakes (son of St. Gregory the Enlightener) and took part in formulating the Nicene Creed.

It also appears that he led the extremely self-denying life of a hermit.

Strong traditions surrounding his life have reinforced his personality in the minds of Armenians over the centuries.

With a prevailing controversy among churchmen over the question of which mountain it was where Noah's Ark came to rest (the Scriptures read *"on the mountains of Ararat,"* Gen. 8:4) Patriarch St. James of Nisibis sought to reach the summit of Mt. Ararat to find the remains of the Ark, and thus put the controversy to rest. Tradition has it that after several failed attempts to reach the summit, an angel appeared before him and gave him a piece of wood, advising him that it was from the Ark. That relic today sits in a golden triptych in the museum to the rear of the Altar of the Cathedral of Echmiadzin.

Tradition also has it that St. James was endowed with supernatural powers. It is said that once when he was passing through the village of Artamed he saw that while the young women of the village were washing clothes in the stream, they had allowed their legs to be uncovered. For punishment, St. James cursed them, and caused their hair to turn white. Even today, it is claimed that women of Artamet have tufts of white in their hair. Artamet is on the southeast shore of Lake Van.

The supernatural powers ascribed to St. James of Nisibis served the people of Nisibis very well in protecting them from the attempted invasion by the Persian monarch Shapuh.

The reverence shown by Armenians everywhere toward "Surb Hakob Medzbna Hayrapet" though he is thought to be Assyrian is a measure of the deep love Armenians have for their church.

၆၁

St. Gregory of Narek
(Narekatsi)

The deepest traditions of the Armenian Church call for monks to remove themselves from the immediate cloisters of the monastery and live apart and alone as hermits. Best known, and best loved and revered of these solitary monastics was the hermit/monk, St Gregory of Narek, whose prayerbook, often called *Book of Lamentations*, or simply *Narek*, was possibly the most desired and loved book in a typical, early Armenian household in the homeland.

He was born in the Province of Vaspurakan (Van) probably in the second half of the tenth century. His father was a theologian who was later ordained a bishop after his wife died. Gregory studied at the monastery of Narek and was early ordained a celibate priest, becoming a teacher in the monastery. He quickly earned the reputation of being a learned teacher, and also a man of godly virtues. He was very much in demand also outside the monastery. His words, both spoken and written, had high intellectual and spiritual content.

In time, wishing to dedicate himself totally to a spiritual existence, disdaining physical comforts, he isolated himself and chose the lonely life of a hermit.

Doing so did not diminish the reverence with which the people esteemed him. Indeed, it enhanced his godly image. There is a legend that tells of the level of that popular belief in his holiness. According to this popular belief, monks at the monastery resented Gregory's forsaking the monastery and becoming a hermit. On an occasion two monks had gone to where Gregory stayed. It was a Friday, a day of abstinence. Yet they found Gregory roasting two pigeons on a spit over a fire. When the visiting monks upbraided Gregory for violating the rules of abstinence, he pleaded innocence, saying he did not know it was Friday. Then, as the legend has it, Gregory asked forgiveness of the pigeons and urged them to fly away. And the pigeons did so.

In his "Book of Lamentations" St. Gregory of Narek, known popularly as "Narekatsi," wrote with a profound sense of self-debasement. In his pleadings to God he lamented that his sins were so manifold that he was unable to live up to God's standards, and could not be forgiven.

His prayers are introduced with the phrase, "From the depths of the heart, a word with God." In Armenian (Classical) that would appear as

Ի ԽՈՐՈՑ ՍՐՏԻ, ԽՕՍՔ ԸՆԴ ԱՍՏՈԻՕՈՅ

Here is a partial translation of Prayer #5 of Narek.

"Here I, an earthborn man, taken with life's meaningless things and drunken with the wine of insanity, who everlastingly falsifies and never speaks the truth, with such reproachable characteristics by what effrontery shall I appear before thy judgment, O fearful, inexpressible, unutterable, most powerful God."

"Each time I display the ungratefulness of my sinful soul toward thy kindnesses I enhance thy greatness and weigh down my iniquity forever."

"Thou adorned with thy words, brightened with thy breath, enriched with thy mind, gave growth with they wisdom, strengthened with thy intellect, set us apart from the animals, endowed us with an understanding soul, crowned us with self-control, fathered us, nurtured us, attended us as Lord."

"Thou planted a thankless one as I in thy garden, thou watered with the water of life, cleansed with the coolness of the basin, gave root with the river of life, fed with the heavenly food, sated with thy godly blood, subdued the untouchables and the unreachables, gave courage for me to lift my earthly eyes toward thee, and filled me with the light of glory. Thou drew unto thee the earthen fingers of my unclean hands, and esteemed the vile dust of my mortal self as a ray of light. ..."

St. Gregory of Narek was the voice of a devout people.

❧

Mkrtich Khrimian, Catholicos
(1820-1907)

Catholicos Mkrtich Khrimian, revered by the people and popularly known as Khrimian Hayrik, was born in 1820, in Van, Province of Vaspurakan, in historic Armenia.

Though he received his education in the monastic environment of seminaries, he taught in secular schools.   Shortly after his marriage had borne a daughter, he fled to Constantinople to avoid being conscripted into the Turkish army.   There, becoming well known as the "Teacher from Armenia" and as a tireless worker, he made people aware of the physical and spiritual deprivation of the Armenians of the Turkish interior to the east.

At the age of 33, he returned to Van only to find that all his family had died.   Grief-stricken, he found solace by turning back to religion, becoming ordained a celibate priest in 1854.

Imbued with western ideas of freedom and the pursuit of education, Khrimian sought to convert the monasteries of the east into centers of education.   But he was rebuffed by the over-conservative monastics, and so he returned to Constantinople.   There he found genuine acceptance of his liberal ideas, and was motivated to expound on the sufferings of the Armenians.   He returned to Van, and with modest printing equipment started to publish the "Eagle of Vaspurakan" (1858), the first Armenian newspaper to be published in the interior.

As primate of Taron, he was responsive to the sufferings of his people, lodging complaints to government officials, and also to the Patriarch of Constantinople. It was in becoming the fearless champion of the Armenians that Khrimian was popularly called by the simple honorific "Hayrik" (Little Father).

When elected Patriarch of Constantinople (1869) he said, "Do not look upon me as the Patriarch of Constantinople. I am the picture of the sufferings of Armenia."

As Patriarch, Khrimian began to press authorities concerning the widespread exploitation of the Armenian people. But because he was in constant conflict with the government and oft-times disappointed in his efforts, he resigned.

With a Russian victory in the Russo-Turkish War, the treaty of San Stefano (March 3, 1878) provided favorably for the Armenians. However, the European powers, troubled by the Russian gains, forced a new treaty at the Congress of Berlin (July 13, 1878). Khrimian led a delegation to it to assure protection of Armenian rights under the Ottoman Empire, but the effort proved ineffective. The new treaty provided for the six great powers to supervise reforms that the Sultan was to carry out. But, "what was everybody's business became nobody's business," as Khrimian later declared.

Khrimian's disappointment was expressed by his famous metaphor portraying the Congress of Berlin as a European banquet of "herrisa," where Armenians with only their "paper ladle" could not get their fair share.

Khrimian had become very articulate in Constantinople in exposing the unbearable conditions in which his people lived under Ottoman rule. Exiled to Jerusalem for his actions, the tireless advocate of Armenian rights declared, "the eagle has been imprisoned in a sparrow's cage."

In 1891, Khrimian was elected Catholicos of All Armenians. "Hayrik," the little father, became the big father of Armenians throughout the world.

As Catholicos, Mkrtich I was faced with a strong challenge to better the plight of Armenians everywhere. His years were fraught with many disappointments along with his successes. His greatest contribution was probably to instill in his people worldwide an undying spirit of courage, tenacity, and a desire to preserve their heritage of church and language.

Mkrtich I, Khrimian, Catholicos of All Armenians, died in office October 29, 1907. His tombstone on the grounds of Echmiadzin bears the epitaph (in Armenian), 'Voice of the Sorrows of the People of Armenia.'

೬〇

Garegin Hovsepian, Catholicos
Author-Archaelogist-Linguist-Soldier-Philologist-Pedagog-
Administrator-Churchman
(1867-1952)

𝕬 true son of Artsakh, brave and bold, he was the epitome of a
courageous scholar-theologian.

After completing his studies at the Seminary of Echmiadzin, Garegin
Hovsepian continued his studies at the Universities of Berlin and Leipzig
where he earned the doctorate degree in philosophy. In the meantime he
had two prize-winning books published.

He was ordained to the priesthood of the Armenian Church at age 32,
and in four years he was named Abbot of the St. Sarkis Monastery of Tiflis,
and Vicar General of the Diocese of Georgia.

He returned to Echmiadzin as lecturer.

In 1917 he was ordained bishop, but his church duties did not prevent
him from participating heroically in the Battles of Sardarapat (1918) and Kars
(1921).

Recognized through his writings for his erudition Bishop Garegin was
appointed in 1920 as Professor in the newly opened University of Yerevan.
He was also appointed to the Academy of Sciences, becoming co-editor to
the Armenian scientific journal "Banber."

In 1927 he became Primate of the Diocese of Crimea and Nor
Nakhichevan (Russia).

When dissension arose in the Armenian Church in America, in 1933,
with the consequent split of the American Diocese into two, Bishop Garegin

was sent by Catholicos Khoren I as nuncio to America with the specific mission of reuniting the two segments. He arrived in the United States in 1936. Though he was unsuccessful in his committed effort to unite the two segments, he nevertheless won high admiration by all for the strong leadership, both spiritual and cultural, he gave to the Armenians of America. Two years after his arrival in America he was elected Primate of the American Diocese.

As Primate of the North American Diocese he immediately brought it new life and vigor. He instituted a plan that has become a tradition, to observe October each year as Cultural Month.

When the throne of the Great House of Cilicia became vacant he was elected Catholicos, in 1943, a position he held until his death in 1952. It was not until 1945 that he was able physically to take over the position because of the difficulties in traveling from America to Lebanon brought on by the hostilities during World War II.

Under the dynamic leadership of His Holiness, the Catholicate became a center for religious and cultural activities, and began to give the Armenians of the Diaspora a new center for the training of clergy for the Armenian Church.

Archbishop Garegin Hovsepian, the late Catholicos of the Great House of Cilicia, led a rich life. He gave the Armenian Church strong administrative, cultural, and spiritual leadership. But in addition, he was a true scholar in his own right. Among his accomplishments was the publication of seventeen books and countless articles, as well as a substantial volume of unpublished works.

Catholicos Garegin Hovsepian, of blessed memory, stands as an intellectual giant among the men of the Armenian Church.

∞

Maghakia Ormanian, Patriarch
(1841-1918)

$\mathfrak{H}$e was a towering figure in the Church.   As a high-ranking churchman, superb scholar-historian, and principled theologian, Patriarch Maghakia Ormanian left his indelible mark on the Armenian Church.

Although born, raised, schooled, and ordained in the faith of the Roman Catholic Church, Ormanian guided his own destiny with his clear and resolute thinking. It became his uncompromising decision to move from the Roman Catholic Church to the national Apostolic faith of the Armenian Church.

At a very early age he showed extraordinary aptitude at the Mekhitarist School in Constantinople, the city of his birth. He was entered into an Armenian Catholic monastery in Rome, and before he was 18 years of age he was ordained to the clergy.

On completing his studies there, when not yet 24, he was given the distinction of a public examination, an honor reserved only for the supremely gifted students.

At about that time a controversy was shaking the Catholic Church. It was the matter of the claim of infallibility of the Pope. Ormanian opposed that concept intensely. He resented the incursion of the Roman Catholic hierarchy into the administration and religious affairs of the Armenian Catholic community.

That concern led to his desire to turn his commitment to the Armenian Church. The transition of fealty took place smoothly over a period of a few years. As a celibate vardapet in the Armenian Church he was assigned as preacher in a large church in Constantinople. He very rapidly gained recognition and esteem.

Soon after, he was named Primate of the diocese of Garin (Erzurum) in 1880 where through his administrative ability and his religious zeal he was able to bring new spirit into the religious life of his flock.

The aftermath of the Russo-Turkish wars had brought serious problems in that some Armenians of Garin were being imprisoned by Turkish authorities for pro-Russian activity. Primate Ormanian, through his statesmanlike actions, was able to mitigate the sentences.

Ormanian was called to the Holy See of Echmiadzin (1887) to bring his administrative skill to strengthen the seminary. But his successes did not find favor with the Russian officials, and Ormanian, still an Ottoman subject, was sent back to Constantinople (1888).

In 1889 he was named superintendent of the Armash Seminary, which he guided with outstanding success, until his election as Patriarch of Constantinople (1896).

Ormanian served as Patriarch for twelve years. They were not easy years, both because of the Ottoman persecutions of Armenians and because of the harrassment by a small group of Armenian terrorists. That troubled relationship with the terrorists continued to grow in intensity. On Christmas morning, January 19, 1903, while he was celebrating the Divine Liturgy, a shot was fired at Ormanian, hitting him in the shoulder. Despite that attempt on his life Ormanian continued unabated to serve his people.

With the overthrow of the Sultan in 1908 by the Young Turks and the consequent disorder in the established structure of the Patriarchate, Ormanian found it necessary to resign from his position as Patriarch.

During his tenure as Patriarch, Ormanian brought about many improvements to the religious, social, and material life of the Armenian Community of Constantinople.

Ormanian's life of ten years after his resignation was spent mainly in writing. His chief contribution was the monumental work "Azgapatum" (National History), a three-volume work on the history of the Armenian people through the Christian era, with emphasis on the men of the Church.

Ormanian's death in 1918 brought to a close a life of total commitment to his church, nation, and people.

80

Cardinal Aghajanian
(1895-1971)

$\mathfrak{B}$orn Ghazaros Aghajanian in a small village near Tiflis in the Caucasus, Cardinal Gregory Peter XV Aghajanian was a highly respected and learned churchman, who was twice regarded as the leading non-Italian candidate for election as Pope. Rumor has it that he was, in fact, once elected by the College of Cardinals, but that he declined to assume the position as Pope.

His early education was under the Catholic fathers of Tiflis, who sent him to Rome for further study and training. Ordained as priest in 1917, he returned to Tiflis to serve the Armenian Catholic population of the area.

With the Sovietization of Georgia, he went back to Rome where he became vice rector of the Armenian College (1921), becoming Rector in 1935, when he was ordained bishop. He attained the academic degree of Doctorate in Theology, Philosophy, and Jurisprudence. He also attained mastery of Armenian, Russian, Italian, French, English, Latin, Classical Greek, German, Spanish, and Arabic.

In 1937 he was named Catholicos-Patriarch of All Catholic Armenians, worldwide.

He was named Cardinal in 1946, at age 50, being the youngest member of the College of Cardinals.

Recognized for his universal capabilities, he was appointed as head of the Congregation for the Propagation of the Faith, putting him in charge of the worldwide mission of the Roman Catholic Church.

In 1962 he resigned as Patriarch of the Armenian Catholics so that he might devote himself entirely to his mission for the Propagation of the Faith.

Though committed to the missionary activity of worldwide Catholicism, Cardinal Aghajanian maintained his identity as an Armenian, and often wore the robes and vestments of a high-ranking Armenian churchman.

જી

H.H. Vazgen I
Catholicos of All Armenians
(1908-1994)

He Restored the Faith

𝕬s successor to St. Gregory the Enlightener, the first of a long, unbroken line, the Armenian people chose, for number 130, His Holiness Vazgen I, Catholicos of All Armenians.

He served as the exalted Pontiff of the Armenian Church for forty years, the fourth longest in duration. Elected Supreme Patriarch on September 30, 1955, he ascended the Throne of St. Gregory at Holy Echmiadzin, and gave the world's Armenians their much-needed spiritual and moral leadership and uplift, until his death on August 18, 1994.

H.H. Vazgen has left his powerful impact on the spiritual life of Armenians everywhere.

Serving during the repressive years of Communist domination in Armenia, he nevertheless was able to put the Church in a respected position in the anti-religious eyes of the Soviet hierarchy. He succeeded in doing so even though his two predecessors had been persecuted by the Soviet authorities for their even lower level of religious and patriotic attitudes.

Much loved by the people of the Fatherland, H.H. Vazken I led the Armenian Church worldwide into a spiritual re-awakening.

He was born in Bucharest, Rumania, to a religious family named Baljian, and christened Levon Karapet. He was educated in the German Evangelical School in Bucharest, and was graduated from Bucharest University in the fields of educational science, psychology, and social science. He taught in the Armenian schools of Bucharest. His strong interest and studies in Armenian history led to his being ordained as a priest in the Armenian Church. Ordination was on September 30, 1942, in Athens, by the hand of the Primate of the Diocese of Greece, who named him Vazgen.

Ordination as Bishop occurred in July 1951, at Echmiadzin, and he was named Primate of the Diocese of Rumania.

After his ascension to the Throne of St. Gregory in 1955, he quickly brought new life to the Supreme Spiritual Council, in order to bring better administrative management of temporal, as well as spiritual, affairs to the Holy See of the Armenian Church at Echmiadzin.

Under his pontifical leadership, the Mother See of Holy Echmiadzin was lifted out of the morass of physical and spiritual neglect to a point where the world's Armenians felt new confidence in the viability and strength of the Mother See to fulfill its patriarchal mission.

As a consequence, pious Armenians throughout the world, those who had the means, flocked to the support of H.H. Vazgen I to provide him with the material resources to enable him to embark upon a massive program of restoring churches throughout Armenia, rehabilitating the Mother Cathedral of Holy Echmiadzin and the Veharan (Residence of the Catholicos and Administrative Headquarters of the Church), and building new edifices.

Prime examples are the restoration of the Church of St. Hripsime in the City of Echmiadzin, and the building of a new museum on the Cathedral grounds.

Moreover, the Gevorgian Seminary, in the Cathedral complex, was given new life, and it became once again the primary seminary for the training of Armenian clergy.

To H.H. Vazgen I should be given the appellation of "The Builder."

As Pontiff, H.H. Vazgen I visited the worldwide flock often. He traveled to the world's numerous dioceses and met with leaders and the people. His messages reached the hearts of his listeners, and he was loved and regarded as the compassionate Chief Shepherd.

The story of his travels and meetings with his flocks throughout the world are detailed in a series of published books.

His Holiness, Vazgen I, will live long in his people's loving memory.

෨

Archbishop Tiran Nersoyan
"The Scholar Theologian"
(1904-1989)

𝕬rchbishop Tiran Nersoyan, erstwhile Patriarch, intellectual giant, universalist, rugged individualist, was a bright star of the firmament of the Armenian Church. A Titan he was by any measure. His mind and hand turned out works that explored and elucidated matters in disciplines of theology and beyond.

A son of Aintab, and a graduate of the Seminary of the St. James Monastery of Jerusalem, he was ordained a celibate priest and named Tiran, to replace his baptismal name of Nerses. But he also chose to replace his family name of Tavukjian (Turkish for chicken merchant) to Nersoyan, Nerso being the familiar form of Nerses.

He received a rich education at Kings College, London, after which he returned to Jerusalem, to teach at the Seminary, later becoming its Principal. In 1939, he went to London as pastor of St. Sarkis Church. In 1943, he was elected as Primate of the Eastern Diocese of the Armenian Church of North America. It was in that position, until his resignation in 1954, that Archbishop Tiran showed his administrative and organizational skills. He ordained many new priests, formed the Armenian Church Youth Organization of America, planned for the building of a cathedral in New York, built nearly a dozen new churches, and restructured and modernized the Diocese and its Constitution.

Mindful of the need for better published church materials, such as translations of liturgical texts and music for use by deacons and choirs in the services of the Church; Archbishop Tiran prepared and published such works to fill that need.

In addition to fulfilling the demands of the office of Primate, Archbishop Tiran was a teacher, encouraging and personally participating in weeklong seminars for those who participated in church services.

As Primate, he sometimes came into conflict with the Catholicos and with community leaders who did not always see or comprehend issues with the same clarity that he did. Without seeking to change the formal name of the Church, "The Armenian Church," Archbishop Tiran used, and instructed others to use, the term "orthodox," to mean "correct doctrine," in describing the Church. For doing so, he was severely criticized by some community leaders, and even incurred a formal condemnation by the Catholicos, who only two years earlier granted him the title of Archbishop and praised him for taking courageous steps for the betterment of the Church, even sometimes "deviating from tradition."

With the Patriarchal throne of Jerusalem being vacant, the Brotherhood of St. James overwhelmingly elected him Patriarch, on March 20, 1957. But as a victim of internal intrigue, Patriarch Tiran was forcibly taken and exiled from Jerusalem, then under Jordanian control. Contributing to that expulsion along with internal politics was the perception that Archbishop Tiran was a pro-Communist. That perception was incited by a few opponents who perverted his views expressed in a 1942 monograph, "A Christian Approach to Communism: Ideological Similarities between Dialectical Materialism and Christian Philosophy."

After his exile, Archbishop Tiran returned to America where he was able to realize a long-held dream – the founding of a seminary in America, The St. Nersess Armenian Seminary.

In parallel with his Diocesan duties, Archbishop Tiran frequently participated actively in international theological conclaves.

Upon his death in September 1989, he was interred in a cemetery in Hartsdale, NY, but his body was later exhumed and re-interred in the Holy Savior Monastic Cemetery of Jerusalem on 13 September 1993.

This man of the cloth, Archbishop Tiran Nersoyan, was truly an intellectual Titan among Titans.

&

Armenian Religious Faith
It now comes as Apostolic, Catholic, and Protestant

The national faith of the Armenian people, Christian since the very beginning of the fourth century, and founded by Apostles, remained unblemished for more than one and a half millennia. It was universal, embracing all Armenians. It was not until the early nineteenth century that any significant digression from that faith took place.

With the fall of Constantinople in 1453, and the establishment of the wide-ranging Ottoman Empire (an Islamic religious state), the populous Christians of the Empire could not be full citizens, as only Moslems could. Being far more numerous than the Moslems, the Christians, though subjects of the Empire, were left without a clear status. The solution was to declare them to be a nation within a nation, having its own specific laws and governed by a religious head with both civil and religious authority.

But that enormous body was a "tail that wagged the dog," and the Sultan, Mehmed II, in a smart move, split the Christians into two roughly equal bodies of Greeks and Armenians (and a number of other very small sects), which had divergent theological concepts. Central to that difference was their doctrine on the nature of Christ.   The Greeks accept the Chalcedonian dyophysite concept of two natures, while the Armenians, having dissented from the findings of the fourth Ecumenical Council (Chalcedon, 451 AD) believe in the "one" nature (monophysitism). Exploiting that difference to his own advantage, the Sultan divided the Christians into two separate (and disparate) "Millets," the "Ortodoks Millet" (mostly Greeks), and the "Ermeni Millet" (mostly Armenians). Each millet had its own laws and was headed by a Patriarch with both civil and religious authority, as set by law.

Thus, "eastern Christianity" was being split into two bodies, one as "orthodox" and the other as "dissenting," (the Armenians).

Early in the nineteenth century, the Roman Catholic Church (not then recognized as heading a millet) had begun to pressure Armenians to attend Catholic churches, a "papist" movement, seeking to bring Armenians "back into the fold." However, the law was forbidding the Armenians from going to those churches because as members of the Ermeni Millet, they were obliged to go to Armenian churches, even under police pressure.

At about the same time, Protestant missionaries from the American Board of Commissioners for Foreign Missions, who had first come to convert Moslems to Christianity (and found it could not be), turned their attention to the Armenians, offering them much needed educational and other opportunities, and in so doing, winning converts.

Both movements, the Catholic and the Protestant, later (near mid-century) became recognized as two more millets, the "Katolik Millet" and the "Protestan Millet."

Thus, in the same manner as "eastern Christianity," now "western Christianity" was being divided and classified as "orthodox" and "dissenting."

The consequence was for the four Christian Millets to form a logical alignment, as shown in the chart below:

Alignment of the Christian Millets in the Ottoman Empire

	WEST	EAST
Orthodoxy	"Katolik" (Catholic)	"Ortodoks" (Orthodox)
Dissent	"Protestan" (Protestant)	"Ermeni" (Armenian)

It is in this way that Armenians of Constantinople and of a number of other cities throughout the Ottoman Empire were drawn into one or the other of these "western faiths," and having emigrated to many parts of the world, they carried their new beliefs with them.

ဆာ

Chapter 5

POLITICAL EVENTS

In Memoriam

Yerevan, Armenia

Montebello, California, USA

Bikfaya, Lebanon

The Armenian Question
ՀԱՅ ԴԱՏ
"Hay Tad"

𝕴t is a long time since the "Question" was posed, but no answer has yet come forth.

For nearly half a millennium Christian peoples, especially Armenians, living under the suzerainty of the Islamic Ottoman Empire, had existed in a state of constant persecution. They had been denied the natural human rights of life, liberty, and the pursuit of happiness.

The Ottoman Empire, at its greatest geographical extent, for about 200 years between 1600 and 1800, held dominion over southern Europe, Asia Minor and the Red Sea, and northern Africa - in an unbroken ring around the central and eastern Mediterranean and the Black Sea. All of historic Armenia lay within its sphere.   So too did the Christian peoples of southeastern Europe.

Russia, in its never-ending quest for warm water ports and outlets to the world, together with the nobly stated purpose of freeing Christian peoples from the heavy Islamic yoke, engaged in a long series of wars with the Ottoman Empire (the Russo-Turkish Wars) over a period of nearly two centuries.

Gradually, Christian peoples in southeastern Europe were liberated.

With the Turkish defeat in 1878, the Treaty of San Stefano (March 3, 1878) granted Russia some lands in today's eastern Turkey. In that treaty, Article #16 gave Russia the right to monitor the treatment and the guaranteed rights of Armenians within the remaining lands of Turkey.

Western European powers quickly sat up and took notice of Russia's extended influence in Asia Minor. Concerned, they were able to force a new international conference, leading to the Congress of Berlin (July 13, 1878). The new treaty, annulling provisions of the Treaty of San Stefano, included an Article #61, which left to the European powers collectively to monitor the treatment of Christian minorities (not specifically Armenians) within the remaining Ottoman Empire.

Before the convening of the Congress of Berlin, an Armenian delegation had made visits to representatives of the European powers to plead for the Armenians. The delegation was led by Patriarch Khrimian Hairik, who returned home to Constantinople after the meeting totally dismayed at the heartlessness and unconcern of the European (Christian) powers.

As it has been observed, concerning the collective responsibility of the European powers to monitor the treatment of Christians in the Ottoman Empire, "What was everybody's business became nobody's business."

This circumstance may be cited as the formal birth of "The Armenian Question."

The continuing story of the lot of the Armenians in the Ottoman Empire, and the growth and development of the Armenian Revolutionary Movement and its horrendous aftermath, can be said to be the result, in part, of the recognition that Armenians can never expect to find salvation through the actions or the intervention of the Christian European powers.

The Armenian Question still remains unanswered.

Only by themselves may Armenians one day provide the answer.

Revolutionary Awakening

fter centuries of repressive domination under the heavy heel of the Ottoman overlords, the Armenian people within the Ottoman Empire were awakened to the recognition that it was time to rise in protest. That time was during the second half of the nineteenth century. The leaders of the movement did not know the words, but they felt, as did Patrick Henry when he said, "Give me liberty or give me death!"

What was it that stirred the Armenian people to rise out of their long period of lethargy, and what was it they wanted?

To answer the second question first, they wanted the following: a) an end to the systematic massacre of Armenians in the Ottoman Empire, b) an end to the unjustified arrest and imprisonment of Armenians, c) an end to the cruel punishment of Armenians in custody, d) an end to unjust levying of confiscatory taxes, e) equality under the law, f) freedom of speech and of the press, and g) a variety of other reforms.

A series of events, both in the homeland and abroad, began the awakening process. The French Revolution and the other European movements to gain freedom for the people had begun to impress the Armenians, mainly through the young men who had gone to Europe to study and who were witness to the struggles there. Their writings reached the hearts and souls of their people back home.

Uprisings by Armenians against Ottoman authorities had taken place in Zeitun and Van (1862), in Erzurum (1881), in Zeitun and the bloody Bab Ali demonstration (1895), the short-lived capture of the Imperial Ottoman Bank (1896), and others.

An Armenian National Constitution, promulgated in 1860 and confirmed by the Sultan in 1863, provided for an Armenian General Assembly, which was granted certain powers concerning the religious and cultural life of the Armenians of the Empire. The Ittihadist Constitution (1908) enabled Armenians to be elected to Parliament. These reforms were not enough.

Political parties, and organized resistance groups formed, the principal parties being Armenakan (1885), Hunchak (1887), and the Armenian Revolutionary Federation (1890).

The spirit of the rebellion and resistance among the Armenians was implanted and nourished by the writings of those who were clearly part of the movement. They conveyed powerful messages in their writings, mostly as poems, many of which were set to music and widely sung. Principal among such writers were Mikael Nalbandian, Raphael Patkanian (Kamar Katipa), Hakop Melik-Hakopian (Raffi), Adom Yarjanian (Siamanto).

An essential part of this revolution was armed confrontation between the Armenians and soldiers and police (gendarmes) of several levels of government. They who led such armed events, many of whom paid with their lives, have remained as eternal heroes in Armenian annals.

Among the best known are General Andranik Pasha, Mihran Damadian, Hambardzum Boyadjian, Serob Aghbiur, Hrair-Dzhoghk, Nikol Duman, Sebastatsi Murad, and Gevorg Chavush. Below are short descriptions of the roles played by each of them.

General Andranik Pasha (Andranik Ozanian, 1865-1927)
See separate story.

Mihran Damadian (1865-1945)

Educator from Constantinople turned revolutionary; Damadian early became aware of the Armenian Question and the unreadiness of the European powers to resolve the question. He took part in the demonstration at Kum Kapi (1890), and soon became a fugitive from the Turkish authorities for his provocative activities. He became an effective voice in the revolutionary movement, traveled widely, was imprisoned, suffered torture, but miraculously was pardoned.

Mihran Damadian

The unstable environment in Cilicia in 1920 led to a dramatic occasion when a revolutionary body declared "freed Cilicia" as an Armenian State, with Damadian as Prime Minister. The abortive, one-day (August 5) government was summarily dismissed by the French High Command.

Damadian visited America, and ended his days in business management in Egypt.

Hambardzum Boyadjian (Murad the Great, 1860-1915)

As a student in medical school in Constantinople, Murad was quick to feel the awakening to protest. As one of the organizers of the demonstration at Kum Kapu (to issue a formal protest to the Sultan concerning the mistreatment of Armenians) Murad also became a fugitive. He joined in the First Revolt of Sasun (1894), which was in truth a battle of self-defense. Murad was imprisoned in Mush and in Bitlis and suffered

Hambardzum Boyadjian

torture.   When called from prison and subjected to interrogation in the Sultan's palace, Murad boldly admitted his revolutionary activity and protested the Sultan's persecution of Armenians, after which he was again imprisoned and tortured.

With help from other revolutionaries, Murad was able to escape from prison.   In 1908, he was in New York where he created enthusiastic fervor among Armenians.

With the promulgation of the Ittihadist Constitution (1908), Murad returned to Constantinople and was elected a member of the Turkish Parliament.   But the events of 1915 led to his arrest and torture.   Later, subjected to a sham trial, he was hanged (August 24, 1915).

Serob Aghbiur (Vardanian, 1864-1899)

A stalwart and fearless young man, and son of a prosperous family, Serob responded very early to the revolutionary call.   His exploits throughout middle Armenia spread terror among his adversaries, all the while eluding arrest.   It was not until the Turkish authorities concentrated all their efforts in middle Armenia to apprehend Serob, believing that with him out of the way, the Armenian revolutionary movement would end, that he was caught through treachery.   He was

Serob Aghpiur

beheaded, and his head was paraded through the streets of Mush and Bitlis. Later, the diocesan primate, Bishop Eghishe, retrieved the head and buried it at the side of the church, under a mulberry tree.

Hrair-Dzhoghk (Armenak Ghazarian, 1866-1904)

Small in stature, yet a giant as an intellectual, Hrair-Dzhoghk, of the region of Mush, wrote powerful articles to awaken the revolutionary spirit, even being critical of the political parties of which he was a member.

Hrair was married and had two children.   But to serve as an example to other revolutionaries, he left his family so that he might devote himself fully to the cause.

Hrair-Dzhoghk

The revolutionaries were not always united in their plans.   Hrair was often in conflict with others who, he felt were too reckless in their methods.   Though he was sincere in his policy of patience and caution, he was criticized by the others, even to the point of questioning his loyalty. While defending a village that was being attacked by the enemy, Hrair was killed by a stray bullet that found its fatal mark.

Gevorg Chavush (Ghazarian, 1870-1907)

Gevorg Chavush

Destiny overruled the ardent wish of the parents of this fiery and restless son to become a priest. After a fitful stay at the seminary where his father had left him, Gevorg left the seminary, and home, to join other revolutionaries. In a defensive battle in Sasun, Gevorg was captured, beaten, and imprisoned. He succeeded in escaping by secretly digging a hole in the wall and escaping into the stormy night.

With numerous military engagements, Gevorg emerged as a most experienced and audacious fighter. He was sometimes under the command of General Andranik.

A guiding principle for revolutionaries – fedayis – was that they should not marry. Notwithstanding, Gevorg was unable to drown his intense love for the daughter of a village chief. After many difficulties, the two were married secretly. However, when the fact was revealed, Gevorg became the object of much scorn.

Death came to the hero in the intense battle at Sulukh, north of Mush.

Murad of Sebastia (Khrimian, 1878-1918)

Born of gypsy parents (probably from the Crimea), Murad left the nomadic life of his family and turned to serve the Armenian people. A famous sharpshooter and frequent hunter, Murad in his youth engaged in competitive wrestling. Disdaining formal schooling, Murad worked as a farm hand for a wealthy family. Love shared between him and the daughter of that family led to their desire to run off and marry. But in an encounter he

Murad of Sebastia

had with two Turks who tried to kill him, Murad succeeded in killing one and routing the other. As a consequence, he had to leave the village, going to Constantinople, where he joined in anti-Turkish terror. Having become a fugitive, Murad went to the Caucasus where he joined a group transporting arms, a very hazardous operation. His brave exploits brought him fame. He urged the people to arm themselves.

Murad was the proud owner of a fine horse that was subject only to him. Poet Daniel Varoujan "baptized" the horse and named it "Pegas" (Pegasus), writing a poem about it.

To apprehend Murad, the governor of Sebastia tried by treachery to entrap him. But Murad outwitted the governor and avoided a plot to kill him. Murad's death came in a battle in the defense of Baku.

Nikol Duman (Nikoghayos Ter Hovhannisian, 1867-1914)

Teacher – revolutionary Duman was a son of Artsakh. His revolutionary activity consisted early of organizing fighting groups in Persia (Tabriz), then in the Caucasus under the unsympathetic Tsarist rule of Russia.   Duman interrupted his teaching to lead an arms transport group into Turkey. In the process, his group was repeatedly attacked, but his amazing feats dumbfounded the Kurds, who even composed a song about him. Duman repeatedly led attack groups to go to the help of besieged defenders, such as at Van.

Death to the hero came through sickness. His spirit was shattered that he could not continue to support the revolutionary movement.

Nikol Duman

The   Armenian   Revolutionary   Movement, aided by world events such as World War I, brought about a total upheaval of the Armenian nation. Even after the virtual annihilation in the homeland arising as an aftermath of the revolutionary movement, the Armenian people have, in effect gained the freedom they had been seeking, but in a wholly different form – Revival in Dispersion.

℘

Shaké Throwing Herself into the Chasm

SHAKÉ

ՇԱՔԵ

"Sisters, there is only one path for us.
That is to die in order not to fall into
the vile hands of the enemy."

With such words Shaké clutched her year-old child to her breast, and looking toward heaven she threw herself into the chasm below.

How often did such tragic events take place? Did they in fact occur at all? The case of Shaké appears to be documented.

It was during the first so-called "Revolt of Sasoun." The revolt was in fact a battle of self-defense. It had come to an end on August 24, 1894, when Armenian resistance fighters had finally given up.

The people of Sasoun had, starting several years earlier, been protesting against the regional Ottoman authorities, seeking freedom from oppression. They asked only for basic human rights. But their demands were being looked upon as a revolt.

Government troops had been systematically attacking the villages of the region to disarm the people and wipe out the Armenian revolutionary movement.

One of the regional villages was Shenik. Its chief was "Grgo." When Shenik was attacked, the villagers held out until their supply of ammunition ran out. Grgo was wounded, captured, and taken away and killed.

Grgo's wife, Shaké, seeing the tragic fate of the village, looked for "freedom" by her brave act. It appears from chronicles of the times that others followed her example.

Shaké's plunge into the chasm has been a much-heralded act during the early days of Armenia's struggle for basic human rights under the oppressive policies of the Ottoman Empire.

Artists have pictured her courageous act, which has been hailed by Armenians as an example of the purity and bravery of Armenian women.

Shaké became a symbol. No one knows how many Shakés there were during the decades of Armenia's revolutionary struggle for liberation.

But their role in the revolutionary movement was much more than to choose to die rather than to fall into the "vile hands of the enemy."

In self-defense battle after battle Armenian women were in the thick of things. They supplied the men with ammunition, fashioned bullets, brought food and water, treated the wounded and even shouldered rifles.

Time and again, a young wife, on finding that her husband had been killed in battle, only redoubled the ferocity of her fighting.

Shaké's act was an act that was characteristic of the women in the revolutionary movement - "deny the enemy."

⚭

"1915"

𝕴t was the nadir, the lowest point in the history of the Armenian existence.

In a fiendish pre-plot, the triumvirate (Interior Minister Talaat, War Minister Enver, and Minister of the Marine Jemal - leaders of the Ittihad ve Terraki party who overthrew Sultan Hamid) executed a plan to remove influential leaders of the Armenian people within the Ottoman Empire in order to carry out their main objective more effectively - the annihilation of the Armenian race.

So it was that the movements of designated Armenian leaders, mostly writers and community leaders, were being monitored by the police, and on the fateful night of April 23, 1915, in a coordinated operation, the leaders were taken into custody. Together, they numbered in the hundreds. Their luminous, but tragic, biographies would all show the year of death as 1915.

Here is a sampling of them:

HRAND (Hovhannes Giurjian): born 1859 in Balahovid.   Writer, public speaker, teacher.

TELGADENTSI (Hovhannes Harutiunian): born 1860 in the region of Kharberd. Writer, teacher, community leader.

AGNUNI (Khachatur Malumian): born 1860 in Meghri. Public   speaker, community leader, reporter.

ZOHRAB (Krikor Zohrab): born 1861 in Constantinople. Attorney, educator, writer. Member of Turkey's Chamber of Deputies.

DAGHAVARIAN, Nazareth: born 1862 in Sebastia. Physician,   naturalist, community leader.

VAROUJAN (Daniel Chubukyarian): born 1884 in Sebastia. (See separate text)

YEROUKHAN (Yervand Sermakeshkhanlian): born 1870 in Constantinople. Writer, public speaker, translator, pedagog.

ARDASHES HARUTIUNIAN: born 1873 in Mulgara.   Public speaker, community leader, reporter.

ROUBEN ZARTARIAN: born 1874 in Kharberd.   Writer, editor, public speaker.

SIAMANTO (Adom Yarjanian): born 1878 in Kharberd. (See separate text)

GEGHAM BARSEGHIAN: born 1883 in Constantinople.   Writer, editor, public speaker.

ROUBEN SEVAK (Chilingirian): born 1885 in Constantinople.   Poet, physician (University of Lausanne).

The fate that befell many of the above-named

Among those taken on that fateful evening was Komitas Vardapet. Miraculously, he was spared through the intervention of a Turkish Poet, working through American Ambassador Morgenthau.   But sadly, the sufferings endured by his people caused Komitas to lose his reason, becoming a victim of dementia (see separate text).

In commemorating April 24 annually as Martyrs' Day, Armenians worldwide want the peoples and nations of the world not to forget the attempted genocide of the Armenians, so that other peoples will not be subjected to the same crime against humanity.

80

The Six "Armenian Vilayets"
Sivas • Erzurum • Van • Bitlis • Diyarbekir
Mamouret-ul-Aziz (Kharberd)

They were central to the "numbers game."
Present-day apologists for what was once the core of the Ottoman Empire deny that any "genocide" of the Armenians took place. Their claim is that their nation was at war (World War I), and that it had to defend itself from internal actions that would benefit its enemy (Russia). As a result, they claim, there was internal conflict, and both sides sustained substantial losses.

But in any case, they say, - and that is central to their claims - the number of Armenians who lost their lives in that era could not have been as large as Armenians claim (1,500,000) because the total number of Armenians in the land was hardly a million.

The six vilayets (states, or provinces) named above have been called the "Armenian Vilayets" because their Armenian population was large: nearly equal to the Turkish population in two of the vilayets, and several times the Turkish population in the other four vilayets. In the case of Van, the Armenian population was more than half of the total population.

How many Armenians, in fact, were there in the Ottoman Empire in 1915?

It is obvious that no truly reliable census data are available. There are several reports and analyses that have been published on the population of Armenians (and others) in the Ottoman Empire in the 1915 era. Highly significant are the two publications cited below. The first gives information from the Armenian point of view. The second is from the Turkish point of view.

"The Armenian Question: Before the Peace Conference," submitted on 12 February 1919 jointly by A. [Avetis] Aharonian, President of the Delegation from the Armenian Republic to the Peace Conference, and Boghos Nubar, President of the Armenian National Delegation.

Sadi Kochash, *"Tarih Boyunca Ermeniler ..."* (The Long-Standing Conflict Between Armenians and Turks Since the Time of the Seljuks)

The first reference offers several tables giving the population of regions, and totals. For the Six "Armenian Vilayets" the report gives the following for 1912.

	Population	Percentage
Christians		
Armenians	1,018,000	40
Other Christians	165,000	6
Moslems		
Turks	666,000	25
Kurds	242,000	9
Other Moslems	270,000	10
Other Religions	254,000	10
TOTALS	**2,615,000**	**100**

For the total number of Armenians everywhere, in 1914, the report gives the following.

In Turkey	2,026,000
In the Caucasus	1,804,000
Elsewhere	640,000
World Total	**4,470,000**

Turkish claims (as set forth in the Kochash reference) attempt to compare figures given by various sources (including Armenian). The claim made there is that the total number of Armenians in the Ottoman Empire in 1914, according to official government figures, was 1,294,851. That number would be in contrast to the count of 2,026,000 (given above), for a difference of 731,149.

If the world population of Armenians in 1914 were 4,470,000, and 1,500,000 perished in the subsequent period, then there would have remained only 2,970,000 Armenians in the world in about 1918.

Musa Dagh
(Moses' Mountain)

heir will to survive led to a bold, defensive stand-off, and that event was later memorialized in a historical novel of epic proportions.

Map of Musa Dagh and Surroundings

It was late summer 1915. The people of several Armenian villages of the region known as Suedia - on the slopes of Moses' Mountain (Musa Dagh) at the northeastern shore of the Mediterranean - had been given the order of deportation by the Ottoman authorities. Some of the people had judged it wise to submit to the order, on promises given them that they would be protected. It turned out instead that those who accordingly heeded the order were slaughtered.

Others, about 5,000 people in all, including women and children, decided otherwise. Despite the extreme shortage of weapons and ammunition they would hold out, preferring to die in battle rather than willingly submit. Word had reached them of slaughter elsewhere, especially in Zeitun, when people submitted to deportation orders.

Quitting their homes, the people took a position on the heights of Musa Dagh. Lying directly west of Antioch (Antakya) and just north of the Orontes River as it empties into the Mediterranean, the mountain reaches a height of 4450 feet. Its western slope descends steeply to the shore of the sea. The region is within the Sanjak of Alexandretta, then part of Syria, for a time under French mandate following the San Remo Conference of 1920, but becoming part of Turkey in 1939.

Having taken defensive positions on the mountain heights, the Armenians were subjected to successive assaults by Turkish troops, in ever more intensive attacks.

The fighting continued over a period of about fifty days, with the Armenian position becoming continually more untenable.

French warships cruising nearby in the Mediterranean in early September observed signaling from the shore and recognized the situation. Through negotiations conducted with a landing party, arrangements were made to evacuate the Armenians. Among the warships used for the evacuation were the cruisers Guichen and Jeanne d'Arc.

Records show that well over 3,000 Armenians were evacuated and taken to Port Said and Alexandria.

The evacuated Musa Dagh Armenians lived in refugee camps for several years, but were able to return to their Suedia homeland after Syria came under French mandate. Later, the whole Sanjak of Alexandretta, which included Suedia, became an autonomous region under French jurisdiction.

Youthful Defenders of Musa Dagh

But Turks, by increasing their population in the Sanjak, were able eventually, through the League of Nations, to force the ceding of the Sanjak to Turkey (1939).

Armenians of the region were then faced with the choice of becoming Turkish citizens, or leaving. An estimated 14,000 Armenians emigrated, most of them going to Beirut.

THE FORTY DAYS OF MUSA DAGH

On an occasion when Franz Werfel was visiting Damascus in 1929 he saw the sorry plight of the maimed and under-nourished refugee children working in textile factories. The experience moved him to the writing of *The Forty Days of Musa Dagh* (1933).

The *Forty Days* became an instant best seller, and the entire world read of the epic stand of the Armenians on Musa Dagh. Werfel wove fictional characters into the epic event, in the process borrowing ideas from the history of the persecution experienced by his people (Jews). In doing so, he used the mystical "forty" of the Bible instead of the fifty days of the epic on the Mountain of Moses. No major commercial filming of the *Forty Days* occurred - Turkey blocked it.

But the world still knows!

ℰ

Sardarapat
(May 23, 1918)

𝔍t is hailed as one of the most brilliant events to be found in the military annals of Armenian history. It was the occasion when the inadequate Armenian army, reinforced by a spontaneously emerging multitude of the people - farmers, workers, intellectuals, churchmen, using whatever implements were at hand - drove the invading Turkish regular army that was trying to break through to Yerevan and beyond.

The highly spirited, enhanced Armenian forces thwarted the long-standing Turkish ambition and dream to link up with their soul brothers of Azerbaijan, thus forming an unbroken band of Islamic Turks from the Mediterranean to the central steppes of Asia (pan- Turanism).

It was May 1918. World War I was still under way, except that the Brest-Litovsk Treaty (March 17, 1918) was to end the conflict between Turkey and Russia, after the fall of the Tsarist government.   The provisions of the Treaty called for Turkey to respect the 1914 border between Turkey and Russia (which included Trans-caucasia).

With the fall of the Tsarist government, and the withdrawal of the Russian forces from eastern Turkey, the three regions, Armenia, Georgia, and Azerbaijan, had been obliged to set up the Transcaucasian Federative Republic, because Turkish forces had already taken back Erzincan, Erzurum, Kars, and Alexandropol, reaching the 1914 border.   Moreover, the threat was recognized that the Turks would try to penetrate beyond.

Mutual mistrust and numerous other factors were about to cause the collapse of the Transcaucasian Federative Republic.

The Memorial at Sardarapat

Those were the circumstances that prevailed on that fateful day, May 23, 1918.

The Turkish forces were ready to violate their agreement as set forth in the Treaty of Brest-Litovsk, by crossing the 1914 border.

They would attack at Sardarapat (and at other points), expecting to push through to Yerevan.

The Turkish forces attacked. But the Armenian forces, under the direct command of Colonel Pirumian, held firm. The Armenians, badly outnumbered, but reinforced in arms and in spirit by the civilian support, forced the enemy to retreat.

The military success at Sardarapat was the signal for successes at other points.

The end of the hostilities was made formal by the Treaty of Batum, signed on June 4, 1918.

With the concurrent break-up of the Transcaucasian Federative Republic, Armenia declared itself an independent republic on May 28, 1918.

Sardarapat stands today as a historical shrine for Armenians. Visitors can now go there and see the stately monument of bells standing there, and the magnificent ethnographic museum that is part of the complex.

The First Republic of Armenia
(1918-1920)

Out of the chaos resulting from the Bolshevik overthrow of the Russian Imperial Czarist government, the peoples of the Caucasus under Russia were thrown into disarray.   The first major action of Transcaucasia (after declaring independence in April 1918) was to establish the Democratic Federative Republic of Transcaucasia, consisting of the regions of Armenia, Azerbaijan, and Georgia.

The Federative Republic, however, lacked unity and was very insecure in the environment created by the continuing negotiations between the warring powers (of World War I), the various peace conferences, and the general instability in the area.

Transcaucasia fell apart very quickly, and out of it came three independent republics in the Caucasus.   Although Azerbaijan and Georgia were able to declare their autonomy under fairly secure military, economic and political circumstances, the conditions for Armenia's declaration of independence,   which   it   was   forced   to   make,   were   desperate. Notwithstanding that, Armenia did declare itself a separate state on May 28, 1918, after a successful, heroic stand-off at Sardarapat on May 23, 1918.

Armenia, as an independent state had thus come into existence after a period of nearly five and one-half centuries of foreign domination. But the conditions under which the fledgling republic had to make do were tragic. It had unsympathetic, or hostile, neighbors. It was land-locked. It had become the unwilling host to hundreds of thousands of refugees from western Armenia (Turkey) fleeing mass extinction, and it was without badly needed resources.

But Armenia did form a government. Heading an initial cabinet was Hovhannes Kachaznuni, as Prime Minister. Later, Avetis Aharonian became President of the Armenian National Council.

With the close of World War I later that year (the Armistice of November 11, 1918) the Armenian Republic tried in vain to woo the victorious Allies for help.

The peace treaty between the Allies and Turkey was signed at Sevres on August 10, 1920.   Article 88 stated, in part, "Turkey ... hereby recognizes Armenia as a free, independent state."   Article 89 states, in part, "Turkey and Armenia ... agree to submit to the arbitration of the President of the United States on the question of the frontiers between Turkey and Armenia..."

President Wilson in compliance with Article 89 did indeed submit a map showing the lands to be awarded to Armenia. The border between Turkey and Armenia, shown on Wilson's map, was an irregular line from the Black Sea extending southward to include Trebizond, Erzinjan, Bitlis, Van, etc.

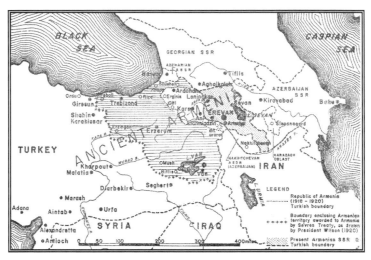

Horizontally-lined area denotes President Wilson's map of Armenia

However, Turkish Nationalist Forces under Kemal Ataturk rejecting the provisions of Sevres, mounted an effective military expedition to the east. The weak Armenian forces were, as a result, obliged to accept the humiliating terms of the Treaty of Alexandropol, December 2, 1920, imposed on them. Thus, Armenia's borders were shrunk back to approximately where they are today.

On that same day, December 2, 1920, the Armenian government (which had been led by the Armenian Revolutionary Federation - ARF) was obliged to resign under the combined pressure of the Turkish forces and the threatening Communist forces, handing over the reins of government to the leaders of the newly created Armenian Soviet Socialist Republic.

As a result, Turkey, having ignored the provisions of the Treaty of Sevres, was able to impose new demands on the Allies, and a new Treaty was signed at Lausanne on July 21, 1923. Thus, the favorable provisions of the Treaty of Sevres had come to naught.

Armenia was thus destined to endure seventy-one years under the repressive yoke of the Soviet Union (USSR).

෨෮

Avetis Aharonian
(1866-1948)

$\mathbb{R}$omanticist and idealist, this statesman led the First Republic of Armenia through its tumultuous years (1918-1920). It was a task beyond the capabilities of any man.

After receiving his primary education at the parish school of his birthplace, Igdir (in the Caucasus), Aharonian attended the Gevorgean Seminary at Echmiadzin. In 1901 he graduated from the University of Lausanne (France), Department of Historical Philosophy, and then studied in the Department of Literature at the Sorbonne.

He served on the editorial staffs, and as contributor, to several periodicals in Paris until he took a position as superintendent of the Nersisian School of Tiflis.

For his political activity there (the Transcaucasus was then under Russian control) the Tsarist government imprisoned him. But on gaining his freedom in 1911 he left the Caucasus.

Aharonian's literary activity began early, in 1887, and continued until late in life, but with a temporary lapse during his intensely active political life in the Armenian Revolutionary Federation and the First Armenian Republic (1918-1920).

A well-known early work is *Patkerner Verchin Tarineri Tajkahayots Kyankits* (Vignettes in the Life of Armenians of Turkey of Recent Years). Other works included novels, philosophical writings, tales, personal experiences, poems, etc.

Though a poet-writer of significance, Aharonian's place in history is secured more as a result of his life as a statesman.

In 1907 he submitted a plea to the Second Peace Conference at The Hague (Netherlands), in behalf of the Armenian Cause.   That plea was turned aside.

In 1917 he was elected President of the Armenian National Council, a group designed to act as a legislative body for the Armenians of Russia. This was the body that would, in May 1918, declare the independence of Armenia.

In 1919 Aharonian was elected a member of the Armenian Parliament, and later its President, as such, as President of the Parliament of the Republic of Armenia, Aharonian held the highest position in the government.

Aharonian headed the delegation to the Paris Peace Conference of 1919-1920.   It was Aharonian who signed the Treaty of Sevres (1920), and he participated in the Lausanne Peace Conference (1922-1923), continually defending the Armenian position.

With the fall of the First Republic of Armenia (Treaty of Alexandropol, December 2, 1920), Aharonian left Armenia with other members of his government.

Avetis Aharonian lived in Paris until his death in 1948.   He is remembered as the poet who became President of Armenia.

ℬ

The Second Republic of Armenia
(1991 and Counting)

With the collapse of the Soviet Union, the People of Armenia came out on September 21, 1991, to vote in answer to the ballot question: "Do you agree that the Armenian Republic be an independent, democratic nation outside the structure of the USSR?" Of the 2,182,150 eligible voters of Armenia, 95.63% voted. And of those who voted, 99.31% voted YES.

While the First Republic of Armenia arose out of the trauma of war and revolution, the Second Republic of Armenia burst forth out of political turmoil.

In the second instance, Armenia was in a better position to take on the responsibility of being an independent state and joining the world's family of sovereign states. In assuming that role, it was as in the first instance confronted with serious obstacles. It was still land-locked. It was still surrounded by unfriendly or hostile governments. And in addition, it had suffered severe loss resulting from the disastrous earthquake of 1988. It was also engaged in the movement to wrest Nogorno Karabagh, an Armenian enclave, from Azerbaijani control, the consequence of which was to be subjected to a ruinous blockade that virtually shut down its commerce and industry, to say nothing of creating terrible hardship for the populace. Moreover, nations

Mother Armenia

of the world were not sympathetic to the Republic's having helped Karabagh succeed in its military actions that, for the present, had given de facto freedom to Karabagh.

In its plan to create a democratic state, a vigorous program of privatization of commerce and industry, as well as farming, is being put into action.

A critical factor contributing to the difficulty faced by Armenia in establishing a viable economy of its own arises, in part, from the following situation. The Soviet Union's decision to dedicate a disproportionately large amount of capital to industrialize Armenia was a boon to the country. Unfortunately, by design, no major industrial product was produced entirely in Armenia. Instead, Armenia was dependent on other republics of the Soviet Union for critical components needed in the industrial products manufactured in Armenia.

In diminishing its ties to Russia, as well as to the other emerging states of the Commonwealth of Independent States (CIS, essentially the former USSR), Armenia has turned towards the west. This shows up in many ways. Foreign capital has entered the country in substantial amounts, and foreign companies have established offices and some operations in Armenia, especially in Yerevan. The American University of Armenia, where teaching is in English, operates under the auspices of the University of California. English has nearly replaced Russian as the second prevailing language, as on street name signs, store fronts, advertisements, etc.

Levon Ter Petrosyan,
The First President of the Second
Republic of Armenia

The governmental structure of the Republic of Armenia consists of three essentially autonomous branches, namely, Executive (President and Council of Ministers), Legislative (National Assembly), and Judicial (with courts in successively higher administrative levels from municipal to the Supreme Court, as well as special courts such as the Constitutional Court, and military courts). This tri-branch structure, as provided for in the national constitution adopted by referendum in July 1995, serves to provide for checks and balances in governmental operations.

As a sovereign state, Armenia has become a member of the United Nations, has embassies in many nations with which it maintains diplomatic relations (including the United States) and hosts embassies of foreign states, has established its own monetary system with the unit of currency being the "dram" (Armenian word for "money"), and maintains a national airline that operates international flights.

Bird's Eye View of Republic Square in Yerevan with the Hotel Armenia on the Right

The Emblem of the Second Republic of Armenia

Armenia enables foreign nationals to become citizens of the Republic of Armenia while retaining their previous nationality and foreign residency. Certain restrictions apply.

Armenia has been receiving foreign aid from the United States as well as from other foreign countries.

The new, independent Republic of Armenia enjoys a warm, cordial relationship with the Mother See of Holy Echmiadzin and with the Armenian Church generally, in sharp contrast to the very uneasy and barely tolerable relationship that existed with the former government, the Armenian Soviet Socialist Republic, under the Soviet order.

The Republic of Armenia has proclaimed itself to be a democratic nation. However, it has yet, both as a government and as a body of people, to learn how to be a democratic nation to the fullest extent of that idea. The prognosis for attaining that status, however, is good, for the fledgling republic has the stability and the will to succeed.

℘

Chapter 6

LANGUAGE
AND
LITERATURE

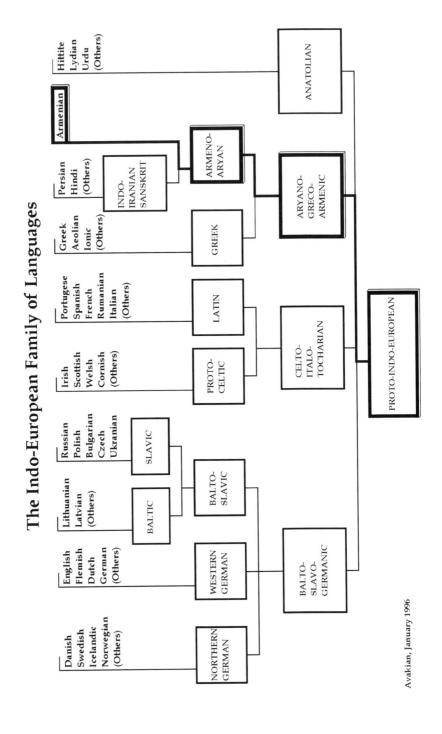

The Indo-European Family of Languages

Avakian, January 1996

170

The Armenian Language

rmenian belongs to the Indo-European family of languages. How do we know that, and what is its significance?

Linguists examine languages and compare their grammar (morphology), vocabulary (lexicon), phonetics (phonology), and sentence structure (syntax). The degree to which any two languages have these elements in common is a measure of how closely they are related.

Accordingly, languages of the world are grouped into major families. The languages belonging to a given family form sub-groups according to the higher degree to which they share these elements. And languages belonging to a given sub-group may be found to form even smaller groupings because of even greater sharing of the elements that make up the language.

World-class linguists have interested themselves in Armenian, and it is their findings that have led to the conclusion that Armenian is one of the Indo-European family of languages.

Several foreign linguists who have made major contributions to this conclusion are Schroder (*Thesaurus linguae armeniae*, 1711), Pott (1833), Petermann (*Grammatica linguae armenicae*, 1837), Windischmann *(The Basis of Armenian in the Aryan Family of Languages*, in German, 1846), Bopp (1833), Muller (1870), Hubschmann (1875), and several more of more recent date.

The Indo-European family is conveniently charted as a tree. The trunk is labeled as the Proto-Indo-European (PIE) tongue (a postulated language that is supposed to be the father of all members of the family). Four main branches are labeled Germanic, Italic, Anatolian, and Greco-Aryano-Armenic. The last branch then divides into two lesser groups, Greek and Aryano-Armenic, which in turn further divides into Armenian and the large Aryan grouping called Indo-Iranian languages.

It must be pointed out that Armenian existed as a spoken language possibly one thousand years before the invention of the Armenian alphabet at the beginning of the fifth century. And with the translation of the Bible, the language became more formally structured (and stable).

A very important criterion for judging the closeness of one language with another is the number of words common to the two. One speaks of 'loan' words, but it is not always clear which of the two languages is the lender and which the borrower. It is often the case that two such related languages have not 'borrowed' at all, but have a common ancestor (such as the PIE).

In tracing the origin of words, and comparing between languages, much attention must be given to consonant shifts and phonological changes. These are changes that follow a pattern consistently. The linguist Grimm (known also as the recorder of fairy tales) has stated a 'law' governing shifts in consonant 'stops.' In its simplest part the law states that the Greek letter 'p' ('pi') becomes the letter 'f' in English, and 'h' in Armenian (as additionally stated by Vernor). Example (three of many): 'pente' (G), five (E), and 'hing' (Arm); 'pyr' (G), fire (E), and 'hur' (Arm); and 'pater' (G), father (E), and 'hayr' (Arm).

The formalized language emerging from the translation of the Bible is called "grabar" (written). The popular speech, or vernacular, evolved continually and varied geographically. The emergent form (in all its dialectal variations) is called "ashkharhabar" (worldly). It was already recognizable in the popular speech by the eleventh century. But it was not until the late eighteenth century that the variant forms (regional) of ashkharhabar became more formally structured, and relatively stable, when a new literary freedom began to arise in Armenia, and writers gave the language more precision, albeit different regionally.

Of what significance is it that Armenian is an Indo-European language? Since language is an exceedingly strong indicator of a people's culture, it follows that the native culture of the Armenian people bears much in common with the cultures of the peoples whose languages are closely related.

$\wp$

Mesrop Mashtots
(The Invention of the Armenian Alphabet)

$\mathfrak{A}$t the beginning of the fifth century Armenia had already been a Christian nation for one hundred years. However, though Armenians had a fairly well developed language of their own, they did not have a written language.

Christian worship was being impeded by the absence of the Scriptures, the writings of the early church fathers, and homilies written in the people's own tongue. Moreover, only a few monks, and fewer parish priests, knew Greek or other languages in which the needed Christian literature was available.

The then Catholicos, Sahak, was eminently aware of the serious situation. Christian education of the people was limping. In consultation with the Armenian king, Vramshapuh, it was determined that a deliberate step should be taken to remedy the situation.

The monk Mesrop, surnamed Mashtots, was called upon to undertake the task of devising an Armenian alphabet. Mesrop, because of his educational background, was the most appropriate choice. The principal source of the history of this undertaking is the writings of Mesrop's pupil Koriun, and also Khorenatsi's History of the Armenians.

Koriun writes of the king's having learned that an Assyrian bishop named Daniel was in possession of the Armenian alphabet from ancient times. These letters were put to test by using children who were to learn the use of the alphabet. It appears that the alphabet had no vowels, and it was found to be inadequate in other ways. The search needed to be continued.

For several years Mesrop traveled to the learned centers of the then civilized world. Edessa (present-day Sanli Urfa) was one of the most important of such centers.

In time, Mesrop and his colleagues devised an alphabet. It consisted of thirty-six letters, seven of which were vowels. Two more letters, (the Armenian equivalent of "O" and "F") were added in the 12th century.) The order of the letters was the same as in the Greek alphabet, but with additional letters inserted. Those additional letters (sounds not in the Greek alphabet) were needed for those Armenian words whose source was mainly Indo-Iranian.

Here are the two alphabets, both in normal order, shown paired vertically. The equivalence is well established through the translation of the Bible done by the Translators. Proper nouns (names of places and persons) were transcribed letter for letter.

The Armenian and Greek Alphabets

Աա	Բբ	Գգ	Դդ	Եե	Զզ	Էէ	Ըը	Թթ	Ժժ
Αα	Ββ	Γγ	Δδ	Εε	Ζζ	Ηη		Θθ	

Իի	Լլ	Խխ	Ծծ	Կկ	Հհ	Ձձ	Ղղ	Ճճ	Մմ
Ιι		Κκ					Λλ		Μμ

Յյ	Նն	Շշ	Ոո	Չչ	Պպ	Ջջ	Ռռ	Սս	Վվ
	Νν	Ξξ	Οο		Ππ		Ρρ	Σσ	

Տտ	Րր	Ցց	Ււ	Փփ	Քք	Օօ	Ֆֆ		
Ττ			Υυ	Φφ	Χχ			Ψψ	Ωω

There is a lovely legend telling of a vision that came to Mesrop in which he saw an angel displaying a tablet with seven Armenian vowels:

Ա Ե Է Ը Ի Ո Ւ

A plausible rationalization of this beautiful legend is that Mesrop, through inspiration, concluded that the best choice for Armenians was to lean toward western culture (Greek alphabet, with vowels) rather than toward the eastern culture (Assyrian alphabet, with no vowels). Moreover, the story about the inadequacy of the alphabet in Bishop Daniel's possession provides some reinforcement to the rationalization of Mesrop's vision.

With the new alphabet in place, Mesrop and his "army" of scholars set about feverishly to translate the Bible, using the Greek Septuagint text. Interestingly, according to Koriun's account, the translation was begun not with Genesis, but with the Book of Proverbs, which begins with "To know wisdom and instruction, to perceive the words of understanding." These, then, were the very first words ever written in Armenian. They would have appeared thus:

ՃԱՆԱՉԵԼ ՁԻՄԱՍՏՈՒԹԻՒՆ ԵԻ ՁԽՐԱՏ, ԻՄԱՆԱԼ ՁԲԱՆՍ ՀԱՆՃԱՐՈՅ

These words have been written in what we today recognize as "capital" letters. Mesrop's alphabet consisted only of those. "Lower case" letters were not devised until centuries later.

It must be pointed out that, in time, there have been some changes in the phonetic values of the letters.   However, the spelling has remained unaltered.

℘

The Title Page from the First Armenian Printed Bible
Amsterdam 1666

The Bible in Armenian

The invention of the Armenian alphabet was undertaken specifically to permit the creation of written materials for Christian worship, not only the Bible (Old and New Testaments), but also other texts of Christendom (liturgies, prayers, homilies) needed in worship.

With the Mesropian alphabet of 36 letters in place very early in the fifth century, a group of scholar-monks, called "Targmanichnere" (The Translators) set about translating the Bible.

At first the Translators started with an Assyrian translation of the Old Testament in Hebrew. That effort was aborted, however, because the language structure (Semitic linguistic family) was too different from the Armenian (Indo-European family).

Consequently, the version used was the Greek Septuagint (*Yotanasnots*), meaning "seventy," the traditional number of scholars who translated the Old Testament from Hebrew to Greek.

The work of translation into Armenian was initially completed in the second decade of the fifth century, and the finally accepted text is believed to have been completed in the year 438. Of course, the language of that Bible was the "*Grabar*," (Classical Armenian).

The Armenian word for the Bible is *Astvadzashounch* (Breath of God).

There are some differences between the commonly known versions of the Bible (King James, Revised Standard, etc.) and the Bible as it is known and used by Armenians. The books of which the Armenian Bible is comprised include some that are usually taken to be part of The Apocrypha (non-canonical books), and excludes some other portions of text.

An important thing to recognize is that the Armenian Church does not use a "Whole Bible," but uses selected segments designated for the several daily offices (services) throughout the liturgical year, day after day. As such, it employs a large portion of the Old and New Testaments, and, in particular, all of the texts of the Gospels.

The meanings of words used in the early classical Armenian at the time of the translation apparently remain little changed today. As a result, the scholars who reworked the Apocrypha of the Revised Standard Version (Thomas Nelson edition) found it helpful to refer frequently to the Armenian text as they tried to extract the intended meaning of the original text. The fact that they have done so has been so stated.

Notwithstanding that the Armenian Church does not normally use the whole Bible in its traditional composition, many such manuscript compilations were produced by scribes in monasteries. The four Gospels were most frequently copied as illuminated manuscripts.

With the advent of printing, Armenian Bibles (grabar) were printed. At least nine such editions exist, with the first printed in 1666 in Amsterdam, with possibly the last in 1895 in Constantinople.

Nevertheless, it was not until very recent times that an Armenian household would have an Armenian Bible, in either classical or modern Armenian.

With the growth of the Armenian Protestant movement starting in the third decade of the 19th century, it became necessary to have the full text of the Bible, in traditional form and in modern Armenian. As a result, a number of translations were undertaken. The earliest printing was in 1822 for the Gospels only and the New Testament in 1825 (in Paris).

The first complete Armenian Bible in modern Armenian was published in 1853, in Smyrna. Since then there have been a number of translations into modern Armenian based on different versions.

The Bible in classical Armenian has been hailed as a superb rendering, for its euphony and clarity in meaning. It has been declared to be "The Queen of Translations."

ℰℑ

The Golden Age of Armenian Literature

The small Christian Armenian nation burst upon the world literary scene at the beginning of the fifth century like a supernova with the creation of its own alphabet, and the continuing century of feverish literary activity. The fifth century, marked in Armenian history as its "Golden Age of Literature," gave immediate birth to a vast body of Armenian writings. The translation of the Holy Scriptures, immediately upon the creation of the alphabet, gave precise form to the extant spoken Armenian language, establishing its phonology, orthography, lexicon, grammar, and syntax.

Today we call the emergent language, full grown, the "Grabar" (written form), or Classical Armenian.

With the language having emerged instantly, fully matured, there came into being a number of scholars, mainly in the monasteries throughout Armenia. They were stirred to put into writing all their knowledge in theology, history, law, liturgics, philosophy, etc. They translated the important writings of the then civilized world. They enriched the Armenian treasury of recorded knowledge and understanding. They made the fifth century truly a Golden Age.

Supporting these scholar-authors were the scribes, a small army of them, who painstakingly lettered the parchment pages to produce the manuscript volumes. Within a few centuries this art of calligraphy would evolve into a very high level of beauty, producing magnificent illuminated manuscripts.

Who were the fifth century principal players in the great drama that was the Golden Age? We list them here and tell what they did.

SAHAK PARTEV (348-439): Catholicos (387-439), who recognized the need for Armenians to have their own written language, and initiated the action to develop an alphabet.

MESROP MASHTOTS (361-440): Scholar, linguist, and monk, who led the effort of developing the Armenian alphabet, and who guided the small army of Translators of the Holy Scriptures.

VRAMSHAPUH (?-414): King of Armenia (389-414), who approved the plan to develop the Armenian alphabet, and gave strong support to the effort.

Sahak Partev, Catholicos   King Vramshapuh

YEGHISHE (ELISAEUS) (410-475): Author, who wrote the history of the Vardanants Wars.

EZNIK OF GOGHP (fifth century): Translator and researcher, who gathered literary works of other peoples.

KORIUN (fifth century): Monk, later bishop, leading pupil of Mesrop Mashtots, who wrote his teacher's biography and the story of the discovery of the Armenian alphabet.

MOSES OF KHOREN (KHORENATSI) (fifth century): Bishop, who wrote the comprehensive History of Armenians, including much of legendary character.

LAZAR OF PHARBE (443-?): Who also wrote the history of the Vardanants Wars, and of an extended period before and after.

HOVSEP HOGHOTSMETSI (?-454): Catholicos (437-454) at the time of the Vardanants Wars.

HOVHANNES MANDAKUNI (410-490): Catholicos (478-490) at the time of the Treaty of Nouarsak (484) with Persia.

֍

The Silver Age of Armenian Literature

Three great churchmen shone brightly as stars in the firmament of Armenian Cilician prominence in the twelfth century. They together created a vast body of literature that adorns the Church and enriches the faithful spiritually and intellectually.

The three were St. Nerses Shnorhali (1100-1173), Mkhitar Gosh (1130-1213), and Nerses Lambronatsi (1152-1198).

Far to the west of the heartlands of Armenia surrounding the slopes of Mt. Ararat was Cilician Armenia arcing around the northeast shores of the Mediterranean. It became a brief but brilliant episode in Armenia's long history. After the Seljuk invasions of the eleventh century drove Armenians out of the east, especially Ani, glorious capital city of the Bagratids, Armenians established a new kingdom in Cilicia where a colony of Armenians had already planted roots. There the Armenians formed the Rubenid dynasty named after the first prince, Ruben (1080), ending with the death of the last, King Leon V (1393).

The Holy See of the Armenian Church, having repeatedly moved to be where the civil authority was located, remained in Cilicia for 336 years, until its return to Echmiadzin in 1441.

During that period, the great churchmen of the Armenian Church produced an expansive body of literature, both religious and secular. It is because of their combined scholarship and writings that the twelfth century has been aptly called the "Silver Age of Armenian Literature," in acknowledgment of the transcendence of the fifth century "Golden Age of Armenian Literature."

St. Nerses Shnorhali (Full of Grace) created by far the greatest amount of hymns, chants, and canticles of the liturgies of the Armenian Church.

Mkhitar Gosh, an intellectual giant, though ordained a celibate priest, is best known for his *Corpus Juris*, a compilation of civil and canon laws. In this undertaking Mkhitar Gosh, having recognized the deplorable condition of the Armenians

St. Nerses Shnorhali

suffering because of the absence of national jurisprudence or a body of laws, sought to establish civil rights for Armenians who were being subjected to arbitrary, unjust, and inequitable treatment by the prevailing foreign authorities.

A monastery in Ichevan, Armenia, has been named Goshavank, after Mkhitar Gosh.

Goshavank (Named After Mkhitar Gosh)

Nerses of Lambron, of royal birth, had the benefit of a very broad linguistic education, in Greek, Latin, Hebrew, and Assyrian. He was ordained a celibate priest, made an archbishop at the age of 23, and appointed Primate of Lambron and Tarsus, in Cilicia.

Nerses played a very important role in defending the Armenian Church against repeated attempts by both the Roman Catholic Church and the Greek Church to recapture the Armenian Church into their fold.

His best known work is *Interpretation of the Divine Liturgy* (Meknoutiun Khorhrdo Pataragi). He also wrote an interpretation of the Book of Proverbs, and of the Book of Revelation, as well as a series of commentaries on the canons of the Church.

The very rich body of Armenian literature from the "Silver Age," together with that of the "Golden Age," attests to the intellectual might of Armenia's writers.

Nerses of Lambron

ℰℐ

An Etymological Safari
(Stalking Etymological Game)

Cognates! Linguistic cognates, that is. What are they?
Words that are recognized to have arisen either as borrowed or as loaned words of other languages, or when they have a common ancestry with words of other languages are cognates. Cognate words normally have a similar appearance. To see that similarity, however, calls for recognizing certain consonant shifts that have arisen when a word travels from one language to another. One of the most familiar of such shifts is found in Latin words beginning with "p" (or the Greek letter "pi"), which appears in the cognate Armenian words as the letter "Հ" (h). Examples are found in the Latin words: penta, pyro, pater, panis, pastor, pax, puteo, and pons. Their Armenian cognates in the same order, are: Հինգ (five), Հուր (fire), Հայր (father), Հաց (bread), Հովիւ (shepherd), Հանգիստ (peace), Հոտ (smell), and Հուն (bridge).

Though English and Armenian both belong to the Indo-European family of languages, though somewhat remotely from one another, they have numerous cognates, derived from a somewhat tenuous path along different branches of the postulated Proto-Indo-European (PIE) language tree (see page 170).

A few examples may be seen in the following cognates: կատու (katu), cat; կով (kov), cow; դուռ (dur), door; դուստր (dustr), daughter; նաւ (nav), naval; ամպ (amb), umbra; լուանալ (lvanal), laval/wash; Հեր (her), hair; ագռաւ (agrav), crow; կարմիր (karmir), carmine; ագարակ (agarak), acre/agriculture; լոյս (luys), lune; and լու (lu), louse.

A pleasing correspondence exists with the words "mouse," and its derivative "muscle" (meaning "little mouse"). The Armenian words are մուկ (muk), mouse and its derivative մկան (mkan), meaning muscle.

But two other examples are especially tantalizing. They are the words "aegis" and "elegy," which bear a surprising kinship to the Armenian.

<u>Aegis</u>: The Armenian word for goat is այծ (aedz), which is also the Greek word, nearly. In ancient times a shield used in hand-to-hand combat was often made of goatskin (light and tough) stretched over a wooden framework, as an effective way to parry a blow from an adversary's sword. Hence, the goatskin offered protection. That led to using the word "aegis" (taken from the Greek) to mean "protection," or "sponsorship," as in "under the aegis of …"

Elegy: The well-known Armenian pre-Christian poem describing the birth of Vahagn, the Armenian pagan god of war, tells of his birth, which was to rise with smoke and flame out of a reed in a sea in travail. The Armenian word in that poem for the reed is եղեգ (egheg), where the ղ (gh) in Armenian is the lambda (λ) in Greek, or the (l) in Latin. In ancient times panpipes were fashioned from reeds (tubular) cut to different lengths and clustered together, four or more in number. Such a panpipe, when played by blowing across the tops, produced a lamenting tone, appropriate for a dirge to be played at a funeral, or also at an occasion of praise. It is in this way that the word *elegy* came to mean a song of lament, or praise, and it derives from the Armenian word that means *reed*.

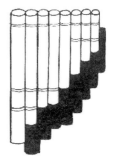

Panpipes

࿇

The Literature and Music of the Armenian Church

𝕿he Armenian Church has developed for its faithful a very rich body of written material and music for religious worship.

The sources for the texts are the Holy Bible, Prayers and Litanies out of the liturgies for early Christian worship, and hymns (called "sharakan") written by early fathers of the Armenian Church (from the 5th to the 15th centuries).

The supporting music for the texts arose from native and regional musical forms.

Liturgical services in the Armenian Church consist of seven daily services (or "offices"), namely, Night, Morning, Sunrise, Midday (which expands into the Sacrament of the Divine Liturgy, or Holy Mass, the "Patarag"), Evening, Peace, and Rest Services. There are also a number of special services such as "Blessing of Waters" on Theophany (being the Feast of Nativity and Revelation), and "Washing of Feet" on Maundy Thursday. Each liturgical service is precisely structured and ordained with designated texts. The outlines of each of the Daily Offices are contained in a Breviary (in Armenian, "Zhamagirk," - Book of Hours).   The special services are contained in a book called "Mashtots."

The Divine Liturgy in the Armenian Church, performed regularly and normally on Sunday mornings, is structured on the ancient liturgies for early Christian worship, the St. Basil Liturgy modified according to the St. John Chrysostom Liturgy.

But what is unique and characteristic in the Armenian Church is its vast body of "Sharakans." They are contained in an enormous compendium of hymns that are inserted into the liturgical structure of a service and are specified for all the days of the liturgical year (Theophany, January 6, through Eve of Theophany, January 5 of the following calendar year). These sharakans are of several kinds. Some are specific for the Night Service, called "Orhnutyan Sharakan" (Lauds). Some are specific for the Morning Service, of which there are four kinds, namely, "Harts" (Faith of the Fathers), "Medzatsustse" (Magnificat), "Voghormya" (Miserere), and "Ter Herknits" (Lord in the Heavens). Some are for the Midday Service, called "Jashou" (literally, the midday meal).

All of these were written by the early fathers of the Armenian Church, and their textual contents (in Classical Armenian), in poetic style, are dedicated to the theological nature of the day (such as Theophany, Easter, Feasts of the Holy Cross, Ascension, Pentecost, Assumption, and numerous lesser feasts and saints' days).

Each sharakan is chanted in a musical mode (or scale), of which there are eight. Most books of the sharakans show musical markings, or neumes (in Armenian, "Khaz"), along with the words. Skilled chanters can sing the sharakan by knowing the designated musical mode, and by being guided by the neumes which give only a partial indication of the musical pattern.

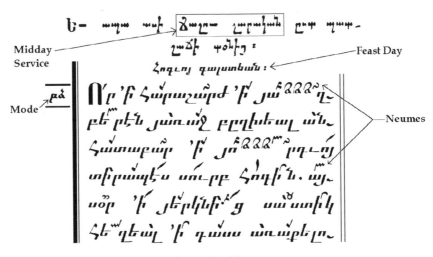

Armenian Neumes

Because the Divine Liturgy in the Armenian Church has become the central form of worship for the people, its music has become more formalized. It is now written in modern musical notation, and harmonized for part singing. Moreover, though early chanting of songs and sharakans was done without accompaniment of musical instruments, modern choirs all sing the music of the Divine Liturgy accompanied by the organ.

Though ancient in origin, the Armenian Church can be justly proud of the music of its Divine Liturgy as it is performed in the contemporary environment.

℘

St. Nerses Shnorhali
(Full of Grace)

𝔄mong its long line of Catholicoi the Armenian Church has produced many great men.   And they, in turn, served the Church meritoriously, enriching it spiritually, intellectually, materially, and administratively.

Outstanding among them was St. Nerses Shnorhali (1100-1173), often called St. Nerses the Graceful. Pontiff from 1166 to his death he was No. 64 in the succession from No. 1 (St. Gregory the Enlightener) to No. 131 (His Holiness, Karekin I). St. Nerses was known also as St. Nerses Klayetsi, meaning that he was from Hromkla, site of the Holy See of the Armenian Church, in Cilicia, from 1147 to 1283, when it moved to Sis.

Nerses was one of four sons of the royal household of Pahlavuni. An older brother, Grigor, preceded Nerses as Catholicos. During Grigor's time a heretical group had been challenging the Armenian Church in doctrinal matters. Grigor called on his brother to prepare a response. Nerses wrote a formidable answer, denouncing the heretical movement and refuting the charges, defending the Church's position in doctrinal issues, such as the dual nature of Christ.

With Catholicos Grigor's failing health, Nerses agreed under pressure to become co-Adjutor. On Grigor's death Nerses became Catholicos, at age 66.

Nerses had already attained widespread fame in his literary and theological writings. He displayed rare skill in lyric poetry.

His first encyclical, "Tught Undhanrakan" (Universal Paper), remains today as a gem in style and content. It concerns church reform, worship, ritual, conduct, and canons.

A letter written earlier at his brother's request to the Byzantine royal house on the doctrinal philosophy of the Armenian Church had impressed the Byzantine King. The King invited Grigor to visit him, to discuss the letter. But Grigor had died. Nerses, as the new Catholicos, wanted to avoid meeting the king, knowing that the king would press for closer union between the Greek and Armenian churches. Nerses knew that such a union would weaken his Church. Yet, he did not want to offend the king or impair the relationship between the two churches. Therefore, he composed a skillful letter that both flattered the king and yet made it quite justifiable for him not to visit the king.

The Armenian Church is very rich in the quality and volume of its church literature. Liturgies of the church, in addition to using the Scriptures and writings of church leaders of all Christendom, also use a vast amount of writings of Armenian churchmen over the centuries. Of all such contributors, St. Nerses Shnorhali has written by far the most songs, hymns (sharakans), and prayers used in Armenian Church liturgies.

Characteristic of his writings is the extensive use of the Armenian alphabet in initial letters of successive verses of a hymn, or of spelling out his name.

Some of the best known of his voluminous output are the following. In "Aravod Louso..." there are 36 three-line verses, with each of the three lines starting with letters of the alphabet in order. It is the same with "Ashkharh Amenayn..."

His "Aysor Anjar..." has 36 verses. Each starts with letters of the alphabet in order. It is the same with "Astvadz Anegh..."

In his "Norasteghdzeal..." the initial letters of the verses spell his name:

ՆԵՐԱԵՍ   (though it should be   ՆԵՐՍԵՍ).

Here and there he used poetic license where a letter needed to be changed. In his song "Nayats Sirov..." initial letters of the verses spell (in Armenian) "Nerses' song."

There is much more, including "gematria," in which words or phrases have hidden meaning through the numerical values their letters represent.

In his contribution to the spiritual and intellectual life of the Armenian Church, St. Nerses Shnorhali was a giant.

ॐ

Nahapet Kouchak
(15th - 16th Century)

Very popular as a minstrel, and yet obscure as an individual, Nahapet Kouchak was of the earliest of Armenian poet-singers. He was evidently of the region of Van, though his numerous quatrains were known and loved widely. He wrote in a quaint language, possibly a very local dialect, more like that of Akn (on the Euphrates between Kharberd and Erzinjan rather than that of Van).

"Ashough" (Minstrel) Kouchak is believed to have been born toward the end of the 15th century. He was buried, as it is commonly believed, in the courtyard cemetery of the St. Theodosis Church in Kharakonis (probably his birthplace) on the northeast shore of Lake Arjak (Erchek) immediately east of Lake Van. Tradition has it that he climbed to the rooftop of the church, and said to those with him that he was to jump off the roof, and that he was to be buried at the spot where he landed. That did become his grave.

The poems, mostly quatrains, attributed to Kouchak number well over 200. However, it is possible that some of them were not written by him, but by other poets even more obscure as individuals than Kouchak. As an extreme point of view, it has been said by some scholars, that Nahapet Kouchak represents no more than a conceptual idea that encompasses a collection of poems of a style, time, and region.

Khouchak's poems fall into three main categories: sensuality (the largest group, nearing 200), allegory and admonition, and emigres.

The poems dealing with sensuality are often very ardently passionate. The following is an example. (The poet's word "groghe," literally "the writer," has been translated as Satan, for that is approximately the intended meaning).

Your bosom's Adam's paradise; Oh, that I enter and pluck the apple,
That I recline between your two breasts and sleep.
From your lips I would drink wine and become drunk.
Let my soul be given to Satan; let him come and take me.

Of special interest is the fact that the poem-song *Krounk* (best known as set to music by Komitas) is attributed to Kouchak. It is the highly popular song of the emigre asking the migratory crane if it has brought any bit of news from home. Few know that the poem has ten quatrains. Below is the well-known initial quatrain.

Կռունկ, ուսպի° կու գաս, ծառայ եմ ձայնիդ,
Կռունկ, մեր աշխարհէ՛ն խապրիկ մի չունի°ս:
Մի՛ վագեր, երամիդ շուտով կը հասնիս,
Կռունկ, մեր աշխարհէ՛ն խապրիկ մը չունի°ս:

Crane, whence do you come? I would hear your voice.
Crane, what tidings have you from home?
Hurry not, you will join your flock soon.
Crane, what tidings have you from home?

The existence of a rich heritage of early poetry-songs of the Armenian people depends much on troubadors like Nahapet Kouchak, Sayat-Nova (1722-1795), and Ashough Jivani (1846-1909). Their combined output represents an immeasurable cultural wealth.

֍

Armenian Printing

𝕬rmenian typographers were quick to adopt Gutenberg's innovation and bring enlightenment to the Armenian world.

It was not long after Johann Gutenberg had introduced his printing with movable type (Germany, circa 1450) that Armenians in several centers began turning out printed material on presses, using Armenian type faces.

The principal and earliest centers producing Armenian printed material were in Venice (1512), Paris (1537), Constantinople (1567), Lvov (1616), New Julfa (1640), Amsterdam (1660), and Leipzig (1680).

Venice had become a world center for printing. It was there, in the years 1512 and immediately following, that Meghapart Hakob published five books in Armenian, the first ever to be printed using the new technology. The five books were a calendar, a missal, an anthology of poetry, a book on astrology, and a prayer book. Some original copies of these books exist today, here and there. Some of these books have been republished in recent years.

During the ensuing years, several others undertook the task of publishing Armenian books in Italy. But the outstanding accomplishment in doing so must be accorded the Mekhitarist Order on the Island of San Lazzaro, in the lagoon off of Venice, founded in 1717 by Abbot Mekhitar. This monastic order, still in operation as an Armenian press (and a peerless center for Armenian research and scholarship) has produced and published untold numbers of books and journals, some in languages other than Armenian. The quality of its printing is of the highest level, and in full color.

Other centers of Armenian printing in Italy (Rome and Padua, especially) have also published books in Armenian.

Paris may have been the second earliest center for Armenian printing. A bilingual work bears the inscription, 'Paris 1537.'

Constantinople (and some other cities in western Anatolia), having become important Armenian cultural centers for Armenians, very early established a number of presses, and published a very large number of books, continuing into the present century. It was Abgar Tbir, in 1567, who established the first Armenian press in Constantinople. His early books included a grammar book, a calendar, a book of prayers and missal, and a Mashtots (compendium of special services of the Church).

191

It is of special interest to note that Catholicos Mkrtich Khrimian ('Hayrik') established a press at the Monastery of Varag (in the hills above Van, far to the east) in 1858.

In 1616, Elder Hovhannes Karmatanents established an Armenian press in Lvov (Poland). The first book he published was a psalter.

With the large-scale transfer (1605) of Armenians from (old) Julfa on the Araxes River to New Julfa, near Isfahan, Iran, by the Persian monarch Shah Abbas, a strong Armenian cultural center developed there. By 1640 a press had been established in the Amenaprkich Monastery with the first book being a modest work on patristic writings. By the year 1642 a substantial volume of the Church Breviary had been published.

Very important in Armenian printing is the publishing of the complete Bible, in Amsterdam, in 1666. This very well recognized and highly prized work, with thirty or more copies known to be still existing, may be regarded as the flowering of Armenian printing.

Some of the Many Type Styles (Faces) of the Armenian Alphabet

Today, anywhere in the world where there are Armenians, in even modest numbers, there are Armenian presses. Modern computer technology has made it possible for even individuals to produce superb Armenian copy for any and all purposes.

The Mekhitarists

𝕿he Mekhitarist Order of Armenian monks in its nearly 300 years of existence has served the Armenians throughout the world as a fount of learning.   Its diligent scholarship, its vast amount of printing and publishing, and its productive schools have enriched the nation intellectually as well as culturally, spiritually, and morally.

Cloistered in their monasteries, the monks have established and maintained a world-wide reputation for the quality of their output. Though they are an Order within the Roman Catholic hierarchy they enjoy the unequivocal esteem of all Armenians, be they Apostolic, Protestant, or uncommitted.

Today there are two branches of the Order, in Venice, Italy, and in Vienna, Austria.

This is how the Order came into existence.

A young lad named Manuk, born in 1676 in Sebastia (Sivas), having shown at about age 15 a great love of religious studies, and being very pious, was allowed to devote his life to God, especially through the strong support of his mother.

Mekhitar

He took the name Mekhitar (meaning Comforter). After having spent about two years at Echmiadzin he decided to go to Rome, for he had been born in a Catholic family.   However, because of illness he returned to his homeland.

In 1696 he was ordained a priest in the Armenian Church, when he was twenty, and was assigned to teach theology at the seminary at Karmir Vank (in the region of Nakhichevan). For his superior work he was awarded the degree of Vardapet (Doctor).

But Mekhitar was eager to form a new monastic order. In 1700 he went to Constantinople, and with the help of the vicar of the Armenian Patriarch (the vicar was converting Armenian Apostolics to Catholicism), he formed a group of supporters.

Because of opposition he was experiencing, he found it necessary to go to Europe. In 1703 Mekhitar sought approval of Pope Gregory XI to form a new monastic order. On gaining approval Mekhitar started work building a monastery in Modena (northern Italy), completing it in 1708.

However, because of the war between the Kingdom of Venice and the Ottoman Empire (1714-15), the members of the new order were obliged to flee to Venice. There the Venetian authorities looked with favor on the Order, and granted them the Island of San Lazzaro (a former leper colony), in the lagoon off Venice, in March 1715.

The Island of San Lazarro near Venice, Italy

The new Order grew in size, in strength, and in activity.

In 1773, as a result of disagreements over provisions of the constitution governing the Order, a group of monks broke away and established a new monastery in Vienna, still identifying themselves as Mekhitarists.

Today, both groups exist, in Venice and in Vienna. Both engage in the highest levels of scholastic research in theology, linguistics, history, and other fields. They print and publish books, in several languages. They also publish periodicals and maintain and support schools, locally and abroad.

As monastic orders within the pale of the Roman Catholic Church, both Mekhitarist groups have served and are serving the Armenian people without compromising their own hierarchical commitment to the Roman Catholic Church, and without subverting the Apostolicity of the Armenian Church and its followers.

Abbot Mekhitar died in 1749.

֍

The Lazarian Language Institute
(The Armenian Cultural Center of Moscow)

The forced dispersion of Armenians from their native homelands did not deter them from establishing strong cultural and educational centers wherever they were.

Among such educational centers was one very fine one in Moscow, the Lazarian Language Institute.

Opened in 1815 the Institute was founded and supported by the Lazarian family, which late in the previous century had left Persia and settled in Moscow.   The family's wealth was based on a textile manufacturing operation on the outskirts of Moscow. Members of the family also distinguished themselves in service to the state.

At first serving as a secondary school, the Institute later developed into an institution for higher learning. It was highly regarded in Russian circles. At first primarily for Armenian students, later the Institute accepted others as well, in number more than Armenians.

The list of its Armenian graduates, some of whom returned to the Institute as faculty members, reads as a list of illustrious intellectuals in various fields, especially in writing. A partial list includes the following: Raphael Patkanian, Michael Nalbandian, S. Shah Aziz, Hovhannes Hovhannesian, Alexander Dzaturian, Vahan Terian, Mkrtich Emin, Grigor Khalatyants. Many of its Russian graduates also attained fame in their fields.

The Institute enjoyed the luxury of a fine facility consisting of three buildings, two-story and three-story, on a large, uncrowded piece of land just off a major square deep within Moscow. The street on which the entrance faces is called Armianskiy Way.

Having fallen into near abandonment, with a deterioration of the physical facility during the mid-Soviet years, and closed to visitors, it was revived once again during the 1980's. Skilled craftsmen from Armenia spent several years renovating the entire facility. The work was undertaken with great care, and was completed in 1987, converting the former Institute into the Armenian Cultural Center of Moscow.

The newly restored complex now houses offices, meeting rooms, dormitories, a museum, an ornate reception hall suitable for concerts of chamber music, and facilities for the care and supervision of Armenian students studying in Moscow.

This new center enhances the cultural activities of the Armenians of Moscow, approximately 100,000 in number. It also serves as a natural stop-over point for Armenian visitors from afar.

೫೨

Foreign Scholars in Armenian Academic Fields

𝔉oreign scholars having discovered the value of Armenian scholarship, both in its own importance and in its relationship to scholarship in other cultures, have contributed a tremendous amount of academic material pertaining to all fields of Armenian culture. Their output has appeared principally in the last century and a half in the form of books in various languages, as well as countless articles in Armenian and non-Armenian periodicals and journals.

Listed below, grouped by main field of study, are those well-known scholars whose works are readily available for further study.

ARCHITECTURE:

Strzygowski, Josef (1862-1941), Austrian archeologist who worked with Toros Toramanian on Armenian architectural monuments. Books include *Die Baukunst Der Armenier und Europa* (2 Vols., Vienna, 1918*); Origin of Christian Church Architecture* (Oxford, 1930); and *Asiens Bildende Kunst* (Angsburg, Austria, 1930).

Baltrusaitis, Jurgis (1873-1944), Lithuanian diplomat, poet and archeologist. Books include *Etudes Sur 1'Art Medieval en Georgie et en Armenie* (Paris, 1929).

LANGUAGE:

Hubschmann, Heinrich (1849-1906), German linguist. Books include studies in Armenian (in German, 1883), and other works, as well as numerous articles.

Meillet, Antoine (1866-1936), French linguist. Books include *Esquisse d'Une Grammaire Comparee de l'Armenien Classique* (Vienna, 1931), and *Manuel de Langue Armenienne* (Paris, 1948).

Macler, Frederic (1869-1938). French linguist, succeeding Meillet in Paris school of Living Eastern Languages. Published countless articles.

Antoine Meillet

Feydit, Frederic Armon (1908-   ), French linguist, pupil of Meillet, Taught at Sorbonne, and published books on Armenian grammar, as well as countless articles.

HISTORY AND LITERATURE:

Parrot, Friedrich (1792-1840), German traveler.   Wrote of journey to and ascent of Mt. Ararat in 1829 (New York, 1846).

de Morgan, Jean Jacques (1857-1924), French historian.   Books include *The History of the Armenian People* (English trans., Boston, 1965).

Lynch, H.F.B. (1862-1913), British historian.   Books include *Armenia, Travels and Studies* (2 Vols., London, 1901).

Grousset, Rene (1885-1952), French historian.   Works cover the Crusades.

Toynbee, Arnold (1899-1975), British historian.   Books include *Armenian Atrocities, The Murder of a Nation* (New York, 1915).

H.F.B. Lynch

Piotrovsky, Boris B. (1908-1990), Russian archeologist.   Books include *The Kingdom of Van and Its Art - Urartu* (New York, 1967), and *The Ancient Civilization of Urartu* (New York, 1969).

Lang, David Marshal (1924-1999), British historian.   Books include *Armenia, Cradle of Civilization* (London, 1970).

Dowsett, Charles (1924-1998), British scholar.   Works include texts and translated Armenian classical works.

Walker, Christopher J. (1942-   ), British historian.   Books include *Armenia, Survival of a Nation* (London, 1980).

℘

198

Sayat-Nova
(1722-1795)

℧he most widely recognized Armenian minstrel, Sayat-Nova, led a stormy life in Tiflis, the cultural center of the Caucasus. Appointed as palace minstrel, he became enamoured with the king's married daughter, and that illicit love was the spark that led to an outpouring of love songs, and also to his expulsion from the court.

Born in the enlightened and refined environment of Tiflis in 1722, Sayat-Nova (Harutiun Sayatian), learned the craft of weaving as a livelihood. At the same time, he became strongly influenced by the bards of Georgia and the surrounding lands of the Caucasus. He soon began to compose and sing songs to the delight of his audiences.

Though he did not have a formal education, he knew its value and learned the languages of Georgia and Azerbaijan as well as his own. By the age of 27, he was already a well-known and esteemed troubadour who captivated his listeners with his songs.

As court minstrel, he had ample opportunity to be with the king's daughter, who, as a result of a love-less marriage, encouraged the young minstrel's affections.

Sayat-Nova's fervent, illicit love naturally led to entanglements and consequently he was banished from the court. Undaunted and undeterred, the lovelorn minstrel pleaded with the king to be taken back into the palace. The kind-hearted king relented, but Sayat-Nova's return led only to the rekindling of the earlier problem, and he was banished once again.

This time, the banishment was even more of a tragic blow to Sayat-Nova because the king's daughter, feeling the strain of the impassioned but perilous relationship, turned away from him completely.

In his bitterness, Sayat-Nova became insolent towards members of the royal household and assailed them with his caustic pen. In retaliation, the king forced Sayat-Nova unwillingly to become a priest.

Thus, Sayat-Nova, now a priest renamed Ter Stepanos, entered a new phase of his life. He married and had four children. Later, when his wife died, he became a celibate priest. He continued as a poet-minstrel but not with the same intensity as before. He also attained a considerably higher level of education.

His commitment as a churchman was genuine and effective. When in 1795 the Persian Agha Mehmet Khan invaded the region and spread terror, putting to the sword the innocent and cultured people of Tiflis and the area, Ter Stepanos chose to defend the church at Haghbat. Refusing to yield entrance into the church to the attacking invaders, he was slain at the door. His tomb remains today at the door of the St George Armenian Church of Tiflis. Armenian pilgrims visit regularly and pay homage to him.

Sayat-Nova was the most loved of Armenian minstrels. As a poet-singer of love songs, he also promoted spiritual love as a churchman. His heart was filled with humanitarian principles. To make his message reach a wider audience, he created and performed his songs in three languages.

Sayat-Nova's main thrust was to assail the injustice, swindling, and oppression that prevailed in his world.

Sayat-Nova's songs are popularly performed today and exhibit a very characteristic musical quality. The words are chosen in a deep regional dialect and usually include reference to himself by name.

ဆာ

Fr. Ghevond (Leo) Alishan
(1820-1901)

𝔄n intellectual giant, Fr. Ghevond Alishan was poet, historian, philologist, geographer, translator, educator, linguist, antiquarian, and scientist. He was also the embodiment of patriotism, and his name symbolized love of fatherland and of national values.

Born in Constantinople as Kerovpe Alishanian, Fr. Ghevond (Leonides) followed his elementary education locally by enrolling in the Mekhitarist school in Venice when he was only twelve years of age. He joined the monastic order when he was eighteen (1838). He became a teacher in the school in 1841 and was named superintendent in 1848.

For two years (1849-1851) he served as editor of "Bazmavep," the magnificently printed literary, historical, and artistic periodical published by the Mekhitarists at their monastery on the Island of St. Lazar, Venice. For a time Fr. Alishan served as teacher at the Mekhitarist Murat-Raphaelian school in Paris.

After some travel to several academic centers of Europe he returned to the monastery at St. Lazar in 1872. In 1877 he became the Chief Abbott of the Mekhitarist Order.

The visual image left by Fr. Alishan, as he was usually portrayed, was as a full-bearded, withered, frail figure, pen in hand, bent over his desk that was covered with reference books. He was a shy person, preferring solitude. But those coming into his presence were much moved by his goodness and his simplicity of manner. He was indefatigable in his research, study, and writing, and demanded much of his body. He instilled in all a deep sense of goodness, probity, religious faith, and love of fatherland. The advancement of these qualities permeates all of his writings.

The quantity of Fr. Alishan's writings, in all fields of his interests, is enormous. Most of his monumental output was published at the Mekhitarist Monastery. His mastery of many languages, European and Asiatic, enabled him to translate important foreign works, as well as to employ vast resources in his researches.

Included in Fr. Alishan's translations are some works of American poets, especially Henry Wadsworth Longfellow.

Among his most important works is a multi-volume series of historico-geographical books descriptive of the several provinces of historical Armenia. The first volume of the series was *Shirak* (1881), followed by *Sisouan* (1885). *Ayrarat* (1890), and *Sisakan* (1893).

His *Haybousak* (1895) is a comprehensive botanical work describing all the plants (trees, shrubs, vegetables, flowers) native to Armenia, with illustrations and scientific designations. The work encompasses thousands of varieties.

Fr. Alishan wrote many poems that remain popular today. His "Bamb Orotan" ("The thundering blasts from the heights resound over Ararat's plains...") is a stirring "call to arms" for the Armenian people to rally to the cause of Armenian freedom. His "Bulbuln Avarayri" (The Nightingale of Avarayr) is an ode extolling the braves who fought and fell at Avarayr, seeking a repose of their souls.

Fr. Ghevond Alishan was indeed an intellectual giant. It should be said that, in the quality and quantity of his literary output and his patriotism, he stands at the pinnacle of those who have served in the Mekhitarist Order over the nearly three centuries of its existence. Few have had as great an impact on Armenian knowledge as has Fr. Ghevond Alishan.

ဆာ

Khachatur Abovian
(1809-1848)

𝕬 man ahead of his times, Khachatur Abovian, despite his short life span, left his indelible and powerful mark on Armenian literature.

Abovian was born in a village on the outskirts of Yerevan, to a prosperous family. His early education was in the seminary of Echmiadzin. At age 15, he was sent to the Nersessian Academy of Tiflis. He was called back to Echmiadzin to serve as secretary to the aging Catholicos Ephraim, a friend of Khachatur's father. There he was ordained a deacon.

Abovian's life was turned in a new direction with the arrival of Friedrich Parrot in 1829. Parrot had come to Armenia for an ascent of Mt. Ararat, which had just come under Russian rule as part of land ceded by Persia. Parrot needed a guide and interpreter. Abovian, with his knowledge of Russian, filled the need perfectly.

The small Parrot party with Abovian reached the summit of Mt. Ararat on October 9, 1829, believed to be the first to accomplish what up until then had been regarded as an impossible (or "forbidden") undertaking.

During this ascent, Abovian endeared himself to Parrot and that led to his being invited to study at Parrot's institution, the University of Dorpat, in Estonia. Abovian studied there for six years, and attained a command of the Russian, Tatar, Persian, and German languages, in addition to his native tongue, Armenian.

On his return to Armenia, Abovian was impatient to impart to his people the riches of western civilization. Himself imbued with modern, liberal ideas, Abovian opened a school in Tiflis. He found both success and frustration in his efforts. His progressive teachings were well regarded by those ready for it, but condemned by traditionalists.

In 1840, in Tiflis, he wrote what is regarded as the first Armenian novel, *"Verk Hayastani"* (Wounds of Armenia). It was a historical novel, written as a popular epic, and it relates to Russia's wars with Persia that take place in the area of Yerevan. In it, Abovian tells of the suffering of the Armenian people at the hands of the Persians, but it also paints vivid pictures of folk life and customs.

The novel has further importance in that it was the first serious work written in the vernacular, the popular speech that was part of everyday life.

Abovian became a popular and prolific writer. His works include essays, plays, verses, poetry, short stories, fables, and textbooks on language.

His output included translations, especially of the works of great German writers.

Abovian contributed strongly to the enlightenment of his people. Unfortunately, a number of those around him, some of whom held important positions, were considerably less than encouraging. Moreover, the Russian occupation of Armenia had turned out to be a disillusionment. But most depressing was the fact that his marriage was not a happy one. As a result of all these circumstances, Abovian began to grow increasingly ill-natured and gloomy.

On April 14, 1848, Abovian walked out of his house for what was to be a brief errand. He did not return. He was never again seen, nor heard from. His disappearance was complete and enshrouded in mystery.

A brilliant contributor to Armenia's literary wealth, Abovian was not yet forty years old when he was abruptly snatched away.

Khachatur Abovian will be well remembered as one of Armenia's greatest writers. One of Yerevan's well known landmarks, known to every visitor, is Abovian Street which leads from a square whose landmark is an imposing statue of the writer all the way down to Yerevan's Republic Square.

෯

Raphael Patkanian
(Kamar Katipa)
(1830-1892)
"One of Many"

"The pen is mightier than the sword," it is said. That is certainly true in the case of the Armenian people, especially in the second half of the 19th century and its turn into the 20th.

But that is not to mean that their sword was not also mighty. There was clearly an arousal of the revolutionary fighters in the last quarter of the 19th century after Khrimian Hayrik's provocative observation that "Armenians with their paper ladles could not get their share of 'herrisa.'"

Revolutionary fighters, as well as the people were awakened by the revolutionary writers of the period. The people were led to rise against the brutal overlords of the Ottoman Empire.

Unable to write and publish their messages anywhere in the oppressive Ottoman lands, these dauntless writers created opportunities in Russia and elsewhere in Europe, setting up an "emigre press," constantly on the run to escape the diligent pursuers of the Sultan's assassins, who reached out far beyond the boundaries of the Empire to apprehend the "provocateurs."

Typical of these revolutionary writers was Raphael Patkanian, known also by his penname Kamar Katipa. [He chose this as his own pseudonym after it had been a composite of his name following the names of two publishing colleagues, K̲. K̲Ananian, and M̲. T̲Imourian. Thus, KaMaR KA-TI-PA.]

Raphael came of a family of writers and poets. He studied at the renowned Lazarian Academy in Moscow. He started writing poetry while in school. His poem "Araksi Artasouke" (Tears of the Araxes), better known by its opening words *"Mayr Araksi Aperov ..."* (Along the banks of mother Araxes ...) brought him much attention.

For a time he published a periodical "Hiusis" (North), in St. Petersburg, but later returned to the Caucasus.

Patkanian's poetry became popular on the moment of publication, for the people saw in him the "singer of their race."

Many of his poems, both revolutionary and universal, were learned by children in schools, and were set to music. One especially beautiful poem, a lullaby, set to music by P. Ganachian, is "Koun yeghir, balas,..." (Go to sleep, my dear child ...". But his lullabies were not always serene. In his poem (also set to music) "Ari im sokhak ..." (O, my nightingale, come from the garden and sing a lullaby to my child ...), the infant is restless and is not quieted by the song of the nightingale, nor of the blackbird, nor of the dove. It is only the hawk with its war notes that brings contented slumber to the child.

Among Patkanian's poems that awakened the spirit of rebellion in the people is "Himi el lrenk, yeghbark ...?" (Shall we yet remain silent, brother, when our enemy has put his cruel sword at our breasts ...?)

His poem "Togh pche kamin ..." (Let the cold wind blow at my face ... I know that sooner or later spring will come) tells of hope that Armenia will gain its freedom.

To awaken the spirit of the people Patkanian recalls the epic hero Vardan Mamikonian's leadership in resisting the 5th century attack by the Persians. "Lrets. Ampere..." (Silence reigned. The clouds have obscured the moon.)

Patkanian was not alone. Other well-known, contemporary poets served the nation by arousing the people in the same way. Notable among them were Mkrtich Peshiktashlian (1828-1868); Mikael Nalbandian (1829-1866); Bishop Khoren Nar-Bey Galfayan (1832-1892); Raffi (Hakob Melik-Hakobian) (1835-1888); and Alexander Dzatourian (1865-1917).

ℰℭ

Raffi
(Hakop Melik-Hakopian)
(1835-1888)

𝕬head of his time, Raffi (Hakop Melik-Hakopian) gave Armenian literature a new impetus, and led the way to freer expression by writers. He played an important role in bringing about wider readership of Armenian literature, doing so through his skill in writing and capturing popular interest.

Born in northern Persia into a wealthy family, Raffi received his primary schooling there, but at a young age was sent to Tiflis for higher education. There he became acquainted with the works of the world's great writers.

For a time he found it necessary to return to his ancestral home to manage the business affairs of his family. But, having been filled with nationalistic feelings, Raffi recognized that his calling should take him elsewhere.

He traveled widely in Persia and Turkey and became closely acquainted with the sorrowful life of his people that provided him much source material for his literary life.

Having returned to Tiflis, Raffi became closely associated with the intellectuals, and the newspapers, of the area.

Raffi left the Armenian people with a rich literary heritage. He had a very large output, consisting of novels, novelettes, tales, travelogs, commentaries, historical analyses, essays, and poetry. His works appeared in periodicals and in separate volumes. In addition, there remained a tremendous volume of unpublished material in manuscript form. Raffi is best known, however, for his novels.

The underlying theme for Raffi's writings is the emancipation of man.

Chalaleddin (1878) is a novelette that brings to light the tragic plight of his people.

The novel *Khente* (The Fool, 1881) extends the same theme of the pressing need of the emancipation of his people.

One of Raffi's main works is the novel *Kaydzer* (Sparks, 1883). It sets forth the principles underlying the epochal emancipation movement.

Raffi's historical writings include the novel *David Beg* (1882). It tells the story of the 18th century struggle of the Armenians to free themselves from Persian rule. David Beg, a military commander serving the Tsar is called upon to lead the Armenians to victory in their struggle. The story was made into an opera, with music by Armen Tigranian. It is often performed in Yerevan, and is available as a recording.

Raffi's masterpiece is probably his novel *Samvel* (Samuel, 1886). It is generally regarded as a superb piece of writing. It tells the story of the 4th century Armenian king who seeks to substantiate the ethnic identity of the Armenian people, and establish their independence when they become embroiled in the conflict between the mighty powers Persia and Byzantium as they clash over the lands of Armenia.

Raffi is well published, and his works, especially the novels, have been printed in several countries. Some have also been translated into English.

ℰᴑ

Hagop Baronian
(1843-1891)

$\mathfrak{H}$e was born, lived, and died in poverty, but his legacy to Armenian literature was an untold wealth of writings of satire, wit, humor, ridicule, and protest. The targets of his insightful pen were the hypocrites, the dishonest, the swindlers, the larcenists, the extortioners, the greedy. They were to be found plentifully among the Armenian "aghas," or bigwigs.

Baronian's aim was good, too good, it might be said, because his attacks, which were sometimes somewhat irresponsible and without restraint, put him in frequent difficulty.

As foremost Armenian humorist, satirist, playwright, Baronian regaled the Armenians of Constantinople with the output of his pen.

He was born in Adrianople (Edirne, at the Bulgarian border), but his life was spent mainly in Constantinople. He was largely self-taught. His gainful occupation was as a pharmacy clerk, a bookkeeper, a doer of odd jobs, as well as a teacher in elementary schools, until late in his short life. He also served as an official in the Patriarchate, and as secretary of the United Armenian Society.

But it was his deft pen that brought him everlasting fame.

His early plays, comedies, were "Yergu Derov Dzara Me" (A Servant with Two Masters, 1865), and "Arevelyan Adamnapuyzhe" (The Oriental Dentist, 1868). They quickly disclosed Baronian's wit and satire.

Baronian, serving variously as assistant editor or as editor in newspapers, wrote frequently appearing satirical articles dealing with community life, family life-styles and mores, theater news, and current events that brought him fame. He also paved the way for Yervant Odian, successor in satire.

During the closing days of the Russo-Turkish Wars, and the ensuing International Conferences and Treaties (1878), Baronian was strong in his attack on the insidious behavior of the European powers, and their position regarding the Armenian Question. Such strong stories led to the forced closing of papers and periodicals carrying those stories.

Baronian's series "Azgayin Jojere" (The Nation's Notables) starting in 1874, stripped away the facade of Armenian "bigwigs" (contemporary and past - writers, actors, national leaders, high-ranking clergy) to reveal their character and their behavior, with some embellishments, often mercilessly, to unveil their weaknesses and misdeeds.

Possibly the best-known of Baronian's plays is "Baghdasar Aghpar" (Brother Baghdasar), written in 1886, dealing with family morality. It portrays Baghdasar, simple-minded, unlettered, boorish, but with homely wisdom, who is victimized by his unfaithful, betraying wife. This satirical comedy has been played by amateur and professional groups in Armenian communities worldwide. It has also enjoyed performances in translated languages.

Another well-known comedy is "Medzabadiv Muratsgannere" (The Honorable Beggars). Apisoghom Agha, the hero, a man of considerable means, comes to Constantinople from Trabizon. He is promptly set upon by countless beggars (persons in many "honorable" walks of life) who try hilarious schemes to part Apisoghom from his wealth.

Hagop Baronian made people laugh, and cry, and fume. He used his satirical pen to the benefit of the common man, but at the cost of his own comfort.

ഔ

Hovhannes Toumanyan
(1869-1923)

arely has an Armenian poet been so popularly loved and so financially successful as was Hovhannes Toumanyan. He was born in a small village of the district of Lori, in the northern part of Russian Armenia, in the region now bearing his name, Toumanyan. He took up residence in Tiflis, but later became very active in writers' groups in Armenia.

His home in Yerevan has been converted into a museum, a popular attraction for both residents and tourists.

Toumanyan began his writing at an early age. He very quickly showed his poetic skill in his charming descriptions of village life and customs. He was prolific in converting popular moral legends and tales into written poetry. He was widely published. His works, as individual pieces and as collections, appear in numerous attractively printed and illustrated volumes, in Armenian as well as in several foreign languages.

Appearing prominently on the plaza of the Opera House in Yerevan, Armenia, are two magnificent bronze statues of seated figures on individual pedestals. One is the poet Hovhannes Toumanyan and the other is the composer Alexander Spendiaryan.

Toumanyan was very articulate in declaring the importance of the social freedom of the people, and in supporting democratic ideals in the face of the autocratic Russian Tsars. For such activity he was for a time imprisoned.

No brief commentary can cover the extent of Toumanyan's writings. Possibly, his best known work is the poem "Anoush," which became the story of the Armen Tigranyan opera of the same name, frequently performed at Yerevan's Opera House. During normal times no tourist remaining in Yerevan for a week or two was denied the opportunity of hearing that opera. It tells the story of a young rural couple in love who become tragic victims of an innocent act of showing-off that occurs during the festivities of a village wedding.

Toumanyan's telling of the epic tale of David of Sasoun is possibly the best known of the numerous versions that exist. His version, in metered rhyme, has been rendered into English on a line-by-line basis by Aram Tolegian.

The Island of Aghtamar, just off the southern shore of Lake Van, was once the Holy See of the Armenian Church. It also contained a village. How had the island got its name? The legend concerning the name appears in Toumanyan's poem "Aghtamar." It tells of the nightly swim of a young lad to visit his island sweetheart Tamar, who lights a fire at the water's edge to guide her lover. But one dark, windy night, jealous island youths douse the fire to thwart the lovers. The swimmer, bewildered and lost, drowns. In the morning his lifeless body is found on the shore. Frozen on his lips are the words, "Akh, Tamar!"

Toumanian's Residence
Yerevan, Armenia

"The Dove Monastery" poem tells of a lovely miracle. Tamerlane has conquered Armenia. While contemplating his success he sees the monk Ohan walk on the water of the lake. To reward him he offers Ohan whatever he would have. Ohan asks for the freedom of his people. Tamerlane grants it, but only for those who fill the monastery. The people come, and all are able to enter. Then, changed into doves, fly out of the windows to their homes. Thus, all of the people of Armenia are freed.

Toumanyan wrote many popular tales, some in prose, for children, and also to give a strong moral message. Here is a sampling of titles: "A Drop of Honey," "The Dog and the Cat," "The Enlightener's Lantern," "The Old Man and the Servant," "Nazar the Brave," "Gikor," "Unfortunate Merchants," "The Fall of the Fortress of Tmouk," "The King and the Peddler," and many more.

Hovhannes Toumanyan was, and is, a national treasure. The nation has been immeasurably enriched through him, and that literary wealth will never lose its value.

৪১

Yervant Odian
(1869-1926)

"I hear what you say, but I know what you mean!"

He saw through the deviousness of others, and then did not hesitate to tell the world about it, sometimes at the risk of his life.

Possibly the foremost of Armenian satirists, Yervant Khachik Odian disrobed the unscrupulous, the dishonest, the unprincipled, the unconscionable aghas, magnates, grandees, hypocrites, pretenders, exposing them for the falsity of their practices.

Odian was born in Constantinople and attended school there for only a short time. Instead, he was schooled at home with hired tutors, and he used the well-stocked family library effectively, learning a number of languages.

By the age of 18 he was already being published, in the form of newspaper articles. A few years later he was invited to become assistant editor, and in 1896, editor of the "Hairenik" paper of Constantinople. It was in that paper that he began to appear with feature articles, tales, and novelettes. The biting content of many of the articles led to his being declared by Turkish officialdom as "persona non grata."

With the Turkish pogroms beginning in 1896, Odian left Constantinople for Athens, Cairo, Paris, Vienna, London, and Bombay. But with the revolt of the Young Turks and the Sultan's being deposed, he returned to Constantinople.

It was not long before he saw the perfidy in the Young Turk movement. But he was caught up in the 1915 upheavals and deported to Deir-ez Zor.

However, miraculously, eluding the widespread massacres, he returned to Constantinople in 1922.

He continued to move about, to Bucharest, Lebanon, and finally Cairo, where he died in 1926, of cancer.

Odian was creative in conveying his ceaseless message, exposing deceit, dishonesty, and duplicity. The character of "Enger Panchuni" (Comrade Good-for-Nothing) portrays an ignorant, arrogant, and vain person who is being called upon to perform important and responsible work for the people and community.

His unique work, *Abdul Hamid and Sherlock Holmes* (1911) satirically portrays the detective-like effort to bare the bloody despotism of the Red Sultan.

Odian used plays to dramatize his mesages on the theatrical stage, as "Charshele Artin Agha."

Many of his full-length writings were serialized in newspapers, and in this way he was able to reach a wider reading public.

Odian also translated a number of classic works of important authors (from the French into Armenian), such as Tolstoy's important novels, *Resurrection* and *Anna Karenina*.

In turn, Odian's works have been translated into a number of languages.

In his days, Odian made people laugh, and think.

℃

214

Arshag Chobanian
(1872-1954)

$\mathfrak{H}$e was a man of letters - philologist, novelist, poet, essayist, publicist, publisher, editor, columnist, all of these - having lived a fruitful life.

Born in Constantinople in comfortable circumstances, and benefitting from the good educational opportunities available there, he quickly found himself engrossed in the literary field, especially in writing textbooks and publishing periodicals for children. He had the good fortune of working with important writers of the day.

His writings appeared in the publications "Burastan Mangants," "Arevelk," "Masis," and "Hayrenik."

Distressed by the constrictive and obstructive policies of Ottoman officialdom, he moved to Paris where he could write as he pleased.

In Paris, Chobanian quickly established himself in his field, and produced the well-known periodical "Anahit" (1898-1911 and also 1929-1949). "Anahit" enjoyed a world-wide readership, and with it Chobanian gained a high level of recognition and esteem.

A major cultural service he performed for the Armenian community was to acquaint the French people with Armenian literature, through his countless translations of Armenian prose and poetry into French.

Moreover, his translations of important European literature into Armenian, with his informative commentaries thereon, gave Armenian readers an acquaintanceship with that foreign literature.

He enriched the Armenian literary field by publishing contemporary writers. In this way he brought wider recognition and popularity to many writers who later became highly renowned.

Also, by publishing compilations, with annotations, of the works of past Armenian writers such as Nahapet Kuchak, Naghash Hovnatan, and St. Gregory of Narek, Chobanian made classic literature available to a wider readership.

Through his carrying on correspondence with European authors and public figures, he made the Armenian Cause more widely known.

Chobanian gave high recognition to contemporary writers and poets of Armenia. He visited Armenia in 1933 where he, in turn, was accorded deep esteem by Armenia's writers and public officials.

In addition to all of his other attainments in Armenian letters, Chobanian was clearly an important publicist for Armenian writers, past and contemporary, being a source of help and encouragement for them.

He was also a source of help and comfort for Komitas Vardapet, who was confined to his hospice bed in Paris.

The Armenian community of Paris admired Chobanian not only for his literary importance, but also for the public service he provided.

80

Avetik Sahak Isahakian
(1875-1957)

$\mathfrak{A}$vetik Isahakian, lyric poet, was born in Alexandropol (later Leninakan during the Soviet period, but now Gyumri), Armenia in the Caucasus. Though best known as a poet and a political activist, he has much prose to his credit.

His early education was received in the seminary of the Holy See of Echmiadzin. At the age of eighteen, he went to Germany, entering the University of Leipzig as a listener. There, he became acquainted with the works of the great German writers.

After returning to Armenia in 1895, then under Russian hegemony, he was imprisoned for his anti-Tsarist activity. Exiled, he went to Europe again and studied at the University of Zurich. His return to Armenia in 1902 resulted in imprisonment for the same reason. He was able to leave the Russian sphere in 1911 for France and other countries of Europe where he lived until his final return to Armenia in 1936, then a constituent republic of the Soviet Union.

Well received in Armenia, both in literary and political circles, Isahakian became permanent President of the Soviet Armenian Writer's Union, was elected Deputy to the Supreme Council of the Armenian Soviet Socialist Republic, and was a member of the Armenian Academy of Sciences.

His death in 1957 was widely observed, both in the Soviet Union and abroad. Isahakian's literary works have been extensively published, both at home and abroad. Translations have appeared in many languages, principally Russian. He is widely recognized in the international literature.

As a young lad stricken by a deep love for a girl he never married, he wrote many poems on love and on the grief of unrequited love. His continuing works portray his feelings of longing. Hardly has there been an Armenian composer of note who has not set an Isahakian poem to music. Many such songs are popularly sung, though often identified more with the composer of the music than the author of its lyrics.

Possibily his best known work, a long narrative tale in meter, is "Abu Lala Mahari." In it, the poet enters the body of the 11th century Arab philosopher Abu, who disdained life as he saw it. He disposes of all his worldly goods and leaving behind the civilization he despises, sets off with a caravan of camels on an endless journey "soaring towards the sun," to see what the universe might offer.

Siamanto
(Adom H. Yarjanian)
(1878-1915)

He was one of those special "martyrs" - the masters of the pen who cried out against the iniquitous injustice being perpetrated against Armenians by the Ottoman overlords, and who paid for their undaunted courage with their lives in 1915.

Adom Yarjanian (penname Siamanto) was born of a family of merchants in the region of Kharberd (Harput).   At an early age he went to Constantinople with his father where he attended school at Kum Kapi and at the Berberian school in Uskudar.

Because of the carnage of 1895-96 against Armenians, young Adom sought refuge out of the country, in Cairo, Switzerland, and Paris.   He attended classes in literature at the Sorbonne, and maintained a close relationship with the Armenian Students' Association of Europe. It was this environment that developed in him his global view of the status of the Armenian people, his involvement in revolutionary activity, and his strong literary capability.

Siamanto's health was weak, and he spent years recuperating at a Geneva sanitarium.

The 1908 overthrow of the Sultan by the Young Turks and the promulgation of the Constitution signaled Siamanto's return to Constantinople, where he made a living with his pen.

But when the true colors of the Young Turks became evident, he left for

America and became editor of the "Hairenik" newspaper.

Siamanto's ill-fated return to Constantinople in 1915 flung him into the hellish cauldron of slaughter that smote the cream of Armenian intellectuals. Siamanto was then only 37. His artistic and sensitive pen still had the capacity to turn out years of stirring, sharply pointed poems that would rescue the Armenian spirit from oblivion.

Siamanto's poems, mostly dwelling on the effect on Armenians of the persecution they were enduring, appeared in Armenian journals published in various Armenian centers outside of the homeland. His first collected poems appeared in 1902. Called *Dyutzaznoren* (Heroically), it was a collection of poems calling on Armenian youths and wounded souls to recognize that there were still many dawns to come, instilling hope in their minds. Other collections appeared in rapid succession.

Siamanto had developed a literary style that was beautiful and sensitive. He wrote in a style of "free verse," not then common among Armenian poets.

The year 1915 brought sudden darkness to Armenian poets and poetry. The curtain fell on Siamanto, as it did on so many others.

ဆ

Michael Arlen
(Dikran Kouyoumdjian)
(1895-1956)

𝕴ris Storm (nee Iris March) was probably America's best known and most-talked-about fictional character in the mid-twenties.

The creation of Michael Arlen, she was the principal character in the highly popular *The Green Hat*. With it Michael Arlen established himself all at once as the author to read. He had touched the soul of his adoring readers, in England and in America.

The Green Hat, a runaway bestseller, appeared in 1924 when he was only twenty-one. Its success brought him into contact with a great number of prominent people in England, and he always had a circle of friends. America, too, was caught up in adulation of this much-admired, popular writer of two continents.

As a book, *The Green Hat* was followed quickly on stage. In New York, Iris was played by Katherine Cornell against her lover Leslie Howard. Tallulah Bankhead was Iris in London. And in the movie it was Greta Garbo who played Iris.

Though born in Bulgaria, Dikran was raised in England. To escape Turkish massacres in southeastern Europe, the family had moved in 1901 to Southport, England, where there was a large Armenian population.

When still a young man, Dikran put aside what would have been an education in Medicine. He took up residence in London, choosing to enter the literary field. His first book, *The London Venute*, appeared in 1913 when he was only eighteen. In 1916, when he was twenty-one, feeling a nationalistic urge, he wrote articles supporting the Armenian cause. They appeared in "Ararat," a magazine published in London by an Armenian group. He was then writing under the name Kouyoumdjian, but later, in 1922 when he became a British subject, he adopted the name Michael Arlen, a character that he had created in an earlier story.

Arlen's Armenian origin was neither an asset, nor a hindrance to his career, for he regarded his heritage casually. When he came to America in 1925, the Armenian community in New York set up a public gathering in his honor. His address to the audience was not particularly in tune with their expectations. Arlen did not in any way seek to deny his Armenian origin, but he made no attempt to please the audience with remarks that carried a strong nationalistic flavor. After all, Michael Arlen had become part of English high society.

Arlen moved back and forth between England and America. In Hollywood, where he was involved in the filming of his *Ace of Cads* (with leading role played by Adolphe Manjou) he was idolized, especially by women.

All America followed his daily comings and goings. At one time he was probably the highest paid short-story writer, anywhere. "Time" magazine put him on its cover, with a cover story.

Although Arlen continued to write novels (he wrote more than a dozen books), dramas, short stories, and screen scenarios, he never succeeded in writing another *The Green Hat*.

Michael Arlen fell in love with and married Atalanta Mercati, daughter of a Greek Count and an American mother. They had a son, Michael, Jr., and a daughter. In his own book, *Exiles*, Michael, Jr., tells about his father in an expository manner.

In his last days, spent mostly in New York, Michael Arlen's health had begun to fail. Death came when he was only sixty-one.

No other Armenian writer has attained the level of worldwide fame enjoyed by Michael Arlen.

ℰℴ

Vahan Tekeyan
(1878-1945)

He was a poet's poet, but he was also a people's poet. His skill in writing in the newly emerging literary language of the western Armenians gave his poetry a melody of its own. He was clearly a master of language.

Vahan Tekeyan was born in Constantinople, of a family that had come from central Anatolia. He had the good fortune of obtaining a fine education, having attended Constantinople's superb Kedronakan (Central) School, the producer of many Armenian intellectuals.

Tekeyan's life was not an easy one. For his livelihood, it was necessary for him to take odd jobs, which took him to London, Marseille, Amsterdam, and Egypt.

But even in early youth he knew that literature should be his life's commitment. While still in school, at the age of 14, he had two poems published in newspapers.

His stature as a writer, as editor, but mainly as a poet continued to grow throughout his life as more and more of his works were published widely, separately and as collections. However, though he joined a political party, and remained a member, his public life was never significant. He was essentially a shy person.

In his later years his life began to fail him, and his resulting distress caused some bitterness to appear in his later poems. Death came early, in Cairo, at age 67.

Though he had not personally relished the satisfaction of popular accolades during most of his life, it was only just before his death that he was honored publicly and ceremoniously.

Tekeyan's poems were always beautiful, in thought and in flow of language. It is said of him that he worshipped nature's beauty. Yet, within that feeling it was possible for him to express anger and frustration, especially in his later years.

Tekeyan's best-known work is the masterpiece "Yekeghetsin Haykakan" (The Armenian Church). In it, expressing his love and admiration for the Church, he wrote, "The Armenian Church is the birthplace of my soul, like an expansive cavern, pristine and profound..." He ends the long poem with the words, "... and its bells peal out victory." With this oft-recited poem, Tekeyan sings out the glory of the Church of the Armenians.

Another of his well-known poems is "Kantzreve Tghas" (It Is Raining, My Child). The mother is calling on her child to have courage despite his unhappiness; it is part of growing up. The words have been set to music by H. Berberian.

Tekeyan was instrumental in launching a number of literary journals, to which he contributed articles and commentaries, in addition to poems. He wrote of the Great Tragedy of 1915, of the "Goghtan" Singers (early Armenian troubadors). He translated some of Shakespeare's sonnets, and also wrote some poems in Armenian following the form of the sonnet.

A physical affliction had left him in a condition that precluded his siring children, which he had much wanted, and he did not marry. Also, the loss of vision in one eye, as a result of a politically motivated attack, contributed to his low spirits in later life.

Vahan Tekeyan, superb Armenian poet, much admired, is further immortalized by having a world-wide organization in his name - "Tekeyan Cultural Association."

ℰℴ

Daniel Varoujan
(1884-1915)

$\mathcal{A}$las, for this highly talented, very young writer-poet for having fallen victim to the Ottoman sword. With his eloquence, both in writing and in speaking, and his progressive ideas, he could have led the Armenians of Constantinople to become a more contemporary society.

Born in a village near Sebastia (Sivas), where he received his primary education, Varoujan was cared for by his mother in his early childhood for having apparently been abandoned by his father. In 1896 he and his mother went to live in Constantinople. There, he was able to continue his education, after which he studied at the Mekhitarist School in Venice, to age twenty-one. He obtained higher education at the University of Ghent (Belgium), to age twenty-five.

Returning to his native Sebastia in 1909 he taught Armenian, French, literature, and political science. From there he went to Tokat and continued in a teaching career that led to his being named superintendent of an elementary school in Constantinople. He remained in that position until he became one of the victims in 1915 of the Great Slaughter perpetrated by the Ottoman assassins.

Unwilling to be burdened by his family name of Chubukyaryan, and when still a young man of twenty-one years, Daniel chose a pen-name, as many of his contemporary writers did. In choosing Varoujan, meaning a male fowl or a falcon, the strong-willed poet may have wished to convey the idea of boldness and daring.

Varoujan's marriage to Araksi Tashjian in 1911, which had caused a stir because his bride had been engaged at infancy to another, was blessed with three, Veronica, Armen, and Haig (the last having been born just before the death of his father.

In a letter to a friend, Varoujan wrote (in March 1914), *"I had gone to Tokat to teach. My three years in the province was a nerve-wracking battle against prejudice, public ignorance, and political perversity. However, because of financial difficulties imposed by having a large family I am now in Constantinople, and am superintendent of an elementary school."*

Varoujan regarded his mission in life to be to purge the community of its archaic customs, entrenched prejudices, and professional disunity. His approach to accomplishing his mission was through poems, plays, and articles he wrote, and through public meetings he organized.

Varoujan's works include "Sarsourner" (Tremblings, Venice, 1905); "Charde" (The Massacre, Paris, 1906); "Tzeghin Sirde" (The Heart of the Race, Constantinople, 1909); "Hetanos Erger" (Heathen Songs, 1912); "Hatsin Erge" (The Song of Bread); "Diutzaznaveper" (Epic Tales); and many more. A few were published posthumously.

His writings appeared in many periodicals, in particular, "Bazmavep," "Geghouni," "Anahit," "Shirak," "Razmik," "Azdak," and "Azatamart."

Despite his tragically short life, as writer and teacher, Daniel Varoujan used both his pen and his voice to bring much understanding and knowledge to his people.

૪ⅅ

Yeghishe Charents
(1897-1937)

Painting by Martiros Saryan

$\mathfrak{F}$oremost writer-poet of the early Soviet period Yeghishe Charents (Soghomonian) led a very productive, but short and troubled life. Armenians world-wide know him best for his poem in praise and glorification of Armenia, opening with the words "*Yes im anuysh Hayastani arevaham parn em siroum ...*" (I love the sunny words of my sweet Armenia), and closing with the words carved in the Charents arch facing Mt. Ararat, seen by travelers on the way to Garni-Geghard, "... *Yes im Masis sarn em siroum.*" (I love my mountain Masis).

Charents' early schooling was in his birthplace, Kars. But schooling did not continue long, for he was a misfit, partly for his ungainly and disheveled appearance, and partly for his difficult behavior. But he was an avid reader, being deeply influenced by the great writers, both contemporary and classical.

When only fifteen he had his first poem published, and he soon had admiring listeners as he spent his days in a public park talking and reciting poems of his own, some being created extemporaneously. Those admirers collected funds to enable Charents to publish his first book (1914).

That book brought him quickly into wide public attention, making him a celebrity and winning his father's encouragement that had been previously lacking.

Monument to Charents on the road to Geghard

Charents became a volunteer and fought in the Armenian defense of Van (1915). The death and destruction he saw there brought on by the Turks, and the death of his comrades became the basis for poems and a later novel.

Feeling the need for formal study in literature he went to Moscow to attend a university (1916). But the next year he returned to the homeland.

By this time critics had begun to extol him for his original style and new outlook in his poems and other writings.

With the entry of Communism into the Caucasus (1920) Charents became caught up in the new ideology. He joined the Armenian Red Army and took part in putting down an uprising in February 1921 against Soviet rule.

In June 1921 Charents took his new bride to Moscow where he published a two-volume work of "Collected Poems."

Back in Yerevan the following year he, with two collaborators, began to take a strong political position on the nature of poetry and its relationship to the masses and Communist ideology. But some of his writings were found to be inappropriate, especially as it had to do with an attitude toward women.

In 1925 Charents had the opportunity of extensive travel in Turkey and Europe.

His wife's death at the very beginning of 1927 left Charents very much depressed. That may have influenced him in finding it more difficult to toe the Communist line. Although in his poetry he began to revive the spirit of pre-revolutionary days, he was still active in the Writers' Union, and holding positions in the State Press.

Charents' voice had begun to stress nationalism, as against the international character of Communist ideology. A work published in 1933 was found to be unsuitable by the Party, and he was expelled from the State Press.

Throughout his later life Charents, in the intensity of his poetic expression had become dependent on morphine. It may have been precipitated when he had kidney surgery, in 1929. Also, his second marriage was not as happy as his first.

The sad beginning of a sad end came when in 1937, in Yerevan, at a social gathering, Charents had become drunk, and in an ensuing argument with a high Communist official over the attention being given to the official's mistress, Charents had become defamatory of Communist Party actions. Charents was taken into custody and jailed.

In jail, Charents continued to write poetry. But the stress, including the drug addiction that he could not satisfy, led to his death.

Still, Armenia immortalizes this great Armenian writer-poet by naming a city after him (Charentsavan).

෯

An Armenian Miniature Manuscript

Sirarpie Der Nersessian
(1896-1989)

Renowned as a Byzantinologist and specialist in Armenian illuminated manuscripts and art history, she was a scholar's scholar. Sirarpie Der Nersessian was a highly admired woman among all Armenians.

Her early education was at the Essayan School and at an English-language secondary school in Constantinople where she was born. She graduated in the field of literature from the University of Geneva, following which she went to Paris and studied at the Sorbonne in the field of history and art history. That institution awarded her the degree of Doctor of Letters.

In 1930 she took a position at Wellesley College, in Massachusetts, as Lecturer, then becoming Professor of Art, and Director of the Farnsworth Museum at the college.

In 1946 she was appointed Member of the Faculty of Arts and Sciences at Harvard University and Professor of Art and Archeology at Dumbarton Oaks, the research center in Washington, DC, operating under the auspices of Harvard University.

On her retirement in 1963 she was designated Professor Emerita.

In addition to her writings Dr. Der Nersessian was invited often to lecture at various universities in the United States and in France. She won academic distinction in both countries, as well as in Armenia where she was elected to membership in the Armenian Academy of Sciences.

Among her several published works are *Armenia and the Byzantine Empire* (1945); *A Catalogue of The Armenian Manuscripts, The Chester Beatty Library* (1958, 2 vols.); *Armenian Manuscripts in the Freer Gallery of Art* (1963); *Aghtamar, The Church of the Holy Cross* (1965); *The Armenians* (1969); and a catalog of the Armenian manuscripts at the Mekhitarist library at St. Lazar, Venice.

It was Prof. Sirarpie Der Nersessian who in 1967 noticed the announcement in the catalog of Sotheby's, London, of the auction sale of 28 Armenian manuscripts, recognizing them to belong to the Armenian Patriarchate of Jerusalem. Dr. Der Nersessian called the attention of the world to this improper offering to the public of stolen manuscripts.

Sirarpie Der Nersessian, after her retirement, spent her last days with her sister in Paris. She is remembered warmly for her invaluable contribution to the world-wide recognition of the beauty of Armenian illuminated manuscripts.

ℰℂ

William Saroyan
(1908-1981)

"In the time of your life, live -- so that in that wondrous time you shall not add to the misery and sorrow of the world, but shall smile to the infinite delight and mystery of it!"

Saroyan Photographed by Paul Kalinian

Who else would, or could, have written such words other than William Saroyan, author, playwright, humanitarian, and sometime artist, of Fresno, California.

Born within the heart of Fresno's "Armenian Town," in 1908, of parents both of whom bore the name Saroyan, Bill, or Willie as he was sometimes called, grew up in an environment, a locale that was to be a very important influence in his writings. In turn, he left his indelible mark on Fresno, making that otherwise unheralded agri-center (except for its bountiful yield of farm products) known to all the world - "Oh, yes, that's where Saroyan comes from."

Indeed, exactly ten years after his untimely death in 1981, the United States Postal Service, in issuing a commemorative stamp in his honor, chose Fresno as the site for its ceremonies of "First Day of Issue," timed simultaneously with the Soviet Union's first day of issue ceremonies in Yerevan, Armenia, for its commemorative postage stamp, using the same art work as for the US stamp.

Saroyan led a very busy life. In any surroundings, his presence was immediately known, first through his booming voice, and then on sight (in later years) with his "handle-bars" moustache, fitting, one might say, to his movements around Fresno on his bicycle.

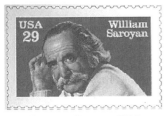

Saroyan Stamp - USA   Saroyan Stamp- Soviet Union

Fresno was quick to recognize its famous writer after his death. It named its main concert hall the William Saroyan Theatre, an action that would have been repudiated by Saroyan's public disapproval.

The William Saroyan Theater - Fresno, California

Repudiation by him of an attempt to bring him honor was not uncommon. When he was declared the winner of the Pulitzer Prize in 1939 for his play "The Time of Your Life," Saroyan rejected it. "...business should not subsidize art ...," he said, in part. That gained him more attention than if he had simply accepted the award. Some have thought that he would even have declined to accept a Nobel award.

Fresno's Metropolitan Museum offers its visitors a comprehensive view of Saroyan, through its permanent, whole-room display of memorabilia that tell of Saroyan and his life.

Fresno's sculptor-painter Varaz, in his privately created Modern Art Museum (no longer standing since the sculptor's death) included a giant-sized Saroyan statue of his head atop a colorful pile of his books in giant size, with titles legible and part of a bicycle protruding from one side.

Varaz and Willie were close companions. Together they were more like a couple of young kids on a lark. Varaz knew Saroyan in a way different from his being an author. As a consequence Varaz wrote "Willie and Varaz," providing a different insight into his close companion Willie.

Saroyan's Bicycle
Fresno Metropolitan Museum

Moreover, Varaz became the medium whereby photographer Kalinian made a series of now-famous photos of Saroyan. One photo adorns the wall of the William Saroyan Theatre lobby. Another became the basis for the picture gracing both the United States and Soviet commemorative stamps illustrated earlier.

Saroyan wrote. He apparently wrote easily. Words came pouring out of his manual typewriter in great volume, despite the fact that he typed while standing.

William Saroyan in His Youth

He has an unbelievingly long list of titles to his credit. His start came in short stories, the first being published in the Armenian English-language newspaper "Hairenik Weekly." The first widely published story was in "Story" magazine, in 1934. His first book (1935) was a collection with the title being the name of that first story, *The Daring Young Man on the Flying Trapeze.*

Experiences while growing up in Fresno and doing odd jobs (telegraph delivery boy), formed the basis for many of his stories. So too did his visits with old-time characters in Fresno.

In later years he maintained an address in Paris, and that stay provided for more stories.

235

Saroyan wrote words for songs. Rosemary Clooney made "Come On a My House" a popular song.

Probably during rare moments of nothing-else-to-do he made free-form line drawings, now a prize to own.

Saroyan visited Armenia several times. He was lionized there. Writers and other intellectuals hovered about him constantly. "My Heart's in the Highlands" (in Armenian) was performed on the Armenian stage.

World War II found William Saroyan in the army (Signal Corps), and at first he was given training as an ordinary draftee. Later, being recognized as a known writer, he was assigned to writing duties in England.

Best known of Saroyan's several dozen titles are *My Heart's in the Highlands* (1939), *The Time of Your Life* (1939), *My Name is Aram* (1940), *The Human Comedy* (1943), and *Places Where I've Done Time* (1972).

William Saroyan's last days were in Fresno, where he began. An unattended cancer had spread through his body beyond the site of its start and claimed the playwright. During his last hours he is reported to have said that people die, "but why me?"

Saroyan's marriage (twice to the same woman, Carol) gave birth to two, Aram and Lucy.

According to his wishes his body was cremated and the remains divided into two parts. One was taken to Yerevan, Armenia, and placed in the Komitas Gardens, a special cemetery for Armenia's greats. The other is being kept in a mausoleum in Fresno (with the intent that when Bitlis, his ancestral origin, is free, those remains are to be taken and interred there).

William Saroyan's remains are, in truth, everywhere, in the many books that came pouring out of his brimming heart, and are now all over the world in languages both familiar and strange.

Statue at the William Saroyan
Grave in Yerevan

℘

Sylva Kaputikyan
(1919-2006)

$\mathcal{S}$ ylva (Sirvard) Barunaki Kaputikyan (also sometimes Gaboudigian), poet, was born in Yerevan. Her innate aptitude for writing poetry became evident very early. Her first published work appeared in 1933. her collection "Im Harazatners" (My True Compatriots) was also published in Russian (1952), for which she was awarded a USSR prize. In later years, she won various other Soviet prizes.

Kaputikyan's poetic works emphasize patriotism and are concerned with the destiny of her people whose path is strewn with both accomplishment and tragedy.

Very early in her career, she enjoyed popular recognition and esteem, both in her homeland and in the world's Armenian communities. She continued to hold a secure position in official government circles despite her courageously outspoken criticism of government wrong-doing that she perceived.

With the Soviet central government's policy of "Russification" (ca. 1965), pressure was being applied to close schools where teaching was being carried on in a language other than Russian or the local native language. Accordingly, those Soviet republics, other than Armenia, with large Armenian populations, which maintained Armenian-language schools were being pressured to close those schools. Kaputikyan bravely criticized that wrong position. She unhesitatingly appeared before government bodies in their official sessions to make her point. In doing so, she won great esteem in the eyes of all Armenians.

In her poem "Khosk Im Ordun" (A Word to My Son), a mother extols the power and magnificence of their mother tongue, and bids her son to keep and protect it. In the closing lines, she says:

> *And see, my son, wherever you may go,*
> *Under whatever skies you may be,*
> *Should even your mother slip from your mind,*
> *Do not forget your mother tongue.*

Though very few Soviet citizens were granted the rare privilege of travel abroad, Kaputikyan was given that opportunity. In 1962-63 she visited Armenian centers in the Near East. In 1973, she visited the United States and Canada. Those two foreign visits led to two books of prose that carry the theme that Armenians, having been driven out of their native lands in 1915 and scattered to the four corners of the world, find their strength and guarantee of survival in the flowering of Soviet Armenia.

Ever mindful of the need for the intellectual development of the child, Kaputikyan has written numerous poems for and about children.

Kaputikyan's poems have been translated into many languages. There are more than twenty collections in Russian.

With the break-up of the Soviet Union, and Armenia's new independence (1991), former strong supporters of the old regime found themselves to be very insecure politically in the new order. Kaputikyan, though she had been fully accepted in the old order (she had been elected as deputy to the Supreme Soviet of the Armenian SSR) and not regarded as disloyal, had nevertheless maintained a strongly patriotic (Armenian) position, being something of a thorn in strictly communist sides. But her unfailing Armenian patriotism put her in a strong position in the new, nationalistic order. As such, she is one of only a few who were able to enjoy continued prominence, esteem and influence.

However, for Kaputikyan, all is not to her liking in the new Armenia. She sees realistically, and declares it - that the new Armenia is being burdened by numerous, nearly insoluble problems: social, economic, and political. But in the end, she is still optimistic.

ℰᴑ

Chapter 7

FINE ARTS

Illuminated Manuscript
Page from Lectionary (Jashots)

Armenian Illuminated Manuscripts

𝕬mong the early cultural arts that superbly endow the Armenian nation today is Calligraphy. In the one thousand years from the time of the invention of the Armenian alphabet (at the beginning of the fifth century) to the time when Gutenberg used a printing press with movable, pre-made type, Armenian scribes turned out many thousands of manuscripts, magnificently lettered and richly illustrated.

Armenian calligraphers, totally devoted to their calling, produced unbelievably beautiful manuscripts illuminated with marginal, partial page, and whole page illustrations.

After many centuries of handling, mishandling, and distress such manuscripts still glow with intense colors - blues, reds, greens, yellows, golds, and blacks - on parchment, and later on paper. Lettering stands sharp and clear, regular, and beautifully written. What kinds of ink were then used to produce such enduring colors? What kinds of pens were then used to produce the sharpest of lines? It was indeed an art that had reached its zenith.

Despite repeated invasions of Armenia by hostile forces that wrought destruction - especially of art treasures - there exist today 25,000 whole volumes of Armenian illuminated manuscripts, many of

Illuminated Manuscript:
"The Presentation of the Infant at the Temple"

them lavishly illustrated. They date from the ninth century on. Fragments of volumes date from the fifth century.

The major collection of these volumes, in number about 15,000, is kept in a special library called the Matenadaran (book repository), located in

Yerevan, Armenia. Built in 1959 the building that is the Matenadaran is unique in that it was the first in the Soviet Union designed and intended especially for the keeping and study of manuscripts.

The nucleus of that large holding is the collection that was once at Echmiadzin, the Holy See of the Armenian Church. That nucleus had been declared state property, and confiscated. But it grew rapidly to the present large collection through numerous acquisitions.

The remainder of the illuminated manuscripts extant is in the hands of institutions and individuals virtually everywhere. Virtually all the national libraries of major western nations have significant collections. Recognition of their worth is made evident by the significant number of published volumes describing such institutional holdings.

Manuscript collections in these institutions worldwide are available for research by individuals. The Matenadaran, in Armenia, is an especially important research center. Interested scholars in the field are enabled to remain in residence at the Matenadaran for their research.

The Matenadaran is equipped to receive casual visitors, at any time. It has on display a great variety of manuscripts, with explanatory comments for public viewing.

In addition to its Armenian collection, the Matenadaran has more than a thousand manuscripts in foreign languages - Persian, Arabic, Georgian, Old Hebrew, Syrian, Ethiopian, Greek, Indian, Latin, etc.

The Armenian literary heritage in the form of manuscripts covers all the fields of knowledge of the times - religion, philosophy, law, history, geography, natural sciences, poetry, and prose. But clearly, the emphasis, as is evident from the quantity and the magnificence of the calligraphy and the illumination has been in the works of religion and especially the Gospel.

Though a small nation measured by the number of its people, Armenia is large measured by its accomplishments in calligraphy and illuminated manuscripts.

&

Matenadaran

Standing prominently on the rising face of the hill at the upper terminus of Yerevan's Mesrop Mashtots Blvd. (formerly Lenin Blvd.) is the Matenadaran.

The Matenadaran is a unique library having a vast collection of ancient manuscripts. It provides for their safe keeping and proper care, and it enables continuing research.

Its collection consists mainly of Armenian illuminated manuscripts, some dating back to the earliest times of Armenian calligraphy. Some fragments date back to the fifth century.

The original collection had been assembled at Echmiadzin, gathered from monasteries and other sources as available. With the Sovietization of Armenia, the Matenadaran collection was declared state property in 1920, and it was expropriated and brought to Yerevan. In 1957 the Matenadaran became the Armenian Institute of Ancient Manuscripts. A special building was designed and built to house the collection, and provide for a research center. That is what is widely known today as The Matenadaran, and it is understood to have been the first building in the Soviet Union designed specifically as a research library with atmospheric controls to protect the valuable collection.

The word Matenadaran is derived from two Armenian words: *matean* and *daran*. *Matean* is the word that means a bound volume, the physical article itself, whereas the common word *girk* refers to its written contents and by extension became the common word for book. The combining form of the word *matean* is *matena-*. The word *daran* means cupboard or closet.

Although there are known today to be about 25,000 whole volumes of Armenian manuscripts extant in the world (and that is despite the great loss of such artifacts during the Genocide of the Armenians), about half of them are in the Matenadaran, as well as thousands of fragments. The number in the collection increases continually, as more and more individual volumes and small collections in private hands find their way "home" to the Matenadaran.

The Matenadaran is open to visitors, and some of the finest examples of the calligraphic and illuminating art are on public display.

Greeting the visitor who approaches the Matenadaran is an elaborate three-level plaza that fronts the building, and where there is a statue of Mesrop Mashtots sitting alongside a large stone panel inscribed with the letters of the Armenian alphabet. The Matenadaran is also known as the Mesrop Mashtots Research Institute of Ancient Manuscripts.

Manuscripts in the extensive collection cover many disciplines: scriptural and other religious texts, especially the Gospel; history; geography; philosophy; the sciences; medicine; jurisprudence; poetry; etc. Included are manuscripts in Persian, Arabic, Georgian, Hebrew, Syrian, Ethiopian, Greek, Latin, Indian, and many other languages.

Numerous volumes and studies have been published, and widely, often with lavish colored reproductions of some of the finest examples of the calligraphic and illuminating art. Such descriptive volumes are readily available.

Anania Shirakatsi Manuscript
(7th Century AD)

Large collections of Armenian illuminated manuscripts exist in Echmiadzin, the Armenian Patriarchate of Jerusalem, the Mekhitarist Monasteries at Venice and at Vienna, and at major museums and university libraries around the world as at London, New York, and Washington, D.C.

The Matenadaran is a jewel of immeasurable worth, and it endows the Armenian people the world over with a sense of pride.

છ૭

Armenian Church Architecture

rmenians, part of all Christendom, had not attended the Fourth Ecumenical Council at Chalcedon in the year 451, for they were fighting the Persians at Avarayr to defend their Christian faith.

Later, in the year 506 at their own Council in Dvin, Armenians rejected the Chalcedonian decisions, because the Council had been in disarray, with the regional bishops quarreling over jurisdiction and preeminence.

In their rejection of the declarations at Chalcedon, Armenians, in effect, were withdrawing from the one body of Christendom, and establishing an independent National Church, the first nation to do so.

It was natural, therefore, for the Armenians to reinforce their independence. And the principal way in which that would become evident was in developing a new idiom of church architecture.

The initial structure that would become the Cathedral of Echmiadzin, built at the beginning of the 4th century, had been replaced, in about the year 480, by a structure with a central plan and pendentives supporting a central dome.

But after the action taken at Dvin, the Armenians began to try various designs for their churches. The church at Avan (now within the boundaries of Yerevan) built at the end of the 6th century (590 A.D.) became a prototype that led to the design concept culminating in the Church of St. Hripsime, in 618 A.D.

The Church of St. Hripsime, in turn, became the basic design concept that has served the Armenian people throughout its history. The Church of St. Hripsime stands, today, in the City of Echmiadzin, not far from the Cathedral.

It represents a design of structural and esthetic magnificence, combining structural integrity and esthetic beauty in a harmonious marriage. The essential structural features of St. Hripsime are that the masonry arches, that support the heavy drum and dome on pendentives, are buttressed by the internal apses. It has been said that if one were in some way to remove the mortar used in binding the masonry blocks together, the building would still stand firm.

The Church of St. Hripsime is an architectural gem.

Seen in the floor plan and in the elevation is the porch with belfry. None of the early Armenian churches had porches with belfries. They were all added in the 17th century, a thousand years after some of the churches had been built.

Armenian churches being built throughout the world today capture some of the essence of St. Hripsime. That is not to mean that they are all simple copies. They borrow elements of design taken from St. Hripsime, but within the limits of the skill of the designing architect they become a harmonious blend of the classical prototype and modern design concepts.

St. Hripsime Cathedral

Interior View of Altar

Plan of St. Hripsime

Section View of St. Hripsime

A major factor in enabling the design of new churches in the "idiom of Armenian Church architecture" is the availability of modern structural materials to replace stone.

One other gem that employs the design features of St. Hripsime is the Holy Cross Church on the Island of Aghtamar on Lake Van. It has won world-wide acclaim.

The distinctive idiom of Armenian Church architecture has helped to uphold the independence of the Armenian Church.

℘

Aghtamar

Lake Van's waters in hues of blue
  Stretching out to infinity;
Surround the island called Aghtamar,
  Giving it a pristine purity.

Rising up from its rocky soil
  Is a work of art - a monument;
Created by man - inspired by God;
  A statement pure and eloquent.

Holy Cross - the Cathedral Church,
  Built by Gagik as the Holy See;
Adorned with carvings on its exterior
  Proclaiming a biblical history.

There, Jesus and Mary, Adam and Eve
  Are frozen in tufa for eternity;
Along with David, Goliath and Saints,
  As a form of sculptural poetry.

And faded frescoes on inside walls
  Attest to a great solemnity,
That took place beneath the circular dome
  Amid such balance and harmony.

Aghtamar is now a lonely place -
  And Holy Cross is an empty shell
The sweet strains of the Mass waft no more
  For Armenians there, no longer dwell.

ℰ

The Church of the Holy Cross - Aghtamar

Aghtamar

𝒜 bout three kilometers off the southern shore of Lake Van is a small island called "Aghtamar."   On it lies a superb architectural monument; it is the Church of the Holy Cross. At one time, the entire island was a vibrant village supporting the cathedral and monastery, which, in fact, was, for a period of time, the Holy See of the Armenian Church.

Throughout the centuries, the Holy See wandered many times from one location to another in response to the relocation of the civil authority of the Armenian nation. From 931 to 944 A.D. the Holy See was at Aghtamar. It was then that the monastery complex was built.

Five Hundred years later, in 1441 A.D. as a consequence of the fall of the Cilician Armenian Kingdom in 1375 A.D., the church fathers decided that the Holy See should cease its wanderings and return to its original site, at Echmiadzin.   But because a strong spiritual authority was not established then at Echmiadzin, the archbishops at Aghtamar declared that the cathedral and monastery complex at Aghtamar was the Holy See.   The same declaration was made by the archbishops at Sis, in Cilicia, that their monastery was the Holy See.

This status of having three concurrent Holy Sees, or Catholicates prevailed until 1895, when the archbishops at Aghtamar voluntarily relinquished their claim, leaving just the two, at Echmiadzin and Sis.

The Cathedral Church of the Holy Cross at Aghtamar is an architectural gem. Built in the unique idiom or style of Armenian Church architecture, its renown stems from the prolific high-relief carvings adorning its entire exterior.

Scenes represented by the carvings are episodes from the Bible, events from Armenian history, and some arising out of fantasy. A few of the carvings have been copied to adorn the exterior walls of St. Vartan Cathedral in New York City.

Much scholarship has been done on all of the carvings, as well as on the frescoes that adorn the interior walls. Several substantial volumes lavishly illustrated with color photographs and architectural drawings have been published.

The Church of the Holy Cross (Interior View)

The magnificent Church of the Holy Cross on the Island of Aghtamar is a much-favored tourist attraction. Access to and from the island is by regularly scheduled motor launch during most of the year. Although the present caretakers protect the edifice and promote it as a tourist attraction of world importance, no effort is being made to protect it from gradual decay, much less to rehabilitate it.

꙼

Ani

A great wall rises from the rocky soil,
  A battered boundary between dark and light;
The guardian of hallowed ground,
  The symbol of past power and might.

To pass beyond through its entrance arch,
  Crowned by a lion - devoid of gate;
Is to pass into the hazy past,
  Where lives and nations met their fate.

Silence is now the rule of thumb,
  And barren is the landscape there;
Shorn of its many vestments grand,
  Through years of pillage, neglect and despair.

The wind blows gently through this emptiness,
  While wisps of grass seek the sun's rays;
Yet, from where they spring lie many buried stones,
  Forever still - now unused - ruins of greater days.

What memories do these stones contain
  Locked within and beneath the ground?
When will they see the light of day
  To let the voices within them sound?

The history that they will tell,
  Of Bagratids and churches grand;
Whose scattered ruins dot this somber soil,
  Whose altars now in silence stand.

Ani, the city of mighty kings,
  Once Armenia's sacred Holy See;
Is now but a shadow - frozen in time,
  Its grandness - only a memory.

℘

The Main Western Battlements (walls) of Ani – Interior View

Ani

𝕬ni is a very important archeological site. Presently uninhabited, it was once the fortified capital city of the Armenian Bagratid (Bagratuni) dynasty from the 9th to the 12th centuries. It was then a prosperous cultural center based on trade and crafts. Known as the "City of one thousand and one churches" it did in fact have about thirty churches and chapels, also palaces, public buildings, inns, mosques, and other structures, as well as residences for a fairly large population.

The site is roughly triangular in shape, situated on a narrow "vee" between two adjoining river gorges (the Akhurian and the Ani or Alaja) which form a natural fortification along two of the three sides. Massive walls or ramparts built of stone are found on the plains forming the third side. The narrow Akhurian River today forms the political border between Turkey in the northeast and the Republic of Armenia. No surface crossings can be made there now, but the remains of an ancient bridge that at one time provided a crossing can be seen.

Ani is recognized at present as an archeological site that cries for extensive research. Knowledge of the entire area is based on excavations and study competently conducted there during the two decades from 1895 to 1915 by Toros Toramanian and Nicholas Marr as well as others.

Ani is situated on a geologic fault that runs along the northern perimeter of Anatolia. The area is subjected continually to earthquakes. The Cathedral that had stood for 1000 years (its dome collapsed in the 1840's) suffered extensive damage to one corner of the main wall during the disastrous earthquake of 1988.

Numerous illustrated books exist in several languages but there has been no recent archeological activity to enhance the store of knowledge concerning this site.

In the second half of the 9th century the Bagratid dynasty had risen to become the most influential of the princely families in feudal Armenia. Ani, as their capital, emerged as the capital city of the nation, and the Holy See of the Armenian Church was there from 992 to 1051 A.D. (having been transferred from Dvin).

The political fortunes for the Bagratids did not last long under successive incursions by the Byzantines and by the Seljuk Turk Alp Aslan. The latter's siege in 1064 A.D. was unsuccessful, except that a severe earthquake destroyed rampart walls, and Ani fell as a result. Later occupation by the Byzantines was replaced by the rule of a Persian king that brought a few years of peace and respite to Ani.

The Ruins of the Cathedral of Ani
(Note damage to corner caused by 1988 earthquake)

Armenian emigration on a vast scale began in the early 14th century as a result of earthquakes and repeated incursions by hostile neighboring nations. Movement was in two segments: south of the Black Sea to the western shores of the Mediterranean, and north of the Black Sea to the Crimea and into Eastern Europe.

Possibly the most important structure in Ani is the Cathedral. It was completed in the year 1001 A.D., and was the largest religious structure built until that time by the Armenians. The Architect-Builder Tiridates (Trdat) needed to solve the aesthetic-structural problems posed by this larger edifice. He did so by employing two architectural features (later extensively used in Gothic Architecture -- pointed arches and clustered columns). Tiridates must have had wide renown, for he was called upon to repair the earthquake damage to the dome of the large Byzantine Cathedral (Hagia Sophia) in Constantinople.

The St. Gregory Church in Ani (built in the name of Tigran Honents in 1215 A.D.) is in remarkably complete condition, with dome intact. Its narthex has been exposed to the weather as a result of earthquake damage from long ago, but the frescoes thus exposed still show vibrant colors.

Access to Ani is from the city of Kars. In Kars stands the abandoned Church of the Holy Apostles built by the Bagratid Dynasty. Long after it was left unattended because of the departure of the Armenians from Kars, it was converted into a museum of Seljuk culture for a time. Today it is empty and unused. Curiously, the church appeared on a contemporary Turkish postage stamp issued to commemorate the 900th anniversary of the founding of Kars.

ക

254

Toros Toramanian
(1864-1934)

$\mathfrak{I}$t was through him that the world awakened to the splendor of Armenian Church Architecture.   Toros Toramanian laid the foundation for the study and research of Armenian architecture.

Born in Shabin-Karahissar, Toramanian's early education in the local schools was followed by higher education in the architectural department of an art school in Constantinople. On completing his studies there, he worked as an architect but was obliged to leave Constantinople because of the 1895 pogroms. He continued in his profession in Bulgaria, and then in Rumania. In 1902 he went to Paris to increase his knowledge in his field. He also traveled to Egypt to study the ancient monuments there.

In 1903, accompanied by philologist Basmajian of Paris, he went to Ani to study the architectural wonders there. He was astounded that so little was known of the architectural treasures there by European scholars, and even Armenian scholars. He was later joined on the site by the noted Russian scholar Nikolai Marr. Together they carried on excavations and studies of the churches, palaces, caravanserai, ramparts, and dwellings.

In 1904 Toramanian went to Echmiadzin where he was asked to study the ruins of the nearby circular church Zouartnots, and conduct excavations and prepare architectural drawings. It was the result of this work that enabled Toramanian to create the well-known "reconstruction" of the circular, three-tier structure. Toramanian's reconstructed Zouartnots was at first rejected by his colleagues as improbable. However, his concept is now generally accepted as valid. After long years of neglect, some work is being done in Armenia toward a partial physical reconstruction of this historical church.

Toramanian's "The Church of Zouartnots," published in 1905, was the forerunner of scholarly works on Armenian architecture. Toramanian followed with the publication of a number of other works, on specific churches, and on the subject generally.

In 1912 Toramanian was invited by Prof. Josef Strzygowski of the Vienna Institute of Art History to submit some of his work for review, for which he received the highest award. Toramanian made an agreement with Strzygowski to work together, and in 1914 went to Vienna, taking with him a thousand architectural drawings, photographs, and negatives for their joint studies. In order to prepare some

Model of Zouartnots Church

additional material Toramanian returned to Armenia. But with the outbreak of World War I, Toramanian was unable to return to Vienna. Strzygowski, however, without Toramanian's approval, published the material in the very fine two-volume work, *Die Baukunst der Armenier und Europa* (The Architecture of Armenia and Europe). It was not until about fifteen years later that Toramanian was able to publish his own, extensive two-volume work, *Haykakan Jartarapetutiun* (Armenian Architecture).

Strzygowski gave a series of eight lectures in Upsala, Sweden, which were later translated into English and published in 1923 by the Oxford University Press under the title *Origin of Christian Church Art*. In it Strzygowski espoused the concept, already enunciated by Toramanian that the Cathedral at Ani, completed in the year 1001 A.D. by the architect Trdat, employed "clustered columns and pointed arches" that served as a forerunner for European Gothic architecture.

It was through Toramanian that Armenian architecture became recognized world-wide as having a distinct idiom of its own. It was also through Toramanian's studies and reconstruction drawings that many of Armenia's historical structures have been physically reconstructed.

Toramanian spent his last years in Armenia where he was very active in the work of the preservation of historical monuments. The Armenian government gave him due recognition for his valuable services.

ℰℴ

Khachkars
(Crosses of Stone)

"The Life-Giving Cross is our Salvation.
With this, we all offer praises."
("Khachn Kenarer ..." from an Armenian Church hymn)

For Armenians the Cross lifted itself out of the abyss of torture and death to the heights of hope and resurrection. Within Armenian churches, inscribed on interior and exterior walls, standing alone, carried in the hand, borne on a staff in procession, sometimes simple, more often decorative, the Cross is everywhere. The Armenian Church does not use the Crucifix - Cross with crucified Christ (although it sometimes may be seen).

A very distinctive form in which Armenians throughout their history have displayed the Cross is the Khachkar, usually a large slab of stone, a stele, a monolith, on which a Cross has been hewn.

Khachkars were used all over historic Armenia. They were placed at crossroads, at church entrances, at cemetery entrances. They were used as grave markers and as votaries. They were often commissioned by someone as a votive offering.

Often, khachkars were carved into the face of a natural wall of rock.

The monoliths are usually man-sized, essentially a vertically standing slab about a meter wide and a half-meter or less in thickness. The top of the front face is usually curved forward. Often there is a slight taper, widening slightly from bottom to top. They are usually mounted on a base, and left standing to the weather.

A Khachkar from Haghbat

257

Though many thousands exist, no two are identical. Yet, they have many characteristics that are the same.

The central feature is a large Cross. Most characteristically the arms curve outward, widening toward the ends. Each corner of the ends of the arms may have a trefoil (pointed loops), representing the Trinity. The outline of the Cross is marked by a continuous bead (often double) that traces the shape of the Cross in an unbroken line. The body of the Cross is covered with a decorative design, and variations are endless.

Out of the bottom of the Cross there is usually a flame-like design that sweeps downward, outward, and upward on both sides.

17th & 13th c. khachkars from the sanctuary of Gayanne Church
Echmiadzin, Armenia

Immediately below the Cross and flame there is usually a large circle, also decoratively carved. It is said that the Cross represents nourishment for the soul, and the circle represents bread as nourishment for the body.

The entire design is usually framed by a wide border of intricate carving; forming continuous beads in faultless basket weave (beads crossing alternately over and under one another).

The sides and back of the khachkar will usually contain information on why the khachkar was made, who carved it, when it was carved, and who commissioned it.

Some of the finest khachkars have been gathered together and are displayed on the grounds of the Cathedral of Holy Echmiadzin.

℘

The Folk Music of Armenia

The indigenous music of Armenia, the native folk music, was most methodically and exhaustively studied and described by Komitas Vardapet. A musicologist of the highest level of expertise, he set forth the inherent characteristics of the popular music of Armenia.

His characterization of that music is to claim that Armenian folk melodies (as well as the sacred melodies of the Church) are as "eastern as Persian-Arabic" [or Turkish] melodies, but that the Armenian is "not the same as Persian-Arabic." It is as to point out that though Armenian is a branch of the Indo-European family of languages, as is Classical Persian (as well as most European languages), it is not the same.

Armenian folk melodies are based not on diatonic scales, but on a chain of tetrachords. A diatonic scale is one that extends over an octave, meaning that the highest end note has a pitch frequency exactly twice that of the lowest end note of the scale. Then, the intermediate notes of that scale are positioned according to simple arithmetic ratios of their frequencies. Incidentally, some of the notes in a diatonic scale for most eastern music are positioned at slightly different frequencies than for western music.

Melodies based on a chain of tetrachords (as is indigenous Armenian music) use notes that do not necessarily form octaves. A tetrachord, consists of four notes with intervals of 1, 1, and 1/2 steps (or in a different sequence). In order to extend the range, or compass, of that short scale of four notes another identical tetrachord is joined to it, the lowest note of the second tetrachord being the highest note of the previous tetrachord. A third, or even a fourth or fifth tetrachord can be joined to the chain, providing as long a range as needed. Notably, a melody extending more than the equivalent of an octave need not necessarily include the note that would be an octave above a lower note in the melody. This characteristic gives the melody a unique quality. Moreover, converting such a melody into a harmonized choral piece for three or more voices requires a wholly new approach.

In general, this characteristic of Armenian folk melodies leads into harmonization with more open chords than would arise in harmonizing melodies that are naturally based on a diatonic scale.

The themes of Armenian folk melodies relate to wedding ceremonies, dancing, plowing, threshing, planting, games, longing, nature, etc.

Armenian composers of the late 19th and early 20th centuries found an unbelievably rich source of material in folk melodies, to be used in generating music for more formal use as in concert presentations. The melodies were typically short, simple pieces. The composers often joined two or more such melodies into more complex, polyphonic songs, often with six or eight parts (voices) rather than only three or four.

Composers who created such harmonized choral music were Komitas Vardapet, Parsegh Ganachian, Romanos Melikian, Grigor Siuni, Anushavan Ter Ghevondian, Alexander Spendiarian, Armenak Tigranian, Christaphor Kara-Mourza, and others.

ℰↄ

Komitas

Orphaned at a tender age,
      And sent to study at Echmiadzin,
Soghomon with his pleasant voice
      Thrived in the musical discipline.

Once ordained a celibate priest,
      He traveled to study musicology;
Learning from the greats of that time
      Composition and forms of harmony.

With formal studies at an end,
      He returned to the place where he began,
To teach to others what he had learned -
      To realize God's Holy Plan.   *(Continued Next Page)*

While there, his greatest works took shape:
    To collect the many songs of his land
And write them down to preserve them,
    As if moved by some divine command.

He then turned his thoughts to the Patarag;
    Arranging the Armenian Liturgy
As if guided by the hand of God
    He gave it a heavenly purity.

His life had many twists and turns,
    And on to Istanbul he went;
Where he showed the world what he had done,
    His arrangements - pure and eloquent.

On a dark and somber April night
    Komitas was led away,
To face a fate unthinkable
    That befell Armenians on that day.

But, no, his fate was not the same
    For Komitas was spared his life
By the intervention of Morganthau
    He lived through all the pain and strife.

After the dirty deeds were done,
    Komitas was still alive;
But his spirit had risen with those who were killed,
    Without it, he could not survive.

Unable to work, a broken man -
    His mind now tortured and wracked with grief -
Komitas languished in a sanitorium
    Until God gave to him His Divine Relief.

℘

Komitas Vardapet
(1869-1935)

Born Soghomon Soghomonian in Gudina (Kutahya, Asia Minor) on September 26, 1869, he was orphaned at the age of eleven. A year later Soghomon was sent to Echmiadzin for study. His singing attracted the attention of the Catholicos. After completing his studies at the Seminary, he taught music there. In 1896, he was ordained an "abegha" (monk), assuming, as is the practice in the Armenian Church, his new name "Komitas." Two years later, he became a "Vardapet" (a clerical title equivalent to a holder of a Doctorate).

Having had his initial musical instruction from the monks, he continued study with the famous composer Kara-Mourza, whose training took him deeper into both religious and secular music.

He often visited Tiflis (cultural center of the Caucasus) where he had the opportunity to study European music under Makar Ekmalian.

In 1896, Komitas went to Berlin for advanced study. After being awarded a doctorate degree in musicology, Komitas returned to Echmiadzin as choirmaster and instructor of music at the Seminary. It was there that he gave special emphasis to the study and analysis of the obscure, ancient "neumes" that were used as musical markers in the hymns (*sharakans*) of the Armenian Church.

Komitas' chief contribution was to rediscover native Armenian folk music. He spent painstaking years collecting and cultivating the beautiful, imaginative, and vibrant music of the village people. He journeyed throughout the provinces, stopping at countless villages to hear the native songs and dances, carefully annotating them for further analysis.

Although Komitas' work in secular music was admired by many of the monastics at Echmiadzin, there were those who criticized him and upbraided him for his emphasis on secular music: they said that he should be working more with "Alleluias" than with "Vay le les."

The opposition grew more intense after the death of Catholicos Mkrtich I, "Khrimian Hayrik" who had actively supported him. Conditions no longer being conducive to performing his work, Komitas went to Constantinople. There, he organized a mixed chorus of three hundred voices, an inconceivably difficult undertaking in the existing social environment.

His magnificent work in arranging and collating the folk tunes he had collected, now having become superb contrapuntal songs for mixed chorus, found expression for the astounded public, long unaware of the existence of true Armenian music. European masters gave glowing praise to the genius of Komitas' arrangements.

Komitas was a purist. He had decried the position taken by some who had been claiming that Armenians did not have their own indigenous music. Impatient with such people, Komitas was harsh in his criticism of them. In turn, he became the object of ridicule to a few.

In addition to his tremendous volume of harmonized and formalized folk music, Komitas also arranged the entire music of the Divine Liturgy (Patarag) of the Armenian Church, for male voices.

During the widespread capture and imprisonment of leaders of the Armenian community in the spring of 1915, Komitas too was taken into custody. Through the efforts of Henry Morgenthau, Ambassador from the United States of America, to the Imperial Throne (Ottoman Empire), alerted by the Turkish poet Mehmet Emin Yurdakul, who admired and esteemed Komitas' work, Komitas was released. But the sufferings of

Stamp in honor of the 100th Anniversary of Komitas' birth

the Armenian people as a result of deportation and massacre exacted their toll on Komitas who became a victim of dementia.

Unable to continue his work, Komitas became confined to a sanatorium in Paris where he remained to his death on October 22, 1935. His remains lie in the special cemetary in Yerevan, Armenia for Armenian greats, aptly named "Komitas Aygi" (vineyard).

Komitas' works have been published widely in Armenia as well as abroad. He is clearly the foremost of Armenian musicians.

℘

Makar Ekmalian
(1856-1905)

hrough him, the music of worship in the Armenian Church took on new color and new brilliance.

Music in the Armenian Church, from earliest times, had been chanted monophonically, and without instrumental accompaniment. It was not until the twelfth century that any kind of written notation was used. The new notation, credited to Khachatur Vardapet of Taron, consisted of neumes (symbols denoting general melody patterns and tempo) which served to identify the music, along with designated scale modes (essentially eight in number).

In the middle of the nineteenth century, "Baba" Hambartzum Limonjian, director of a music school in Constantinople, that was the main training center for church singers, invented a new system of notation. It consisted of symbols (not unlike the earlier neumes, but totally different in meaning). Each symbol represents a note on the scale, without the use of a staff. They bear a one-to-one equivalence to the modern system of notes on a staff of five lines. Baba Hampartzum's system found widespread use and numerous printed volumes were produced, including a superb volume printed in 1875 at Echmiadzin. That volume was of quarto size and consisted of 1,100 pages, containing all the "*sharakan*" (hymns) of the Armenian Church. One may still find some senior deacons in the Church that still use that notation.

The Limonjian system did not lend itself to writing polyphonic music, singing in parts, nor for accompaniment on a keyboard instrument.

It was Makar Ekmalian who broke through that impediment.

Ekmalian was trained in music in St. Petersburg, Russia. His monumental contribution to music in the Armenian Church was to convert the basic melodies of the liturgy ("mayr yeghanak") and harmonize them for part singing, all recorded in European music notation, and arranged for accompaniment on a keyboard instrument. He produced essentially three arrangements of the Divine Liturgy: in three parts for male voices, in four parts for male voices, and in four parts for mixed voices.

At its completion, it was formally sanctioned for use in the Armenian Church through an encyclical ("kontag") issued by the then Catholicos at Echmiadzin, His Holiness Mkrtich Khrimian, dated June 2, 1895.

The complete work was published in a magnificent 264-page volume, in Leipzig and Vienna, in 1896.

A much abbreviated version of this work was published in 1919 by the choir of Holy Savior Armenian Church of Worcester, Massachusetts, the first Armenian Apostolic church in America. Its contents were mainly the arrangement for mixed voices.

With it, the Armenian Church throughout the world continues to this day to sing this version of the Divine Liturgy, in four parts, with mixed voices, and accompanied by an organ.

Other polyphonic arrangements exist for the music of the Divine Liturgy. The one by Komitas Vardapet is in fairly common use, especially in Armenia and in Istanbul. Some competent choirs have the capability of singing in either of the two versions.

More recently, (1985) a third version, composed by Khoren Mekhanejian (former director of the Echmiadzin choir) has been sanctioned for use. It is based on mostly new melodies that differ from the "mayr yeghanak."

Still other arrangements exist, with some bits in use by choirs from time to time, though they have not been formally authorized.

The "Yegmalian" version is known, and used, and loved by choirs all over the world.

છ૭

Krikor Proff-Kalfaian
(1873-1949)

"Proff," as his small circle of friends and music lovers knew him in Fresno, spent his last, sad days without having tasted the adulation of an adoring public that he richly deserved. Though clearly in the public eye as a choirmaster in Fresno's Holy Trinity Armenian Apostolic Church, and the composer and publisher of numerous songs of which he wrote the words as well, Krikor Proff-Kalfaian has not attained the recognition that Armenians of the world should have accorded him.

He was born in Broussa (now in Turkey), but was fortunate in being given the opportunity to study music in France. He was taught by composer Vincent d'Indy, who recognized Proff-Kalfaian's innate artistry.

It was in France that he created most of his musical output. There he published a magazine (in Armenian and French) devoted to Armenian fine arts. It was there too that he composed music for the Divine Liturgy of the Armenian Church, based partly on traditional melodies and partly on wholly new themes of his own.

He was appropriately recognized in France for his mastery of music, and as a result, he was invited by the Ottoman Ambassador to France to become the Director of a Conservatory of Music that the Ottoman government was to open in Constantinople. The Balkan Wars, however, prevented this plan from being realized.

After arriving in the United States in 1913, he became choirmaster in the Armenian churches of Boston, Worcester, and Lowell. In 1918, he was invited to Fresno to become choirmaster of the Holy Trinity Armenian

Church, where he served during two separate periods, there using his own arrangement of the music of the Divine Liturgy.

After an illness of a few months, he died a despondent and lonely man. He was buried in Fresno's Ararat Cemetery, in June 1949.

In addition to the music, Proff-Kalfaian often wrote the words as well. Possibly the best known of his songs is "Nor Oror" (New Lullaby). The intensely rousing lyrics that this strongly patriotic composer wrote seek to stir Armenians to avenge the slaughter the nation had borne. The words of "Nor Oror" are here in translation.

NOR OROR
(New Lullaby)

Dejected, sad, doleful, and forlorn,
Numbed by fear, you sleep - unprotesting.
Wake up, then. It is time for spirited battle.
The Red Beast thirsts for your blood.

Frozen from the cold, faint from hunger, exhausted,
Night and day, you implore in vain.
Why do you cry? Turn away from strangers.
Why do you cry? Evil is the wicked foreigner.

Then hear me well. Cease your weeping and wailing.
Do not defile your brother's blood with your tears.
Take up the knife of vengeance and go forth unbridled.
The God of Armenians will bring you Victory.

℘

Aram Khachaturyan
(1903-1978)

𝔄ll the world knows him as the composer of "Sabre Dance." Aram Khachaturyan, born of Armenian parents in nearby Tiflis, Georgia, rose high in the restrictive view of Soviet authorities who could easily deem a piece of music as "bourgeois," and unacceptable in their ideology. But Khachaturyan, borrowing heavily from Armenian and other Caucasian folk themes, won approbation from the censors. In 1983 the Soviet Union honored him with the issue of a commemorative postage stamp.

Khachaturyan won acclaim for his music not only within the Soviet Union, but also world-wide. In 1968 he toured the United States, conducting orchestras of several cities in concerts consisting entirely of his own compositions. These concerts were eminently successful, but the man himself once said, *"Khachaturyan the composer is not always satisfied with Khachaturyan the conductor."*

Khachaturyan did not study music until the age of nineteen. He went to stay with his brother in Moscow, and entered the Gnesin School of Music, where he studied both composition and conducting, as well as the 'cello. On graduating in 1929 he succeeded in passing the entrance examinations and enrolled in the Moscow Conservatory.

Best known of his works are the ballets "Gayane" and "Spartacus," the Violin Concerto, the Piano Concerto, the Masquerade suite, and the Symphony No. 2.

Khachaturyan lived in Moscow, but he often visited Armenia and his native Caucasus, to be further stimulated by the rich folk themes to be found there.

Although all of his works bear the color of his native Caucasus, it is the music of the ballet "Gayane" that is perhaps the richest in tincture.

It is this ballet that includes the "Sabre Dance," a robust, rousing, rhythmic tune that attained world-wide popularity and fame.

Though not himself a highly acomplished pianist, Khachaturyan's strong instinct of the capabilities of the piano enabled him to create the beautiful Piano Concerto that is widely played, and often recorded.

Khachaturyan was highly regarded in Armenia. He was elected to the Supreme Soviet of the Armenian Soviet Socialist Republic, and in 1939 he was awarded the highest honor of the USSR, the Order of Lenin.

He was also highly regarded by his fellow composers of the Soviet Union in being made Deputy President of the Organizing Committee of the Union of Soviet Composers. As such, he played a significant role in establishing a favorable environment for all Soviet composers.

It was while he was still a student at the Conservatory that he met Nina Makarova, also a student. Their marriage was blessed with three children.

Aram Khachaturyan was probably the Armenian composer of greatest renown. He, like Komitas Vardapet, used Armenian thematic material and gave it the best possible recognition and acclaim.

෨

Alan Hovhaness
(1911-2000)

$\mathfrak{H}$is is the music of the spheres, of nature, expressed through Oriental tunes and intervals and rhythms, and through ancient Armenian religious chants, but yet uniquely his own. He stands apart, as does his music, a fusion of East and West, mystical, beautiful, ceremonial, and celestial.

Alan Scott Hovhaness, born in Massachusetts, son of Tufts College Chemistry Professor Chakmakjian (author of the English-Armenian dictionary that bears his name) and a Scottish mother, very early in life showed his natural gift for musical composition. Even before having had any formal training he had written compositions, and he had experimented on the family pump organ and later an upright piano. Some of his compositions from that early period when he was a young boy were performed in school concerts.

Formal training at the New England Conservatory of Music, winning of several awards, teaching, composing, and accompanying made up his early life. For a time he was organist at St. James Armenian Church of Watertown, Massachusetts, where he became familiar with the rich heritage of Armenian religious music. Clergymen especially knowledgeable in Armenian musical modes were an important resource for him, as was the music of Komitas Vardapet. This was also his "Armenian Period," when he wrote the "St. Vartan Symphony," in addition to other works.

Already well recognized in 1958 for his creative works, Hovhaness was awarded the doctorate by the University of Rochester, and again the next year by Bates College. Years later, he was again so honored by American Armenian International College.

Hovhaness was extremely prolific in composition. But there came a time when he wanted to distance himself from his earlier works that no longer expressed his feelings. To do so he destroyed possibly more than a thousand pieces of music, of various kinds, mainly by burning the manuscripts.

The music of the East - Japan, India, China, Korea, Hawaii, along with Armenia - became his principal source material.

The start of his eastern association came in 1959 when as a Fulbright Research Scholar he went to India. It was a mutually rewarding association - the Indian people loved him, and he their music. While there he wrote a number of compositions that were performed by Indian orchestras.

In 1960 he went to Japan. His stay there was even more rewarding. The people of Japan were already more familiar with his music than Americans. In Japan too, Hovhaness produced works employing its music. Certain accommodations were needed in the music to enable it to be played on western instruments.

His long-time stay in Japan, and also his research and composition in Korea, were enabled by a Rockefeller grant.

An interviewer of Hovhaness (Julia Michaelyan, free-lance flute player, and graduate of Juilliard School of Music) once wrote, *"Hovhaness' ideal music is the giant melody of the Himalayan Mountains, seventh century Armenian religious music, classical music of South India, orchestral music of the Tang Dynasty of China, Ah-ak of Korea, Gagaku of Japan and the opera-oratorios of Handel."*

Hovaness' creative mind and fertile pen produced many hundreds of works reflecting the influences of the music of Japan, India, Korea, and other eastern regions. Among his works that are based on Armenian persons and events are the following: St. Vartan Symphony, Echmiadzin, Mysterious Mountain [Ararat], Lousadzak, Khaldis, Anahid, Sosi, King Vahaken, Armenian Rhapsody.

When the one-hundredth anniversary of the birth of Komitas Vardapet was to be fittingly observed, in 1969, Alan Hovhaness gladly agreed to direct the professional chorus in recording Komitas' works.

℘

Ivan Aivazovski
(Hovhannes Aivazian)
(1817 - 1900)

World-renowned for his dramatic marine paintings Aivazovski captured the sea in all its moods, peaceful, troubled, and in its fury.

Born in the Crimea in a small town on the shore of a gulf off the Black Sea, Aivazovski in his childhood was in constant sight of the sea. His home, on a high piece of ground, commanded a grand view, including ancient fortress walls and ramparts, and other vestiges of a storied past, the devastation of war.   Always in his view were fishing vessels, naval battleships, and whatever else the sea offered.

Even as a child, Aivazovski developed a strong interest in peoples' struggles for independence, and in the romance of heroic feats in sea battles as depicted in pictures that he saw. He himself, very early, showed native skill in drawing.

It was his good fortune, when he was only sixteen, to be admitted to the Academy of Art in St. Petersburg, based on some childhood drawings he submitted. There his skill advanced rapidly, and he was awarded top prizes for his paintings. The awards included the privilege of travel, and he spent two years in the Crimea painting scenes dear to his heart.

When he was twenty-two, he went as artist on a naval expedition. When hostile encounters arose, Aivazovski showed great courage and valor.

After a time in Italy he returned to Russia and was commissioned to paint the Russian naval ports on the Baltic Sea, being designated Artist of the

Naval High Command and allowed to wear the uniform of the Admiralty.

In 1845 Aivazovski returned to his native town in the Crimea where he set up a studio that became his permanent residence. There he witnessed some of the battles of the Crimean War (1856), which gave him inspiration for many of his paintings.

Aivazovski traveled frequently, to Italy, Paris, and other European cities, and also to Armenia and other parts of the Caucasus. He sailed often on the Black Sea, visiting at its shores, as well as on the Mediterranean. These voyages enabled him to accumulate a large number of sketches he made during his travels.

Toward the end of his life he made a long trip to America.

Aivazovski produced more than 5000 canvases, some of which are quite large. He worked very rapidly. His technique is truly distinctive; his works can be recognized by amateurs. Eventhough fairly large collections are found in many places (the

Shipwrecked 1876

Hermitage, most large museums, the Armenian Catholicates and Patriarchates, and in private holdings), his paintings are in very high demand, and they enjoy the highest admiration. The town of Feodosiya, his birthplace in the Crimea, has assembled a large gallery of his works.

Aivazovski served the interests of the Armenian people very well. He was the first to portray nature in Armenia, Mt. Ararat and its plains, Lake Sevan, and many others. His "Tiflis Scene" (1868) was the first in the genre of Armenian life.

Aivazovski enjoyed the esteem not only of the Imperial Russian Government, but also of the Soviet Government. The Soviet Union has issued a series of commemorative postage stamps showing reproductions of a number of Aivazovski's paintings, as well as a painting of the artist himself.

൸

Martiros Sargis Saryan
(1880-1972)

hough born in the refugee community of Nor Nakhichevan (southern Russia), Martiros Saryan, after some wanderings, made Armenia his permanent home (1921), and led the artists of his new homeland into a prolific half-century of works of many genres.

Martiros Saryan's ancestors had been driven out of Ani into the Crimea before their settling in the new Armenian colony of Nor Nakhichevan.

In his early youth, Martiros studied art and sculpture in Moscow where he came into contact with Russian intellectuals, and during which time his occasional travels into the Caucasus led to his fascination with the geography and countryside of Armenia.

In his first creative period (1904-1909), he strayed from traditional art, which gave rise to his works being labeled 'Saryanesque.' Even in that early period, he participated in art exhibits.

During the second period of his work (1910's), he enjoyed having showings in international exhibits. His themes, in contrast to those of his first period, no longer presenting nature, people and animals in fantastic style, were concretely realistic.

The third period of his work began with his final return to Armenia in 1921, accompanied by his family. The period was characterized by his interacting with other intellectuals, both native and repatriate. He was quickly given administrative responsibilities, being named to manage the newly organized National Gallery of Art. He was also chosen as the first president of the Union of Artists of Armenia.

He was the recipient of numerous Soviet and international awards.

Notwithstanding his heavy responsibilities, his artistic output did not diminish. Among his international exhibits was the important one-man show in Paris in 1928. A serious loss of his works occurred with a fire on the ship that was returning his paintings from an exhibit in Venice in 1924.

Saryan's Studio in Yerevan

The year 1967 saw the opening of a three-story museum dedicated exclusively to Saryan's life and works. It is a modern structure on Yerevan's Toumanian Street in which are displayed a very substantial collection of his paintings.

Spring Day (1929)   Avedik Issahakian (1955)

Saryan's works have a very distinct and easily recognized character. He enjoyed very high popularity and esteem, both as a person and as an artist, and was recognized as artist laureate of Armenia.

ℰℭ

Arshile Gorky
(1904-1948)

𝕭osdanik Adoian (Arshile Gorky), son of Van, versatile and gifted painter, driven to bringing fame to his people, achieving limited success, and with his life cut short by a tragic end, was an insufficiently recognized artist on the Armenian American scene.

He was born near Van, in a small village on the southeast shore of Lake Van. Art seemed to come naturally to him. He virtually began to draw even before he started to talk. With his father having slipped off to America (1908) to avoid a Turkish army draft, little Vosdanik was enriched artistically with the help of his family members through their visits to nearby historic sites and the beautiful natural environment.

Vosdanik had been so named to reflect the noble ancestry that was theirs.

When only six years of age, he became acquainted with ancient Armenian paintings in the churches of Van, and also with community life, with Armenian revolutionaries, and with church life.

With the Turks' siege of Van (November 1914) the Adoian family joined the trek of tens of thousands of refugees from the area, eventually, after eight months of torturous marching, reaching Echmiadzin and Yerevan.

Living an impoverished life, with his two older sisters having gone to America to join their father, the remnants of the family suffered from want, especially from hunger. In 1919 Vosdanik's mother Shushanik died, leaving only the orphaned Vosdanik and his younger sister Vartoosh. In later years the artist would lovingly immortalize his mother through his paintings depicting her as she was in his memory.

With their father and sisters in America the two were able to make their way to America also, in 1920, by way of Batum, Constantinople, and Athens. At first living in Watertown, Massachusetts, with their sister, they moved to Providence, Rhode Island, to be with their father.

After a time in the Boston area where he taught art at the New School of Design, and also entertained theatre audiences with quick drawings of presidents, he moved in 1925 to New York where he set up a studio. It was there that he adopted the name Arshile (provincial form of the name Arshak) and Gorky (Russian for "bitter").

Gorky's portrait painting began at this time. His mother and sisters were important subjects for him. He taught art at the Grand Central School of Art. In 1930 he had an exhibit of his works at the Museum of Modern Art.

The times being economically difficult, especially for a young artist, he was taken on in 1933-34 by the Civil Works Administration in the Public Works of Art Project.

In 1935 he began an important task with the Works Progress Administration Federal Art Project, lasting until 1941. His assignment was to undertake the monumental task of painting a mural of more than 1500 square feet for the Newark Airport, depicting "Aviation: Evolution of Forms under Aerodynamic Limitations." As a result of later renovations at the Newark Airport the murals appeared to have been lost. Fortunately, they have now been found.

His first museum purchase was in 1937, by the Whitney Museum of American Art. The piece was called "Painting, 1936-37."

His first one-man showing in New York took place at the Boyer Galleries.

In 1939 he completed murals for the Aviation Building at the New York World's Fair.

During the continuing years Gorky's life was more completely filled with exhibits of his works, painting murals, and occasional teaching of art. Also, his marriage (the second) gave him two daughters.

Throughout his work in contemporary art, Gorky continued to portray his deep-seated love for Armenia's soil, its natural countryside, and its life.

In 1945 an exhibit at the Julien Levy Gallery led to his being hailed by a critic as having produced the most original art in U.S. history.

A disastrous fire at his Connecticut studio destroyed many of his paintings.

The Artist and his Mother (ca. 1926-36)

Despite his successes in being recognized as an important modern artist Gorky was never financially comfortable. Nor was his health strong. In 1946 he had a colostomy for cancer.

Tragedy struck in June 1948. As a passenger in an automobile accident (the driver was his gallery exhibiter Julien Levy) his neck was broken and his arm was paralyzed, leaving him unable to paint. His wife and the two children left him.

Totally despondent and alone in his Sherman, Connecticut studio, he committed suicide by hanging.

Although his life was cut tragically short, his work has left an indelible mark on the American modern art scene.

ॐ

Varaz Samuelian's Statue of David of Sasoun - Fresno, California

Stylized Statue of William
Saroyan - Fresno

"Grape Pickers of Armenia"
(Acrylic on Canvass)

Varazdat "Varaz" Samuelian
(1917-1995)

𝕱 or him Art was language. He "spoke" it in many languages, and on many topics, using brush, hammer and chisel, and pen as well.

Varazdat Samuelian, who signed his works "Varaz," was born in the heart of Yerevan, capital of Armenia, in a family of refugee survivor remnants of the epic battles in the defense of Van in 1915.

Varaz' birth was coincident with the 1917 politico-social upheavals of Russia, and his infancy was concurrent with the Armenian Republic of 1918-1920.

As a youth, growing up in the new politico-social environment of Communism that had pervaded Armenia, Varaz was physically agile, performing in sports, and receptive to education. He became credentialed as an art teacher in 1938, and taught for a short time. But to advance his art he went to Kiev and entered the Art Institute there.

With the outbreak of World War II and the Japanese attack on Outer Mongolia, Varaz joined the Soviet Army to help the Mongols repel the Japanese.

But just before his term of voluntary military service was to end he was drafted to serve at the western front, to battle against the Nazi war machine.

After some months in battle action Varaz was taken prisoner by the Germans. And for the duration of the war his life was a continuity of escape, recapture, sickness, wounding, recuperation, hunger, evading the enemy, suffering, and helping the French partisans.

With war's end he found himself in southern France where a unit of the United States Army was stationed. Through the good offices of US Army officer Capt. Doniguian, Varaz was eventually put into contact with his brothers in the United States. But in the meantime he had been living in Paris, working as a model to eke out a living, and also attending art classes.

Arriving in the United States in 1946 Varaz worked for a time in San Francisco, and in 1957 he moved to Fresno where he set up his own studio.

Working as a sign painter for a livelihood, in parallel to pursuing his art of painting and sculpture, Varaz began to give reality to his life-long dream, that of portraying Armenia's epic heroes.

So it was that he created works of art using his brush and his hammer and chisel, filling his studio and the surrounding grounds with the likenesses of Armenia's historical greats.

The outstanding one of such works is his majestic David of Sasoun astride his horse. This grand statue, fashioned of hammered copper plates, and standing thirty feet high, adorns the corner plot of the Fresno County Court House Park, at M and Tulare Streets in Fresno. It stands as a superb public monument.

On acquiring land at "R" and Merced Streets, across from the Fresno Community Hospital, Varaz built the "Varaz Modern Art Museum." It became a showplace for hundreds of his art works, with paintings inside and sculptures outside, including one high-standing symbolic statue of his intimate friend William Saroyan standing by his bicycle and surrounded by his books.

Classicist, impressionist, modernist, Varaz was all of these, reflecting the dramatic changes in his life.

Few knew Saroyan as did Varaz. The two were frequent companions engaged in recreational activities together, some of which could be called escapades. To tell of these experiences and to describe his friend, Varaz wrote the book "Willie and Varaz," giving the reader a view of the famous author as no one else could.

Varaz himself authored a number of books and pamphlets that in addition to their texts are replete with reproductions of his paintings and photographs of his sculptures. A dominant theme in both his paintings and his writings was to condemn war and to extol peace. Among his books is "History of Armenia and My Life."

Though Varaz carried on his work with ceaseless, and seemingly tireless, energy, it may be that the suffering he bore as a prisoner of war contributed to his untimely and unexpected death, on 7 November 1995, at the age of 78.

Though Varaz was Fresno's own, he was known and esteemed worldwide.

ℰℭ

Reuben Nakian
(1897-1986)

𝕬 native of New York City, Reuben Nakian, an innovative and original sculptor, was a pacesetter in 20th century American sculpture. He is recognized for his pioneering work for which he received several fellowships and grants from a number of foundations, including Gugenheim and Ford. He held major exhibitions in several cities in the United States, Europe, and South America. Several nationally known museums have purchased major works of his for permanent display.

Nakian started his art study at an early age (fifteen), attending the Art Students' League, the Independent Art School, and the Beaux Arts Academy. But after a short period of formal study, he came to the realization that he preferred to learn art as an apprentice working under established sculptors in their own studios.

Nakian became acquainted with Arshile Gorky, who had a strong influence on him.

Initially, he favored using familiar animals for his works, but he eventually turned to figures of mythology and religion. He is said to have revitalized Mediterranean mythology, though he generally stayed clear of surrealism and abstraction. Also, he produced busts of prominent figures in the arts and in public life. From time to time, Nakian was even called upon to design stage sets for New York's theater productions.

His own "Descent from the Cross," in cast bronze adorns the entrance plaza of St. Vartan Cathedral in New York. Mindful of Rubens' great masterpiece of the same title, Nakian chose the same theme, though in his case, decidedly in abstract form.

Descent from the Cross
St. Vartan Cathedral, New York

In his obituary (NY Times) it was stated that Nakian saw himself as a "legatee of ancient Mediterranean tradition. His subject matter was heroic, largely drawn from Greek and Roman mythology, particularly the aspect that dealt with the erotic exploits of the gods."

കൗ

Koren Der Harootian
(1909-1991)

With his chisel and and his skill he transformed shapeless materials into embodiments of Armenia's historical figures and epic events.

Koren Der Harootian, son of a brutally slain priest of a village of Kharberd, miraculously found his way to Worcester (1921) with his mother after an odyssey that took them through the genocide, the collapsing Tsar's army, and the Armenian Republic.

As a very young man Koren was captivated by the paintings and sculptures at the Worcester Art Museum, and he knew at once what his calling was to be. He went to Jamaica in 1930 where he produced a large number of paintings of the lush tropical scenes he found there.

Recognized for his talent by the Museum Director for his talent, he was given a one-man showing of his works.

On a return to Jamaica he began to produce carvings out of the native hardwoods, and decided that sculpting would be his main interest.

His work continued to gain wider and wider recognition internationally. His pieces may be found in a dozen or so of reputable museums, including the Metropolitan Museum of Art of New York, and he has enjoyed more than a dozen one-man exhibitions.

When the original Diocesan complex was built on Second Avenue in New York, his greater-than-life-size full relief of Christ adorned the front face of the building.

Prominently displayed on the grounds of the Philadelphia Art Museum is his 24-foot bronze sculpture of "Little Mher," son of David of Sasoun of the epic cycle. The work was commissioned by the Philadelphia Armenian Bicentennial Commemorative Committee.

Sculpture of Armenian Legendary Figure Mher

Der Harootian's donation of more than 200 pieces of his paintings and sculpture to Armenia reflects his intense pride in his Armenian heritage. His donated works are on display in a special museum in his name.

In 1985 he was commissioned by the government of the Armenian Soviet Socialist Republic to create a stone monument representing "Reborn Armenia." To complete that historic monument Der Harootian lived in Armenia for several years.

Having just returned from Armenia to prepare for an exhibit in New York, and also for a visit to Jamaica, Koren Der Harootian met an untimely death in early 1991 in an automobile accident in upstate New York.

80

Rouben Mamoulian
(1897-1987)

Director of stage and screen par excellence, this Armenian immigrant created gems to delight millions of theatre-goers, and in doing so launched many who became famous stars.

Rouben Mamoulian was born in Tiflis, the art capital and cultural heart of the Caucasus, of a mother who was smitten with the theatre, both as promoter and actress.

Mamoulian's family's activities and moves were just right to give him the opportunity of directing plays and rising in his profession rapidly. His early schooling was in Paris, then back to Tiflis, and then the University of Moscow.

Through a series of very fortuitous circumstances and chance acquaintances Mamoulian was engaged to direct a play ("The Beating on the Door") in London, in 1922. He was then only 25 years of age.

As a consequence of his directing that play in London Mamoulian received an offer from George Eastman to go to Rochester, New York, to help organize and direct an American opera company for the Eastman Theatre. Mamoulian accepted, and there produced several grand operas and operettas (1924-25).

Feeling the urge to be in New York City, and despite Eastman's attempts to dissuade him, Mamoulian accepted the offer to direct a new play "Porgy." It was his first production in New York City (1927).

Although he continued directing in a series of stage plays for many years, Mamoulian decided to try his hand at making motion pictures. His first film was "Applause" (1929), one of the earliest sound pictures. In it he introduced a new technique, joining two sound tracks offering flexibility in producing unique sound effects.

Mamoulian's second film was "City Streets." In it he introduced still another new technique, that of allowing the thoughts of a player to be expressed audibly while the player is seen on the screen without speaking.

Mamoulian's production (1935) of "Porgy and Bess" (the musical based on the original play "Porgy") became an instant success as an American opera.

There followed a long sequence of plays and films directed by Mamoulian. A short sampling of titles is enough to establish Mamoulian as one of the greats. On the stage there were "Porgy and Bess," "Farewell to Arms," "Oklahoma," "Carousel," with repeated restagings. The films included "Applause," "City Streets," "Dr. Jekyll and Mr. Hyde," "Love Me Tonight," "Song of Songs," "Queen Christina," "We Live Again," "Becky Sharp," "The Gay Desperado," "High, Wide, and Handsome," "Golden Boy," "Blood and Sand," "The Mark of Zorro," "Rings on Her Fingers," "Summer Holiday," and "Silk Stockings."

In his productions Mamoulian gave impetus to rising stars. Among them were Fredric March, Gary Cooper, Maurice Chevalier, Marlene Dietrich, Fred Astaire, Tyrone Power, and Greta Garbo.

Mamoulian tried his hand also at writing, and with good acceptance. Two works were "Abigayil, Story of the Cat at the Manger" (1964), and Shakespeare's "Hamlet, A New Version" (1966).

Rouben's was not the only Mamoulian name associated with the stage. Rouben's mother Virginia (Vergine), who had accompanied her son on his early travels, and then, with her husband, was brought to America by him in 1931, is well known on the Armenian stage. Her love for the theatre remained strong throughout her life.

Despite his fame and successes Mamoulian's last years were sad ones, partly because of his wife Azadia's lingering illness, and partly because of his general carelessness in maintaining a healthful household.

Rouben Mamoulian earned his prominent place among the immortals of stage and screen.

℘

ΑΡΜΕΝΙΚΟ ΘΕΑΤΡΟ
THE ARMENIAN THEATER

𝕿wo millennia ago Armenians arriving at one of their theaters to view a drama might well have been confronted with a sign reading "ΣΡΟ" (let us say they would have taken it to mean "Standing Room Only"). The play being staged there might have been written by King Artavasd II, and in Greek (for Armenians were not to have their own alphabet until nearly five centuries later).

The Armenian Theater appears to have flourished in pagan Armenia, even before the first century before Christ.

It is believed that the first theater in Armenia was built in the capital city of Tigranakert (city built by Tigranes) in the middle of the first century BC. A second theater was built by his son Artavasd II, in Artashat.

The dramas presented there were borrowed from the Greek Theater, and Artavasd II probably wrote some, himself. The themes of the dramas were tragedies (*voghbergutiun*) and comedies (*katakergutiun*). The thematic material, especially of the tragedies, borrowed heavily from Armenian mythology, and epics that formed a sub-class of epic dramas (*diutsaznergutiun*).

Artavasd II

Later, when pantomime came to the Armenian Theater, the Armenian language adopted the word for "mime," (*mimos*), which entered the language in the same form. However, when the influence of the Hellenistic (Greek) theater was first felt in Armenia, it was not necessary to adopt the Greek words for "tragedy" and "comedy," for Armenians already had the words *voghbergutiun* and *katakergutiun*, which were retained in its lexicon, providing evidence that the Armenians already had a going theater.

Dramas were presented more in the form of dance and song, rather than by recitation. The player on the stage was called a *gusan*, or a *vartzak* (usually a woman).

With the creation of the Armenian alphabet early in the fifth century, it became easier to write Armenian dramas.

However, with the advent of Christianity in Armenia, the theater was not only disdained by the Church hierarchy, but was also condemned as being harmful to the morals of the people. In later centuries, however, the Church was willing to tolerate those dramas that it deemed to have appropriate content. It may also be that the theater influenced the Church to put more stress on the dramatical aspect of its liturgical services.

When Armenia lost its independence (1375 AD), an end came to the vigor of its ancient and medieval theater.

But the modern era in Armenia brought on a reawakening of the Armenian Theater. The political resurgence of the Armenian people late in the 19th century brought with it a class of playwrights and a viable theater in its main cultural centers of Constantinople and Tiflis.

Hamalir Sports & Concert Complex, Yerevan, Republic of Armenia

Today in the homeland, the Republic of Armenia, there is a thriving theater, with repertoires that include not only the great Armenian plays, but also the world's classical and contemporary plays. They are offered not only in Yerevan, but other cities as well, where one can find Shakespeare and Saroyan in Armenian.

Yerevan boasts superb venues, such as the Opera House (1935) with its back-to-back halls, where world-class operas are staged, the new Sundukian Theater (1966), the Hamalir (Sports and Concert Complex), as well as numerous concert halls. Other cities throughout Armenia also have their theaters and concert halls that play a major role in the cultural life of the people.

Opera House – Yerevan, Republic of Armenia

The Armenian Diaspora has not fallen behind. Throughout the world, where there are large Armenian communities, the theater thrives.

℘

Camera Portraiture

They were only a handful, five of them, but they portrayed the famous figures of the world.

They were artists, but instead of using a brush to portray their subjects they used a glass lens. They attained the pinnacle of prominence with their photographic magic. Their images created with light instead of with paints will endure in themselves as well as in the minds of the people who viewed them.

These are the five camera greats.

- ◆ John Garo
- ◆ Yousuf Karsh
- ◆ Artin Cavouk
- ◆ Harry Naltchayan
- ◆ Paul Kalinian

JOHN GARO (1882-1939). Garo (Hovhannes Garoian) was born in Kharberd, son of a Congregational minister. At age 14 he came to America after his parents had been killed in a massacre. Working as an office boy in a greeting card plant in Worcester, he soon discovered his talent. Moving to Boston and working with commercial photographers there, he, at age 20, opened his own portrait studio on Boylston Street. There he rose with phenominal quickness to become world- renowned. Among the

John Garo

notables that he captured through his camera lens were governors, bishops, opera stars, stage celebrities, and symphony conductors, including Calvin Coolidge, Geraldine Farrar, Ethel Barrymore, Edward Everett Hale, Caruso, and Scotti.

His understudy-successor was Yousuf Karsh.

Yousuf Karsh

YOUSUF KARSH (1908-2002). Born in Mardin, a vilayet of Diyarbekir, the young Yousuf (Joseph) came to America in 1924. After studying with photographer Garo (see above), he opened his own studio in Ottawa. He rose rapidly in fame for his superb portraits of the world's great figures, including Winston Churchill, Albert Einstein, Helen Keller, Jan Sibelius, Pablo Casals, Mamie Eisenhower, John and Jacqueline Kennedy, Richard Nixon, and several members of the British royal family.

Karsh' famous "bulldog" portrait of Winston Churchill was used on the commemorative stamp issued by the United States Postal Service on the occasion of the death of the British statesman. Karsh' autobiography, "In Search of Greatness," appeared in 1962.

ARTIN CAVOUK (1915-1995). Cavouk (Haroutiun Cavoukian) was born in Mersin (Cilicia). The family moved to Cairo where he studied photography under his father. He developed his art in Antwerp, specializing in color portraiture. In 1958 he set up a studio in Toronto where he produced magnificent color portraits, notably of the Queen of England, Prince Philip, Lester Pearson (Prime Minister of Canada), General Charles de Gaulle, Anastas Mikoyan and several other Soviet leaders. Called the "Karsh of Color," Cavouk

Artin Cavouk

died in 1995, twelve hours after the death of his beloved and supportive wife.

Harry N. Naltchayan

HARRY N. NALTCHAYAN (1933-1994). While cycling with his brother in their native Beirut one early morning, the free-lance photographers came upon a large French ship that had grounded just off shore. Their pictures of the panicking passengers brought them instant international attention. Harry came to America in 1958, and with a portfolio of his photos and his fluency in five languages he landed a position on the Washington Post. As White House Photographer, he won many awards.   His photo of four living American ex-Presidents together was widely published. The National Geographic article, "The Proud Armenians" (June 1978) was illustrated with the exciting photos by Naltchayan.

PAUL KALINIAN (1932-   ). Born in Beirut and educated in Damascus, Kalinian entered photography at an early age. He opened his first studio, "Photo Paul," in Beirut in 1961. In 1964 he moved to Montreal and then on to the United States, earning a degree in Professional Photography and Motion Picture Production at the New York Institute of Photography. In 1973, Kalinian opened "Paul's Photography" in Fresno, where he was able to fulfill his long-standing desire to photograph the elusive William Saroyan, through the helpful intercession of their mutual friend sculptor

Paul Kalinian

Varaz. One of the resulting portraits of the writer became the basis for the William Saroyan commemorative stamps issued concurrently by the United States and the Soviet Union on May 22, 1991.

Continuing in his dedication to Saroyan, Kalinian wrote, directed and produced the highly acclaimed documentary film "William Saroyan: The Man, The Writer," which won five international film festival awards, including the Gold Award for Best Documentary at the Philadelphia Film Festival in 1995.

℃

An Armenian Carpet

Magic Carpets

𝕴n the traditional Armenian homeland, it was the hand-woven carpets covering coarse (even dirt) floors and settees that made for a comfortable, homey atmosphere in the household, such as when children gathered around to hear grandfather spin his entertaining tales.

Along with other peoples of the Middle East, Armenians very early developed advanced skills in textiles, and in particular, the hand weaving of carpets.

In its entry on Rugs and Carpets, the Encyclopedia Britannica says, *"Various of the Arab geographers give valuable though meagre information about carpet weaving in the Near East from the 8th to the 14th centuries. Armenia was certainly one of the most productive districts. There were found good wool, clear water, and fine dyes, especially a scarlet made from the "Coccus ilias" called "kermes" and widely exported. Armenian rugs were famous in the 8th century, and we know that by the 10th century such cities as Dvin, Van, Erzerum, Bitlis, Vartan, Aklat, and Tiflis, all produced famous rugs. Marco Polo reported that the Armenians and Greeks in the towns of central Asia Minor (Konya, Sivas, and Caesarea) wove the most beautiful carpets in the world."*

Natural fibers of wool, cotton, and silk, along with vegetable dyes provide the main elements of carpet weaving. The colorful designs of the carpets are very distinctive, being characteristically unique for the people in each large geographical region, or sub-regions, or even small population centers as cities and villages.

Thus, hand-woven carpets and rugs are usually identified by the name of the country (as Persian), or of a region (as Caucasian), or the name of a city (as Shushi). Also, the style of knot used in the weaving process, just as the design, varies from region to region, and is characteristic for any given region. Consequently, a knowledgeable expert in carpets is able, nearly unfailingly, to identify where a given carpet was woven.

Armenian carpets, too, bear their own characteristic designs. Occasionally, they may also include Armenian lettering, or inscriptions telling of the circumstances surrounding the weaving of an individual carpet, and often the date.

The Armenian linguist, Hrachya Ajarian, has posited that the English word "carpet" is in fact a derivative of the Armenian word կարպետ (karpet), though that word, itself, may have been derived from the earlier word կապերտ (kapert). The more common Armenian word is գորգ (gorg).

Although oriental hand-woven carpets are produced over a wide geographical range, our attention will be centered on Anatolian and Caucasian rugs.

The main factors in rug weaving are Yarns, Dyes, Weaves, and Designs.

YARNS: The principal textile fibers used are wool, cotton, and silk. Sometimes, metallic filaments (gold, silver) are included to add extra luster to the finished product. The foundation of the rug is most commonly of cotton yarn for its greater strength.   The yarns are spun in various thicknesses depending on the fineness desired in the rug.

DYES: Vegetable dyes (plants, roots, bark, berries, etc.) are dominant in dyeing the yarns, although some mineral dyes are also used. Fastness of the dyes, besides their brilliance, is a prime requirement. There are more than thirty plants that yield usable dyes. Mixing provides still other tints. The most famous of Armenian dyes is the cochineal red extracted from a worm.

WEAVE: Two basic types of knots are used for locking in the pile onto the foundation. They are the Ghiordes (blind) knot and the Sena (Persian) knot. There is a wide variation in the fineness (density of the knots forming the woven pattern) ranging from 100 knots to the square inch to over 2,000.

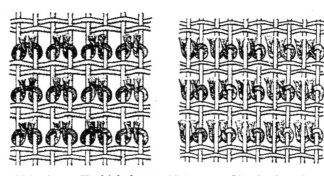

Ghiordes, or Turkish, knot   Սէնաշ որ Բերսիական քնող

DESIGN: The rugs of Anatolia and of the Caucasus feature intricate and delicate designs, in both the borders and in the field.   Field designs are of several types, medallion, animal/bird, garden/flower, landscape, prayer, dragon, etc.

So, let your imagination fly away on a magic Armenian carpet.

℘

Armenian Ceramics
Tiles from Kutahya (Jerusalem)

The name Kutahya is almost synonymous with decorative ceramics. The age-old Kutahya craft of producing ornamental tiles is attributed to Armenian craftsmen who developed the art to its highest level.

For several hundred years the craft flourished in this city in western Anatolia, even before the arrival of the Moslem invaders of the 15th century.

Kutahya (birthplace of Komitas Vardapet) had become a renowned center for both ornamental tiles and illuminated manuscripts.

It was natural that the two would find harmony and a marriage would result. Armenian craftsmen painted their brilliant color glazes on fine clay squares and fired their handiwork in kilns that were virtually never allowed to go cold.

The lavish paintings in Armenian illuminated manuscripts thus found a new medium in which to tell their story.

Armenian churches being built in the Near East were frequently adorned with the beautiful tiles from Kutahya.

Such a craft that revealed the resplendence of the art and the radiance of the faith of the Armenians could not be allowed to continue to prosper under the oppressive policies of the Ottoman Sultans. Armenian churches were destroyed and their ornamental tiles stripped away. The craft seemed to be in danger of annihilation.

But there was reprieve. A number of the families of craftsmen found refuge in Jerusalem, where they set up their kilns and continued in their art.

They are there today, in Jerusalem. One of the finest of the tile shops can be found on the Via Dolorosa, not far from the Church of the Holy Sepulchre. Tourists would do well to visit any of the several shops and purchase tiles of their choice.

ॐ

Armenian Ceramic Tile from Jerusalem in the Kutahya Style

Ceramic Pieces from Kutahya - ca. XVIII c

Coins of Armenia

𝕬s a sometimes sovereign nation, Armenia minted its own coins for the realm.   At other times, when Armenia came under foreign control, the use of other coins was imposed by the controlling nation on the commerce of Armenia. Numismatic scholars have studied these coins, and their comprehensive findings have been published in several important volumes.

Coins in use in Armenia throughout its history by themselves bring that history to light, by identifying the ruling authority as well as the monetary unit in use.

Coins, in general, were stamped out, or cast, of a variety of metals - gold, silver, copper, bronzes, and iron. Some coins, however, were made of other materials, such as leather and wood.

Numismatic studies lead to the following simplified summary concerning coins used at various times in Armenia.

A.   Orontid Dynasty (320-215 B.C.): Silver and copper coins were minted. They bore inscriptions in Greek, naming the monarch on the throne, showing his effigy on the obverse and an eagle or a mounted figure on the reverse.

B.   Artaxid Dynasty (190 B.C. to 10 A.D.): Silver and copper coins were minted. They bore inscriptions in Greek naming the ruling monarch. The very familiar coin bearing the effigy of Tigranes (the Great) wearing the diadem (see illustration) is the best known Armenian coin.   The reverse bears the inscription   in   Greek   "VASILEOS

Artaxid Dynasty
Tigran the Great, 1st c. BC

TIGRANOY" (King Tigran), and shows a figure carrying a palm frond.

C.   Roman Period (10-193 A.D.): Roman coins bearing inscriptions in Latin, meaning "Armenia Conquered" were used.

D.   Arsacid Dynasty (193-430 A.D.): Only Persian coins were used in Armenia.

E. Period of Foreign Domination (Persian, Byzantine, Arab); also Armenian Governors (430-860 A.D., Post-Mesropian Period): Coins were minted by numerous Arab overlords bearing the inscription "Arminiya" (in Arabic).

F. Bagratid Dynasties (860-1080 A.D.): There appear to be no coins minted by any of the Bagratid Dynasties.

G. Rubenid Dynasty/Cilician (1080-1375 A.D.): A rich variety of coins exist from this period. Inscriptions are in Armenian, and the Cross is prominently shown (see illustration). The coins are of gold, silver, copper, and bronzes. Most of the coins have effigies of the ruler minting the coin, together with his title, in Armenian, as "LEVON TAGAVOR HAYOTS" (Leon, King of Armenians).

Rubenid Dynasty-Cilicia
Levon I, 13th c. A D

H. Dark Ages (Ottoman domination, 1375-1918): No Armenian coins.

I. Armenian Republic (1918-1920): Armenian paper currency was in use as well as Russian coins. The monetary unit was the Ruble.

J. Soviet Period (1920-1991): Soviet currency and coins were used exclusively.

K. Armenian Republic (1991-present): A new monetary unit was introduced, called the "Dram" (Armenian "money"), divided into one-hundredths called the "Luma" (classical word for "money"). Coins have been issued for denominations up to 100 Lumas (equals one Dram), but their use is limited because of their small value.

Front of Coin   Back of Coin

Hetumian Dynasty- Cilicia
Hetum-Zabel, 13th c. A D

Chapter 8

OTHER
CONTEMPORARY
FIGURES

Armenian Benefactors in America
A Representative Listing

Arakelian ❧ Berberian

Chamlian ❧ Dickranian

Fesjian ❧ Garabedian

Gulbenkian

Hovnanian Family

Isbenjian ❧ Kavookjian

Kerkorian/Lincy

Manoogian/Simone

Mardigian ❧ Mardikian

Nazarian ❧ Mugar

Peters ❧ Pilibos

Good Samaritans
(Armenian Benefactors in America)

Captains of industry, titans of commerce, wizards of finance, developers of reality, producers of agriculture; they not only employed their acumen in order to generate substantial wealth, they were also Good Samaritans.

They displayed a God-given virtue to share their abundance and support good causes. As benefactors, they also won the genuine respect of the Armenian people for their unstinting readiness to give and give, wherever and whenever the Armenian people, a nation in dispersion, had a need but not the monetary means to fulfill it.

As we read in the Gospel, *"I came that they may have life, and have it abundantly"* (John 10:10). And how does He do that? Through the agency of these generous benefactors.

These Armenian benefactors may be found in many countries around the world. But we have here in this assemblage identified only some who are in America, although their beneficial reach has been worldwide.

What have they done in fact? The list is long, and seemingly endless. They built and maintained Armenian schools. They built churches and cathedrals. They built and stocked museums. They restored architectural monuments. They repeatedly provided and transported needed supplies to ravished Armenia. They rehabilitated hierarchical centers and built seminaries. They endowed academic chairs and offered educational scholarships. Their reach often went beyond Armenian needs into the American public realm, establishing hospitals, libraries, and educational centers for the public good.

The Armenian people are proud to be able to count these agents of Christ in their midst.

❧

Saroukhan's Work

On Armenians and Their Hospitality
"Oh, no, Mr. Garabed, you must have some of this too. I prepared it with my own hands."

On Ascribing Armenian Origins to All Important Figures
*"Truman is Armenian, he just shortened the "ian" ending of his name.
And how about the Manchester Guardian?*

Alexander Saroukhan
(1898-1977)

$\mathbb{P}$ossibly the foremost Armenian caricaturist of all time Alexander Saroukhan brought his wit, perception, humor, and satire to the attention of all the world, evoking admiration and esteem.

Although his regular gainful employment was as cartoonist and satirist for Egyptian newspapers in Cairo, and he occasionally appeared in newspapers elsewhere in the world, he is best known by Armenians for his sharp satire on Armenian mores. He might also be described as the visual equivalent of satirist writers Hagop Baronian and Yervant Odian.

Saroukhan was born in a village near Batum on the eastern shore of the Black Sea. He was sent to Constantinople in 1909 to study art, and was actually given teaching responsibilities at the school even before graduation in 1915.

He was spared the Ottoman Gehenna because his Mekhitarist School was under Austrian protection.

Because Saroukhan knew several languages he served during World War I as a translator for the British Army.

The Armenian humor periodical "Gavrosh" was the first to publish one of his cartoons, in 1921.

His pen served him well also in writing, his articles having been printed in various periodicals and much sought after.

Saroukhan's cartoons on Armenian topics and issues appeared primarily in the newspaper "Arev" (Sun), of Cairo.

His knowledge of Arabic, as well as English and French, along with his insightful nature, led to his being put into the service of the American OWI (Office of War Information) during World War II.

Saroukhan's fame among Armenians all over the world continued to grow over the years. He visited many Armenian communities, including those in America.

Victor Ambartsumyan

Sylva Kaputikyan

Charles Aznavour

Arshag Chobanian

Typical of his satirical cartoons of weakness of character in some Armenians is the pair of cartoons showing a father and mother about to enroll a young son and daughter in a school. They have inquired about the fees to be paid. One cartoon depicts the meeting with the administrator in an Armenian school, and the other in a French school.

The harried male administrator in the Armenian school has stated the fee, a very modest sum that includes books and material, lunch, and five and a half days of school. The parents complain bitterly that the cost is exorbitant, robbery!

The stern female administrator in the French school states the fee, much higher than for the Armenian school, and with books and material extra, and only four days of school. The parents meekly and approvingly compliment the school for being so generous and accommodating.

Saroukhan did indeed comprehend human failings.

&

Roger (Hratch) Tatarian
(1916-1995)

$\mathfrak{A}$s roving reporter, wire service editor, news bureau chief, UPI executive, international news analyst, teacher, columnist, and commentator, Journalist Roger Hratch Tatarian was indeed born to fill those roles superbly.

He was born in Fresno of parents who had only recently married in Bitlis and migrated to the United States. Even in his early teens Roger became a sports writer for the school newspaper (Longfellow Junior High School). He graduated from Fresno State College in 1938, and in a few months was working in the Fresno office of the United Press International. Soon after, he went to the San Francisco office and then on to the Phoenix office, before going on to the Washington, DC, office in 1941.

In 1945 Tatarian was given his first foreign assignment, as Director of the London Office of UPI, and later in Rome. He returned to London as Director of European Operations of UPI, until 1959, when he returned to the United States.

The year 1961 found him serving as Chief Editor in the New York office, and in 1965 he was named Vice President of UPI.

In 1972 Tatarian accepted the invitation to join the faculty at California State University, Fresno, as Professor of Journalism, a position he filled for fifteen years. In that capacity he was named Outstanding Professor, in 1981.

In 1987 he became a regular weekly columnist, appearing in the Sunday issue of the Fresno Bee.

Tatarian was a member of the United States Delegation to Paris for the UNESCO Conference (1980) on International Communications.

During his last years in Fresno he was a regular participant in the Public Television discussion program called Valley Press. He also appeared as TV Commentator. Tatarian was held in very high regard in the entire community of Fresno.

On the day of his death, Sunday, June 25, 1995, his regular Sunday column that appeared in The Fresno Bee on that day happened to be on his roots and the Armenian Genocide.

A major community-wide memorial service was held to honor this widely-esteemed, self-made journalist.

෨

Victor Ambartsumyan
(1908-1996)
"Envoy to the Stars"

e spied on the stars to learn their secrets, and revealed them to all the world.

Victor Hamazasp Ambartsumyan (Hambartsumyan), astro-physicist, won world renown for his pioneering work in the discipline of astrophysics. He probed the secrets of how and when stars came into being, and of what they are constituted. He promulgated theories, and supported them with his telescopic observations and mathematical analyses. He wrote textbooks, which were translated into many languages. He was invited to conduct seminars. He organized academic bodies of his professional colleagues.

He was highly regarded internationally and widely honored.

Astrophysicist Ambartsumyan was multi-lingual, and could conduct his seminars, or serve as guest of honor at a scientific colloquium, in any of several languages.

He was born in Tiflis, Georgia, and completed his formal education at the University of Leningrad (1928). He continued graduate studies in the astronomical observatory, and in 1934 was designated Professor at the University, later also at the University of Yerevan.

He was the founder of the Soviet School of Theoretical Astrophysics.

His status in his discipline could be measured by the positions he held: President of the Academy of Sciences of Armenia; Founder and Director of the Byurakan Astrophysical Observatory; President of the International Astronomical Union (for several years); President of the International Council of Scientific Unions, and much more.

Byurakan Astronomical Observatory Main Building

The Byurakan Astro-physical Observatory is located high on the southern slope of Mt. Aragadz in Armenia, at an elevation of 4950 feet above sea level.   It was founded in 1946, and opened in 1956.   Director Ambartsumyan surrounded himself at the Observatory with a team of gifted astrophysicists, mathematicians, and other scientific specialists.   The Observatory enjoys world-wide recognition and esteem.

Astrophysicist Ambartsumyan's specialty was Cosmogony. Cosmogony is that branch of Astrophysics that is concerned with the evolution of the universe. It involves the study of the origin of stellar galaxies, their stars, and their planetary systems.

Despite his unbelievably deep involvement in his professional field, Victor Ambartsumyan was always active and supportive of public agencies and social commissions.

He truly was one of the great scientists of the twentieth century.

෨ර

Andranik

Like an eagle, he had soared;
 Like a tiger, he had caught;
Like a fox, he had outwitted;
 Like a lion, he had fought.

Many an enemy, had he conquered;
 Many a strike, had he planned;
Many a battle, had he won
 For the sake of his people and land.

Committed to Armenia's liberation
 From the young age of twenty-two,
He had never compromised his principles
 For the selfishness of a few.

From Arakelotz to Zangezour,
 His leadership had been supreme;
He was loved by all Armenians
 Who held him in highest esteem.

General Andranik Ozanian
 Whose life was but a test
Of great resolve and sacrifice
 Was finally laid to rest.

Like an eagle, he had soared;
 Like a tiger, he had caught;
Like a fox, he had outwitted;
 Like a lion, he had fought.

8&

General Andranik Ozanian

Andranik Pasha
(1865-1927)

The first name in the Armenian struggle for national liberation in modern times is Andranik. "Like an eagle he soars over the mountains and ridges."

Andranik Toros Ozanian was born in historic Shabin-Karahisar ("Shabin, the black fortress," 80 miles northeast of Erzurum). He was destined more, perhaps, than any of the other Armenian revolutionaries, to provide leadership, rationality, acumen, prudence, and effectiveness to Armenia's rising up against the brutal Ottoman oppression.

Even during his adolescence Andranik recognized the pattern of Ottoman oppression and the sufferings of his people. So it was that at the tender age of 22, having lost his wife and two children, Andranik joined a partisan group formed in his native town.

Inspired with the ideals of liberation for his people, Andranik went to Constantinople to meet those who had already been deeply involved in the liberation movement. He readily accepted tasks assigned to him.

When the leader, Serob Aghbiur, of a fighting group which Andranik had joined, was killed, Andranik was named leader.

It was in 1901 when his fighting group held out in the Arakelots Vank against an overwhelmingly superior force that Andranik's name became famous for his effectiveness as a revolutionary leader.

There were many more similar occurrences to come.

Andranik, at first, joined the Hunchak party; it was through party organization that he could be effective in securing men and materiel with which to carry on. But disagreement with party policies led Andranik to leave the Hunchak ranks and join the Dashnak party. There too, when that party engaged in practices judged to be wrong in principle, Andranik resigned.

During the period 1907-13 Andranik committed his energies to helping the Bulgarian liberation movement. In it he created an Armenian division, which brought honor to itself by its effective participation. For his efforts Andranik was decorated and commissioned an officer.

With World War I under way (1914-1918) Andranik went to the Caucasus and assisted in organizing Armenian battle units to fight the Turks alongside the Russian army units.

In 1915 Andranik was named commander of all Armenian volunteer units within the Russian army.

The overthrow of the Tsarist regime in Russia (1917) and the consequent collapse of the Russian imperial army found Andranik on the side of the working class out of which the social revolution in Russia had arisen.

Early in 1918 he began to organize a separate army to liberate western Armenia. Made a Major General, Andranik had many thousands under his command, Armenian soldiers from the old Russian army, and many thousand Armenians who had volunteered from all over the world.

Gen. Andranik with his Men

However, short on resources and back-up military fighting units, Andranik had to abandon his plan to take Erzurum.

With the collapse of the Tsarist Russian government an independent Armenian Republic was set up in May 1918. Andranik was in sympathy with the social principles that came with the new Russian order and desired to maintain amicable relations with Russia. However, Armenia's ruling party, the Dashnaks, did not favor such a relationship. As a result Andranik once again had a falling out with them.

The brilliant defense of Zangezur (1918-19) under Andranik's command marked the end of his military career.

Leaving Armenian lands he traveled to Europe and eventually to America (1922), finally settling in Fresno, California, with his new wife. His name and fame enabled him to be effective in fund-raising activities in America for aid to Armenian orphans.

His life in Fresno, with frequent visits elsewhere in response to calls, was spent very much in the public eye. But his health was failing. While seeking to regain strength in a sanatorium in Chico, California, the death that he had eluded in his many years of fierce battle encounters now finally caught up with him. The date was August 31, 1927.

Citywide public attention was accorded him at his funeral in Fresno, where he was interred (September 7, 1927) in the Ararat Cemetery.

A few months later Andranik's remains were exhumed and taken to Paris (accompanied by his widow) for a second funeral service and interment.

Few heroes have been as well acclaimed during their lives as was Andranik.

ഇ

Cymbals By Zildjian

𝖂here else, other than from the Avedis Zildjian Company, would a fine symphony orchestra, or a top-rated band, buy their cymbals? For tone and timbre, for brilliance and color, for crash and power, no other cymbals can match a "Zildjian."

When the opportunity presents itself (at, say, intermission time), go to the percussion area of an orchestra in concert and look at the cymbals there. Look (and find) stamped on the cymbals the company's distinctive logo.

The first of three Avedis Zildjians to head the family enterprise was the inventor and founder alchemist of Constantinople, in 1623. Having fashioned an alloy of copper and zinc, and having devised a process for casting and spinning the alloy into cymbals, that first Avedis, nearly four centuries ago, established the family tradition, and earned the delineating surname of "Zildjian" (maker of "zils," cymbals).

Avedis Zildjian

That family enterprise continued operations unabated, and gained the unchallenged worldwide recognition of being the makers of the "one of a kind," the "only" cymbals to have.

In time, after three centuries of manufacture, and because of political instability, the center of the family's operations moved (1927) from Constantinople to America, to Quincy, a coastal city of Massachusetts.

It was in America, under the third Avedis in the lineage, that the company and its superior product became more widely recognized and esteemed.

Although the company managers and their craftsmen were the unquestioned masters of their art, they nevertheless established, as a policy, a very close and cooperative relationship with hundreds of famous musicians, orchestra conductors, and band masters, to learn what each was looking for in the sound cymbals make for their particular type of music. For the company's craftsmen's skill in fashioning cymbals was so great that they could create cymbals virtually on a custom basis. They could design and make to order cymbals with various combinations of 'pitch,' 'response,' 'sustaining power,' 'crash,' 'splash,' 'ride,' 'swish,' 'ping,' 'sizzle,' or other characteristics sought by performing groups.

The list of musicians with which Avedis Zildjian, III, had such cooperative contact is long and includes the great and famous.

The Zildjian Trademark

It is a striking fact that other makers of cymbals have been unable to match a "Zildjian." The principal reason for this is that the Zildjian process employs proce-dures that remain a company, or family, secret, handed down and carefully guarded for nearly four centuries. What secrets! It is the Zildjian secret of how to prepare the alloy, how to cast it, how to spin it, how to apply the tonal grooves, how to temper and age it. And there are other secrets concerning obscure requirements that others would not even suspect exist.

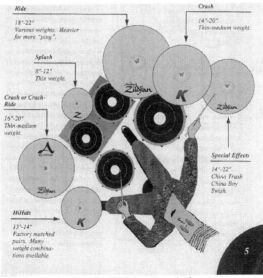

Avedis Zildjian Cymbals

Expect to find Zildjian cymbals in the finest orchestras throughout the world, from Armenia to Zanzibar.

☙

"Mr Five Per Cent"
(Calouste Sarkis Gulbenkian)
(1869-1955)

He led the world in recognizing the economic and political power of petroleum. And he took action to acquire and wield that power.

Calouste Sarkis Gulbenkian exploited that power to become one of the world's richest men. He did so virtually single-handedly, waging battles against governments, potentates, industrial giants, and the upheavals of wars. His was a case of David against a swarm of Goliaths.

Calouste Gulbenkian was a graduate engineer, a financier, an industrialist, a diplomat, a philanthropist, an art connoiseur, and, incidentally, an admirer of beautiful women.

Born near Constantinople in a wealthy family (Gulbenkian on both sides) already in the business of oil, Calouste went on for higher education in France, and then in London where he was a top graduate in civil engineering. He entered his father's oil business (in Baku). He published technical materials (book and magazine articles) on oil and its economic and technical employment, and conducted research for the Ottoman government and for Russian oil interests. He established contacts with British oil interests and finance people.

Soon (1897) he obtained oil concessions from Persia, and began a dizzying sequence continuing over the next twenty years of negotiations and deals with the giant oil companies of England, Holland, Turkey, Persia, Iraq,

317

Russia, Germany, Venezuela, France, and Mexico, creating a variety of alliances in which he always included himself with a substantial interest.

In 1931 he had the opportunity for a profitable oil concession in Saudi Arabia. However, the British government effectively blocked it. As a result, American interests succeeded in getting into Saudi Arabia's enormous oil resources (Aramco).

The disruption caused by World War II, for a time, compromised Gulbenkian's five percent interest in the Iraq Petroleum Company. However, through legal maneuverings, he succeeded in restoring his five percent.

In parallel with his intense activity in complex international negotiations involving governments, industrial firms, and political entities, Gulbenkian developed into an avid collector of art. He became world-renowned for his insatiable appetite for acquiring famous, high-priced art, outbidding other celebrated buyers.

Through the foundation he established in his name, Calouste Gulbenkian became, and continues to be, the benefactor for numerous Armenian and non-Armenian causes. One of the earliest such benefactions was to build and endow the Armenian Church in London.

He was the President of the Armenian General Benevolent Union, 1930-1932.

The phenomenal success attained by Gulbenkian in amassing a wealth of several billion dollars is now memorialized by the monumental cultural center in Lisbon, Portugal, created, maintained, and operated by the CALOUSTE GULBENKIAN FOUNDATION.

The enormous complex of modern buildings on spacious grounds that not only displays his superb collection of art in many forms, serves also as the center of cultural life in Lisbon. The center supports numerous cultural activities in music, drama, and visual arts on a continuing basis. It also hosts meetings of groups of many kinds, domestic and international. For its fame it attracts visitors from all over the world.

The name Calouste Gulbenkian evokes feelings of awe and admiration - awe for his spectacular accomplishment, and admiration for the use to which he has put his success.

℘

Khachadour Oskanian
(ca.1818 - 1900)

The true beginning of Armenians in America is marked by Khachadour Oskanian's arrival in 1834. We must go back a few years and trace the dramatic events that led to it.

The American Board of Commissioners for Foreign Missions had missionaries stationed in Beirut and Jerusalem. It was there that the American missionaries had first contacts with Armenians (c. 1820). The Board had directed missionary William Goodell to go from Beirut to Constantinople to work with Armenians. He would be joined (1832) by Henry Dwight who had just visited Armenia, with Eli Smith.

The two missionaries opened an academy in Constantinople and found ready students from the education-starved Armenians of Constantinople. They organized an Evangelical Union (1836) and carried on correspondence with the Armenian provinces. This activity may be said to mark the birth of Armenian Protestantism.

Among the students was a bright lad, Khachadour Oskanian (age 16). He was sent to New York for continued study under the aegis of the Board. After six years of study he returned to his native Constantinople, and in 1840 established a periodical "Azdarar Biuzandian" (Byzantine Monitor). He had a sharp pen and attacked the Armenian bigwigs. As a consequence, his publication folded.

He was elected a member of the Patriarchal Assembly. Through that position he was introduced to a high-ranking Turkish official who sought his advice on "how to make the Turks better known to Americans." Oskanian's flippant answer was, "Open a Turkish bath in New York."

Feeling the urge, he returned to New York in 1854. On the ship during passage he met and found friendship with the editor of the New York Herald, James Bennett, thanks to knowing a few European languages, to having a silver tongue, and to having had journalistic experience.

Oskanian made a name for himself in journalism, his articles appearing frequently in the New York Herald.

Despite his having been sponsored by the Protestant Board he had the principled courage to criticize the Protestant assertions that the Armenians and their Church were backward and heathen. He labeled Armenians "Yankees of Asia Minor."

Oskanian won praise for his stalwart position in defense of Armenians and their culture. His home had become a gathering place for Armenian newcomers, who were beginning to arrive in considerable numbers.

James Bennett, Oskanian's friend and mentor, had formed a favorable opinion of him, and of Armenians generally. Bennett owned a large piece of land in Ohio. He suggested that that undeveloped land be developed into a city for Armenian newcomers. Bennett also offered to build a house for Oskanian, and to pay the cost of educating his children. Oskanian pondered over this offer, but ultimately declined, partly because his American wife did not want to leave the lush life of New York.

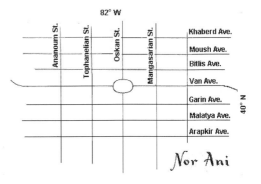

Oskanian's Possible Concept of "Nor Ani," Ohio

But years later (c. 1880), Oskanian, along with Armenian friends, planned to encourage a large movement of Armenians to America, offering lands under the prevailing homesteading laws. They laid out a city that would be called "Nor Ani" (New Ani). The east-west streets would be named Van, Moush, Zeitun, Garin, etc., and the north-south streets would be named Oskan, Tophanelian, Mangasarian, etc.

The ambitious plan did not materialize, however, mainly because the plan was inadequately structured and managed.

Khachadour Oskanian, nevertheless, continued in his very busy and productive life, well regarded by those with whom he worked. He died in 1900.

જી

"Citizen" Cartozian

In 1925 a dramatic event took place in the United States, one that threatened the right of Armenians to become naturalized citizens of the United States of America. The event galvanized the attention of Armenians throughout the land. It was the trial of the United States of America vs. Tatos O. Cartozian, in which the United States was suing Cartozian to relinquish his acquired citizenship on grounds that he was an Asiatic, and not a "free white person" in the meaning of the law of the land then in force as requisite for naturalization.

The threat felt by the Armenian community was that if the United States position were upheld by the court, then untold numbers of Armenians in America would be shorn of their citizenship.

Of course, Armenian leaders throughout the country became intensely interested. Newspaper men, lawyers, and others flocked to the Federal Courthouse in Portland, Oregon, to follow the legal proceedings.

New York Times (July 28, 1925)

Mr. Tatos [Tateos] O. Cartozian was a rug merchant in Portland. He had sold an oriental rug to a State Senator.

The Senator, apparently feeling that he had been cheated in his purchase of the rug, and not finding satisfaction in his claim against Cartozian for restitution, prevailed upon appropriate Federal agencies to sue Cartozian, to strip him of his citizenship on grounds that he, as an Armenian and a native of Asia Minor, was not a " free white person."

The verdict was to be given by United States District Court Judge C.E. Wolverton following a hearing that took place in July 1925.

The defense attorneys had arranged for a number of depositions earlier obtained, to be submitted at the hearing. The depositions had been taken from qualified anthropologists and other authorities. These depositions declared that Armenians were of "Alpine stock," and not Asiatic in the usual sense of that word, even though they came from Asia Minor. It was being declared that Armenians were the "Yankees of Asia Minor."

Also, there were paraded before the judge a number of persons, Armenians, who were of very light complexion, and with European facial features. It was even submitted that one "beautiful" Armenian woman was married to a prominent non-Armenian physician from Seattle, to show that Armenians were accepted into American society.

The statement made by Judge Wolverton at the opening of the hearing on July 27, 1925, was as follows:

> "...Defendant is a native of that part of the Turkish Empire known as Turkey in Asia, or Asia Minor, having been born in Sivas, which is located in western Armenia, towards Anatolia and is of Armenian blood and race. It is alleged that he is not a free white person within the meaning of the naturalization laws of Congress. No charge of fraud is made, and sole question to be determined is whether defendant is to be classed, for naturalization purposes, as a 'free white person'..."

The judge's decision was reported in the New York Times on the next day [July 28, 1925, page 12] as follows.

> "Armenians are eligible to naturalization as American citizens, Federal Judge C. E. Wolverton decided today. In the Cartozian case the judge handed down a decision that was a victory for the Asia Minor people ... The government contention was that Armenians are of Asiatic descent and therefore not eligible to naturalization."

8◯

Postscript

Our "Journey" has come to an end. It was a quick trip, touching only a few high spots here and there. But, as it is with many first-time trips, the experience serves mainly to whet the appetite for learning more on later visits.

A generation ago, young Armenians bent on learning about their people's past decried the lack of sources in English, out of which they might glean the facts of their storied heritage. Fortunately, for today's crop of young Armenians, there has been an explosive growth in the number of works published in English on Armenian topics. Moreover, there are many dealers of books that stock a good selection. Today, one can obtain catalogs of available works for sale by NAASR, the AGBU, the several church headquarters, individual churches, print shops, etc.

Furthermore, these works exist at all levels, between being written for a child's level of comprehension, all the way up to the highest level of scholarship out of Armenian study centers at universities.

We would point out that this particular work can serve in two ways. In one sense, it is a quick reference to many significant topics relating to the Armenian presence on the world scene for three millennia. In the other sense, it serves as an introduction to topics that a reader may want to explore further.

The Author

ՀԱՅԵՐԸ

Երկնքի խոնարհումն երկրի քարերուն
Հաղորդում մ՚է փնսորինած Աստուծմէ.
Եւ հողը կը դառնայ արգաւանդ սերմանող
Իր բազմափեսակ նիւթերէ:

Հսկայ ժայռեր կեցած շարան շարան,
Դէմ առ դէմ են դալար խոփերուն,
Որ յամառօրէն կ՚ապրին, կ՚աճին
Սնունդ քաշելով արմատներով փոկուն:

Օձապտոյտ ժայռափոր գետաձորեր
Կ՚անցնին ծայրէ ծայր այս երկրին հնոյ.
Արգասաւոր արոփներ Ալյեան կեանքով
Սննդող են արարածներուն Աստուծոյ:

Լայնածաւալ ու բազմափեսակ այս երկիրը,
Իր խաչքարերով մաշուած հեղեւանք օղին,
Որ, մարդադաշտ կեանքի եւ մահու,
Տունն է այս հպարտ ու ազնիւ ազգին:

Յառաջագոյնն է Քրիստոնեայ ազգերու շարքին,
Եւ մարդող պաշտպանելու հաւատին,
Իբրեւ ապացոյց՝ փաշուած քարերէ
Փառահեղ երկեր կարուցին, կերտեցին:

Դարերով արշաւող անարդար հրոսակներ,
Ունակոխելով հողը սրբազան,
Ջարդ, աւեր, նախատինք սփռեցին,
Բայց իրենց ողջ ոգին մարել չկրցան:

Չախողութիւն երբէք չվհատեցուց
Այս ժողովուրդը իր կամքէն.
Եւ զօրացուած իր հաւատքով Աստուծոյ
Յառաջդիմեց յամառօրէն:

Այսօր դեր կան աննոնք աշխարհիս վրայ
Մինչ այլ ազգեր կային ու անցան.
Հայեր իրենց փոկուն արմափներով
Կը սպասեն նոր արշալոյսի ծագման:

Եւ իբրեւ թէ հզոր, հսկայ խորհրդանիշ,
Միշտ նայող բարձրէն, վերէն
Մասիսները իբրեւ օգնող աշ մը փուլող,
Կեցած, կանգնած երկինքը կը համբուրեն:

Գրեց՝
 Արա Յովհաննէս Մովսեսեան

Թարգմանեց՝
 Արա Աւագեան

325

Index

General Works on Armenian History

Ananikian, Mardiros H., *The Mythology of All Races*, Vol. VII. New York, Cooper Square Publishers, 1964

Arlen, Michael J., *Passage to Ararat*, New York, Farrar, Straus & Giroux, 1975

The Armenian People From Ancient to Modern Times, Vols. I,II. (ed. by Richard G. Hovannisian)

Arpee, Leon, *A History of Armenian Christianity*. New York, Armenian Missionary Association of America, 1946

Bournoutian, George A., *The History of the Armenian People*, Vols. I,II. Costa Mesa, California, Mazda Publishers, 1993

Chahin, M., *The Kingdom of Armenia*. New York, Dorsett Press, 1987

Dadrian, Vahakn N., *The History of the Armenian Genocide*.

Deranian, Marderos, *The Village of Hussenig*. Boston, Baikar Publishing House, 1981

Deranian, Martin, *Worcester Is America: The Story of the Worcester Armenians: The Early Years*, Worcester, 1998

Dzeron, Manoog, *Village of Parchanj, General History*. Fresno, Panorama West Books, 1984 (trans. by Arra S. Avakian)

Haig, Vahe, *Kharpert and Her Golden Plain*. New York, Mekhitarist Press. 1959 (in Armenian)

Hoogasian-Villa, Susie, *100 Armenian Tales*. Detroit, Wayne State University Press, 1966

Hovannisian, Richard G., *The Armenian Republic*, Vols. I-IV. Los Angeles, University of California Press, 1971

Kaloustian, S., *Saints and Sacraments*. Fresno, A-1 Printers, 1959

Katchaturian, Chahen, *Armenian Artists*. Yerevan, Armenian National Gallery

Mirak, Robert, *Torn Between Two Lands*. Cambridge, Harvard University Press, 1983

Morgenthau, Henry, *Ambassador Morgenthau's Story*. New York, Doubleday, 1918

Novello, A.A. et al, *The Armenians: 2,000 Years of Art and Architecture*.

Samuelian, Varaz, *Willie and Varaz*. Fresno, 1985 (trans. by Arra S. Avakian)

Toriguian, Shavarsh, *The Armenian Question and International Law*. Beirut, Hamazkaine Press, 1973

Uvezian, Sonia, The Cuisine of Armenia. New York, Harper & Row, 1974

Bibliography

Ararat (quarterly), numerous issues. New York: AGBU

Armenian Affairs (quarterly), Vols. 1-4. New York: Armenian National Council of America, 1949-50

The Armenian Digest (monthly), numerous issues. New York

The Armenian Review (quarterly), numerous issues. Boston: Hairenik Ass'n

Atamian, Sarkis, *The Armenian Community*. New York: Philosophical Library, 1995

Avakian, Arra S., *The Armenians in America*. Minneapolis: Lerner, 1977

Chalabian, Antranig, *Revolutionary Figures* (English edition). Privately printed, 1994

Der Nersessian, Sirarpie, *The Armenians*. New York: Praeger, 1970

Elisaeus, *Vasn Vardanay ev Hayots Patmutiun* (On Vardan and the War of the Armenians). Mekhitarists, Venice, 1859 (in Armenian)

Encyclopedia Brittanica, numerous entries. Chicago: 1971

Geghouni (annual), numerous issues. San Lazzaro: Mekhitarist Fathers

Hay Endanik (monthly), numerous issues. San Lazzaro: Mekhitarist Fathers

Haykakan Sovietakan Hanrakitaran (Armenian Soviet Encyclopedia), numerous entries. Yerevan: 1986

Khorenatsi, Movses, *History of the Armenians*. Cambridge: Harvard, 1978 (trans. by Robert W. Thompson)

Koriun, *The Life of Mashtots*. New York: AGBU, 1964 (trans. by Bedros Norehad)

Lang, David Marshal, *Armenia, Cradle of Civilization*. London: George Allen and Unwin, 1970

Lynch, H.F.B., *Armenia: Travels and Studies*, Vols. I, II. London: 1901

Moushegh, Bishop, *Amerikahay Taretsuyts* (Almanac of the Armenians of America). Boston: 1912 (in Armenian)

Ormanian, Malachia, *Azgapatum*, Vols. I-III. Beirut: 1959 (reprint in Armenian)

_____, *The Church of Armenia*. London: 1912 (trans. by Terenig Poladian)

Personal Correspondence

Tzaynkagh Sharakan (Hymnal). Jerusalem: St. James Press, 1914 (in Armenian)

Walker, C.J., *Armenia, The Survival of a Nation*. London: 1980

Zhamagirk (Breviary). Jerusalem: St. James Press, 1915 (in Armenian)

About Author/Poet
Ara John Movsesian

Ara John Movsesian is a graduate of the University of California at Berkeley and a California state registered architect who resides in Fresno, California. In addition to writing the poetry found in ARMENIA: *A Journey Through History*, Mr. Movsesian has written several other works, two of which are published by The Electric Press.

Pearls of Love
How to Write Love Letters & Love Poems

"Short of having a friend named Cyrano, you can't beat this guide to writing ... Love Letters ... and Poems."

--Patricia Holt
S.F. Chronicle Book Review

ISBN 13: 978- 0-916919-40-5 • L/C No. 84-147625 • POD Softcover
$17.95 • THE ELECTRIC PRESS/BOOKSURGE
Individual Copies available through AMAZON.COM
Retail, Institutional & Library orders may be placed through BOOKSURGE.COM

ॐ

Love Poems for Cards & Letters

187 short love poems express many romantic emotions, including anticipation, yearning, excitement, hope, friendship, joy and love. You can use the poems as they are or change them to fit your own needs. Excellent for use in creating your own personalized greeting cards

ISBN 13: 978- 0-916919-04-7 • L/C No. 88-81507
$10.95 • THE ELECTRIC PRESS/BOOKSURGE
Individual Copies available through AMAZON.COM
Retail, Institutional & Library orders may be placed through BOOKSURGE.COM

Arra S. Avakian, Sc. D.
(The Author)

Arra S. Avakian has been deeply involved in Armenian community life and in the study of the Armenian culture for many years.

Dr. Avakian was graduated from Massachusetts Institute of Technology, and on completing graduate study in 1935 was awarded the degree of Doctor of Science in the fields of Mathematics and Physics. For many years, he served with distinction in scientific research and engineering, especially in the area of Aerospace technology.

Responding to a call, Dr. Avakian was appointed Professor of Armenian Studies at California State University, Fresno, in 1970. Several years later, he took a similar position at the newly formed American Armenian International College, in La Verne, California. Dr. Avakian initiated the Armenian studies programs at both institutions. He continues to maintain a highly visible profile in the dissemination of knowledge of the Armenian cultural heritage through his authorship of newspaper and magazine articles and his public lectures on Armenian subjects. In addition, he has been, for many years, a presenter in the Elderhostel program on the cultural history of the Armenian people. His book, *The Armenians in America,* is used as a reference text in public schools. He has made a specialty in the translation of Armenian works, books and articles, into English.

On invitation, he taught graduate mathematics at the American University of Armenia, in 1993.

Dr. Avakian has held leadership positions in such community organizations as the Armenian Students' Association of America, the National Association for Armenian Studies and Research, the Armenian Assembly, the Knights of Vartan, and the Armenian Church at both parish and diocesan levels. Among his special interests are the music and liturgy of the Armenian Church, in which he has served as Choir Director for many years. His published manual for choir directors is readily available.

In 1995, Dr. Avakian was elected a delegate to the National Ecclesiastical Assembly at the Holy See of the Armenian Church, at Echmiadzin, for the election of Karekin I, Catholicos of All Armenians. Also, in that same year, he was awarded the St. Sahag-St. Mesrop Medal of Honor by the Catholicos, together with an Encyclical (Gontag) commending him for his long years of fruitful service to the church.

Dr. Avakian has traveled extensively, with visits to Armenian centers throughout the world, especially in historic Armenia (Anatolia) and the Republic of Armenia, often forming and guiding tourist groups.

He makes his home in Fresno, California.

৪১

ARMENIA: A Journey Through History
THE ELECTRIC PRESS/BOOKSURGE
Individual Copies available through AMAZON.COM
Retail, Institutional & Library orders may be placed through BOOKSURGE.COM

11083598R1

Made in the USA
Lexington, KY
09 September 2011